ADVANCE PRAISE

"*The Power of the Only* by Angela Chee is a profound exploration of how to turn being 'the Only' into a source of strength and leadership. Whether you're the only woman, person of color, or someone with a unique perspective, Angela shows how to leverage your experiences to break barriers and create meaningful change. This book empowers readers to tap into their inner power, embrace their uniqueness, and thrive in any environment. A must-read for those ready to shift the status quo and become bridge builders for the next generation of leaders and innovators."

—**DR. MARSHALL GOLDSMITH,** Thinkers50 #1 executive coach and *New York Times* bestselling author of *The Earned Life, Triggers, and What Got You Here Won't Get You There*

"*The Power of the Only* is a game changer. Angela Chee redefines what it means to be 'the Only' in the room—transforming it into your greatest strength. With authentic storytelling, deep insights, and practical strategies, this book is a must-read for every woman, leader, and innovator. Through powerful stories, real-world examples, and scientific research, Angela equips you with the tools to communicate with confidence, lead with purpose, and thrive in any environment. More than a book—it's a movement. Discover how to create the future you deserve while leading the way for others. As I always say, when purpose meets passion, you're unstoppable. A must-read!"

—**SHELLEY ZALIS,** founder and CEO, The Female Quotient

"Angela Chee's *The Power of the Only* isn't just a book; it's the start of a movement; it's your precise GPS for turning what sets you apart into what sets you ahead. Angela's personal journey and wisdom shine in *The Power of the Only*. Her ability to connect her stories and those of other Onlys with actionable strategies makes this book an essential guide for anyone navigating environments where they feel different. It is a masterclass in leadership, communication, and self-discovery. As someone who has written extensively about 'distinction,' I can promise that Angela Chee redefines what it means to stand out. She challenges us all to embrace the transformative power of being 'the Only.' *The Power of the Only* can unlock unparalleled opportunities for growth, innovation, and impact. This is a must-read for anyone seeking to embrace their individuality and amplify their influence."

—**SCOTT MCKAIN,** author of *Iconic* and member of the Professional Speakers Hall of Fame

"Angela Chee's *The Power of the Only* is the book I wish I had during my own 'Only' journey. Angela seamlessly blends her personal challenges and triumphs with insights from other trailblazers, making you feel seen and heard. With her deep expertise in communication and leadership development, she offers more than just inspiration—she provides insights and actionable strategies to help you find your voice and your power. This must-have book is more than a resource—it's a call to action. If you're ready to speak with confidence and navigate environments with grace and authority, this book is for you."

—**DEEPA PURUSHOTHAMAN**, bestselling author of *The First, the Few, the Only*

"Angela Chee doesn't just talk about being 'the Only'—she's lived it. From growing up in an immigrant household, like I did, to her successful career in media, Angela shares her personal journey along with the powerful stories of other changemakers. Her five principles provide a relatable, research-backed road map for turning your uniqueness into your greatest strength and shifting your mindset from one of scarcity to abundance.

For anyone who's ever felt like they didn't belong, this book shows you that being the only one isn't a weakness—but can be an opportunity and the key to your success. Angela empowers you to break through fears, embrace your voice, and thrive in every area of your life. *The Power of the Only* is a vital guide for personal and professional growth—and a reminder that you're not alone on this journey."

—**FARNOOSH TORABI**, financial expert, author, and host of *So Money*

"Angela Chee beautifully captures what it means to be a trailblazer. In *The Power of the Only*, she shows us that being the 'only one' in the room isn't a limitation—it's an opportunity to stand out and make an impact. The book is relevant, relatable, and an inspiring read. Angela's stories make you feel like you're right there in the room with her. It's more than a collection of experiences—it offers a clear flow of how to learn, take action, and reflect, with practical exercises that are easy to understand."

—**GINA GOMEZ**, founder and CEO, Arista Management Group

"*The Power of the Only* isn't just a book—it's an awakening for those of us who refuse to fit the mold. Angela Chee shows you how to turn the challenge of being 'the Only' into your greatest asset, offering inspirational stories and a road map to honor your power, trust your intuition, and break through barriers. If you're ready to stop playing small, claim your space, and step fully into your greatness, *The Power of the Only* is a must-read."

—**ALI BROWN,** founder of The Trust

"Finally, a blueprint for being the Only without feeling lonely! This book is for anyone who's ever walked into a room, saw zero familiar faces, and thought, 'Here goes nothing.' Angela Chee's journey shows us not only that being the first in the room is possible, but powerful. A must-read for all the bold and brave 'firsts' who are charting the path."

—**HENNA PRYOR,** workplace performance expert and author of *Good Awkward*

"*The Power of the Only* is a transformative guide to unlocking your full potential. Angela Chee turns what many perceive as a challenge—being 'the Only'—into a powerful opportunity for leadership, innovation, and impact. Her insights not only inspire but equip you to thrive personally and professionally by embracing the strength of who you truly are. Angela provides the tools to help you reframe challenges, celebrate wins, connect with any audience, and create a bold vision for the future. It's a must-read for leaders ready to step up, and for any company committed to supporting them."

—**JENNIFER MCCOLLUM,** CEO of Catalyst and author of
In Her Own Voice: A Woman's Rise to CEO

"*The Power of the Only* is a must-have for anyone who has ever felt like they didn't quite fit in. Angela Chee goes beyond stories and inspiration—she equips readers with practical strategies and mindset shifts that help you go from feeling like an outsider to embracing your true self. Through insights and case studies from trailblazing leaders and everyday clients—Angela shows you how to own your voice, communicate with presence, and lead with confidence. She shares her wisdom and actionable tools to help you nurture self-awareness, quiet your inner critic, connect authentically, and celebrate your wins. If you're ready to thrive and step into your fullest potential, this book is the empowering guide you've been waiting for."

—**TRICIA MONTALVO TIMM,** author of *Embrace the
Power of You: Owning Your Identity at Work*

THE POWER OF
THE ONLY

THE POWER OF THE ONLY

OWN YOUR VOICE
THRIVE IN ANY ENVIRONMENT

ANGELA CHEE

IDEAPRESS
PUBLISHING

WASHINGTON, DC

IDEAPRESS
PUBLISHING

Ideapress Publishing | www.ideapresspublishing.com

All trademarks are the property of their respective companies.

The author is not engaged in rendering professional medical advice or services to the individual reader. The ideas and suggestions contained in this book are not intended as a substitute for consulting with your mental health care provider.

Cover Design: Faceout Studio, Spencer Fuller
Interior Design: Jessica Angerstein

Cataloging-in-Publication Data is on file with the Library of Congress.

Hardcover ISBN: 978-1-64687-170-4

Special Sales
Ideapress books are available at a special discount for bulk purchases for sales promotions and premiums or for use in corporate training programs. Special editions, including personalized covers, custom forewords, corporate imprints, and bonus content, are also available.

1 2 3 4 5 6 7 8 9 10

To my parents, the original "Onlys," and all my ancestors.

For every Only,

Know you are seen, heard, and valued.

You are the change you have been waiting for.

CONTENTS

PRINCIPLE 5 OWN YOUR FUTURE

Introduction

THE POWER OF THE ONLY

I'm eight years old, kneeling in front of the TV, and the green shag carpet presses into my knees. I'm waiting for the *den den den den* music and the broadcast announcer's deep voice: "This is the Channel 2 News update."

I lean closer. She's about to come on the screen.

My neck strains as I try to get closer still, smiling wide at the screen.

There she is. Connie Chung.

My dad, sitting in his '80s leather recliner behind me with his feet propped up, says, "Hey, you could be like Connie Chung!"

I look back at him in shock and then wide-eyed at the screen.

Who, me?

Connie Chung, one of the first Asian American newscasters, was the evening anchor at KNXT Channel 2 and became the first woman to coanchor the *CBS Evening News*. To the world, Connie Chung was a broadcasting icon, but to me, she was the lady in the box who made me feel less alone.

As a child, I noticed that no one looked like me. No one on TV or in my neighborhood. I was the only one. My dad's suggestion that I could be like Connie Chung set my imagination on fire. I became fascinated with the power of television, and seeing another "Only" planted a seed in me that became my North Star. At the time, I didn't even realize it. This idea was germinating and waiting for the right moment to bloom.

I wanted to be like Connie Chung.

On December 3, 2001, nineteen years after my dad's suggestion, I started my first day as an on-air reporter at Channel 2 News in Los Angeles, now called KCBS—the same station on which I first saw Connie Chung.

In broadcasting, many of us hope to make it to the top. The road to my dream was filled with hard work, sacrifice, competition, rejection, and adventure. Achieving this dream in the Los Angeles TV market—ranked only behind New York—and in my hometown at age twenty-seven was the greatest accomplishment of my life at the time. My dad could sit in the same chair and now watch me on the screen every night.

But this dream almost didn't happen; I talked myself out of it so many times.

Growing up in the suburbs of Los Angeles, I was a sweet, shy Chinese American girl with a bowl cut and glasses—the only Asian in the neighborhood. All I wanted was to fit in. Neighbors were friendly; kids, not always. I did whatever I could to survive and not stand out. I hated having shoes clutter the welcome mat because we didn't wear them in the house. I'd whisper at the supermarket because I didn't want others to hear me speaking Chinese. I didn't want Chinese food; I wanted pizza and McDonald's. I didn't want straight black hair when everyone around me was blonde. I wanted to hide all the things that made me . . . *me*. The last thing any child wants to be is the "Only" anything, right?

Even after I survived the typical journey of awkward adolescence, I kept getting mixed messages. My dad had said, "You can be like Connie Chung!" but when I told my parents that I actually wanted to go into news, they tried to stop me by saying, "It's too hard," especially for a Chinese girl. Don't get me wrong, my parents are my biggest supporters, but as immigrants from Taiwan, they played it safe—safe from failure—and they wanted me to play it safe too. I was often reminded not to stand out or speak up, which to me, meant that being an Only was not safe or secure.

They said those things to protect me. They had no concept of the ripple effects of their well-meaning intentions.

In college, I was ready to take on the world. But at a career talk, a reporter did not share her wisdom; instead, she shared horror stories about being an Only, leaving a trail of venom to follow. I now understand where she was coming from, but just as words can easily lift someone up, words can easily crush their ambition, too. The experience left me deflated.

That day, I decided my dream wasn't worth pursuit. So, instead of interning at the local TV station, I tried advertising and public relations. After graduation, I worked as an assistant at Paramount Pictures in Hollywood, helping launch *Entertainment Tonight China*. Close enough to TV, but still far from my original dream. Despite some success, I always felt that tug to play bigger. To dream bigger.

Have *you* felt that tug? To do more and be more? Maybe the tug that called you to pick up and read this book?

After years of working hard, I realized I was no closer to my dream and started to feel a deep sense of regret. I was sick of saying, "It's too hard," or "I wasn't ready." I was tired of listening to the voices of the past, the voices in my head that had been cultivated by society, my culture, and those who said I couldn't do it.

I wasn't afraid to be the Only anymore.

It was now or never.

I started moonlighting for free at local cable stations to get on camera and accumulate some sample tapes for my reel. I took broadcast journalism classes at UCLA at night. I went to journalism conferences, met with agents and reporters, and tried improv comedy. I mailed out letter after letter and sent my reel to news directors nationwide. I even drove to cities around the country to deliver them personally if the opportunity arose.

I eventually landed my first on-air job in Palm Springs as a weekend reporter. I couldn't afford to leave my full-time job, so I worked seven days a week for about a year; five at Paramount and every weekend in Palm Springs, two and a half hours away. Saying *yes* as an adult to my "childhood dream" was a major turning point in realizing that I had power all along.

Eventually, I moved to another small market, Bakersfield, before getting back to Los Angeles, where I started as a dayside reporter in the Inland Empire before becoming part of the "Dark-30 club" of morning news (up by 2:30 a.m. and on air by 5 a.m.).

And then, after hundreds of stories and years in the business—from anchoring a four-hour morning show to being on HGTV, E! Entertainment, and more—there was another shift in my career. It was time to leave the news. After my son was born, I stepped into being the Only again and launched my professional emcee and speaking career, as well as a coaching business.

This shift is what led me here, to you.

Several years ago, on the night before a business mastermind/conference, I met with my friend, Dr. Valerie Rein, a fellow speaker and author. While sharing stories, I mentioned that as a keynote speaker, I'm often the only woman and usually the only Asian on stage. In fact, most of the time, I'd been the sole Only in the room.

> **I realized being an Only wasn't a weakness; it was my greatest strength.**

Even as a communication/media coach, I've found only a few role models in the professional development space who look like me or have my lived experience.

And yet, it no longer bothered me to be the Only.

I realized being an Only wasn't a weakness; it was my greatest strength.

Have you ever had your life flash before your eyes? Like a movie montage during my conversation, I saw the wins, milestones, and challenges of growing up in a predominately White neighborhood and working my way up in the competitive entertainment and news industries. In each case, I overrode the negative messages I received, moved past my initial fears of being an Only, navigated the environment, and learned from those challenges. I felt powerful; I was no longer buying the narrative that it's sad to be an Only.

I turned to Valerie and said, "There is power in being the Only. It's time we step into it."

She gave me a powerful gaze and touched my arm. "Wow, I got chills hearing you say that."

In that moment, there was a shift inside me, like a ray of light had ignited something in my soul. I didn't know exactly what it meant and couldn't stop thinking about it. What if every Only

We don't have to wait for the world to change to step into our greatness.

could feel that power? Why can't people see the power they have being an Only? And more importantly, how can we all step up and harness the Power of the Only?

In the wake of the 2016 US presidential election, the #MeToo movement, and polarizing headlines, there was an energetic shift in our world. People were starting to stand up, show up, and be counted. Then, after the 2024 presidential election, another seismic shift. The barriers we Onlys face are not imaginary and can't always be overcome with just our mindset and determination. They are real and detrimental, so we must work hard to remove them. I am thankful for those who take on the system every day to make it better for everyone.

I also realized then that *we don't have to wait for the world to change to step into our greatness*. It's in fully embracing and celebrating being an Only, despite the often challenging environment we operate in, that we *can* change the status quo. We can create new rooms from the outside, but we also need to shift the room from the *inside*. It's time to shift from the mindset of scarcity to abundance, bring others in, and carve a new path for more Onlys to follow.

After 2016, I embarked on a journey to explore these questions; I started *The Power of the Only* podcast, interviewed Onlys about their experiences, and researched strategies and tools to help Onlys thrive. I continued to discover Onlys wherever I went, highlighting their stories and gathering their insights. I did soul-searching to put the wisdom I shared with others into my own day-to-day life. The culmination of that quest is this book, and the five principles included here will help you step into and harness the Power of the Only.

THE POWER OF THE ONLY

The Power of the Only is seeing, understanding, and feeling what others don't. It's leveraging this unique perspective to achieve your goals and create change for yourself and others. It is cultivated through years of navigating challenges and different situations as an Only—whether you are the only woman, person of color, LGBTQ, neurodivergent, or the only voice or person in the room who sees things differently and wants to shift the status quo, break through barriers, and create something new.

The Power of the Only allows you to make the most out of every opportunity available, regardless of your environment. When you step into this power, you know the value you bring to every interaction. You don't second-guess yourself. You know what you want and don't want, what you are willing to do and what you are not, and you don't accept that these decisions are unavailable to you. You will thrive in any environment and be the bridge builder for the next generation of leaders, ideas, and innovation.

So, where does this power come from?

It's already inside us. You already have everything you need. If you are an Only, all the things that may have been challenging in the past, such as the act of hitting barriers and either breaking through them, going around them, or forging a new path, are what have helped shape you. You had to figure it out to survive. While doing so was probably draining at times, it helped you cultivate many skills. If at first you felt like being an Only was lonely and hard, it has since evolved into a strength: the ability to connect with others, be empathetic, and understand the bigger picture. It's these experiences that shape you to see beyond, understand, navigate, process, empathize, and innovate.

Your power is already inside you waiting; all you have to do is tap into it.

I personally didn't step into the power of being an Only during one singular moment or one grand act. It happened over a series of moments that started to chip away at the once impenetrable wall of my past and the stories I had heard and told myself. Having both good and bad experiences allowed me to gain a new perspective and the skills I needed to know I could not only survive but *thrive* in any situation.

Your power is already inside you waiting; all you have to do is tap into it.

Growing up as the only Chinese American girl around taught me how to navigate conversations, be comfortable, and connect with different groups. Working in competitive industries like Hollywood and TV news helped me hone my skills and know how to be seen and heard, despite others telling me it would be too hard. When I was younger, I felt like I had to hide parts of myself; now, I am comfortable in my skin. It took time and various experiences to step into all parts of my Only. Once I truly embraced being an Only, it started to make a difference in my life.

There's no doubt that it is hard being an Only. But you understand hard; you have already been through a lot of challenges and learned how to navigate them. To access the power inside you, you must honor your journey and recognize your challenges as strengths. You have developed them through years of navigating things you may not have necessarily wanted to but polished you like a beautiful stone that is now ready to shine.

THE FIVE PRINCIPLES OF THE POWER OF THE ONLY

To harness the Power of the Only, we must break through barriers, both internal and external. We must see what those barriers are, understand where they came from, and redefine them so that they are no longer obstacles but strengths. Through my research, experience, and years of interviewing Onlys who have stepped into their power and thrived, I've identified five guiding principles to harness the Power of the Only:

1 **Own Your Opportunity.** You recognize your value and don't wait for opportunities to come to you or think you can't have something yet. You know that nothing is stopping you from taking the opportunity in front of you.

2 **Own Your Power.** You already have everything you need inside you to succeed. You don't need permission to take up space and don't need to change to fit in. You have internal status and agency.

3 **Own Your Voice.** You don't have to find your voice; you already have one. You know what you say matters and that the words you use about yourself and others matter too.

4 **Own Your Communication.** You communicate in a way that truly connects with your audience. In short, it means to be heard and felt so you can create the change you need and want.

5 **Own Your Future.** To own your future, you need to focus on thriving, not just surviving. You understand that the mindset, habits, and skills that got you to where you are now may not be sustainable or get you to where you want to be. You bring new people in and carve a path for others to follow, amplifying the effects of your Power of the Only.

To access the power inside you, you must honor your journey and recognize your challenges as strengths.

In the following chapters, I dive deeply into each of these five principles. By the time you finish this book, you will have gained the awareness, tools, exercises, and strategies necessary to own your voice, thrive in any environment, and unlock your full, imagined potential.

But it's not just my story that will help you navigate your own journey; you'll hear from a powerful list of Onlys—leaders and innovators who have shattered barriers and redefined industries. From Deb Liu (CEO of Ancestry) to Gail Becker (founder of CAULIPOWER, who disrupted the $5 billion US pizza market with her gluten-free cauliflower crust). You'll learn from Wall Street veteran Carla Harris (one of *Fortune* magazine's 50 Most Powerful Black Executives), Dany Garcia (chairwoman of The Garcia Companies and owner of the United Football League—the only woman in the US with majority ownership of a large sports franchise), and Dave Noll, the creative force behind Food Network's *Chopped*, who rose from humble beginnings (growing up on subsidized school lunches) to pitching hit TV shows in Hollywood.

I also share the stories of trailblazers like philanthropist Melinda French Gates, actor and producer Reese Witherspoon, and director Ava DuVernay who are reshaping the landscapes of entertainment and philanthropy. You'll also hear from my everyday corporate and entrepreneurial clients, whose challenges, victories, and hard-earned lessons show how they've applied the five principles in their own lives. Their experiences offer inspiration and practical insights on how you can harness these principles to navigate your own path to success.

In each chapter, exercises help you reflect on and apply the principles. You can try them immediately or come back to them at any time. Consider me your personal cheerleader and coach

Being the Only may seem lonely at times, but you are not alone.

through this process. Being the Only may seem lonely at times, but you are not alone.

AWAKEN YOUR VOICE

I want to change so many things in the world but I can't tackle them all. That is not my gift. My gift is to help you recognize your own brilliance, awaken your voice, and empower you to take meaningful action. I aim to inspire you to not only pursue your goals but also live them fully, find sustainable success, and spark positive change in others. You have the power to do this, but first, you must claim it.

Some have always felt the calling to claim their power and step into their Only, but some of you may not feel as bold. You are the trailblazers, innovators, and thought leaders who haven't quite stepped into your full potential or created the impact you envision. Maybe you don't feel ready or find barriers are holding you back. Or maybe you don't know how to navigate the systems and the resources around you or how to communicate to move forward. However you feel and whatever the *why* behind this feeling, it is okay. These fears and barriers don't have to define who you are.

Stepping up doesn't look a certain way and there is no right or wrong way to do it. It doesn't matter how big or small your actions are. You don't have to prove anything. You get to decide and create what comes next. By stepping into your imagined potential, everyone wins. When

Onlys embrace their power—not power *over*, but power *within* to uplift themselves and those around them—they generate transformative energy. This energy can be harnessed by companies, organizations, communities, and entire societies to see the world from new perspectives, take innovative actions, and reimagine our future.

We need Onlys more than ever.

We need *you*.

It's time to step up into the gift you were given.

PRINCIPLE 1

OWN YOUR OPPORTUNITY

Chapter 1.1

OWN YOUR
OPPORTUNITY

Never be limited by other people's limited imaginations.

—MAE JEMISON

With my heart pounding, I pulled out of the KCBS-TV studios in Los
Angeles and onto the streets of Hollywood. It was rush hour and I was the
noon anchor and reporter in Bakersfield the following day. Bakersfield is
only about two hours away from LA, but that day, the drive was one of
the longest of my life.

My contract, my job, my savings, and my childhood dream were all
on the line.

As I cruised along the I-5, I pondered all my hard work over the years.
Through the winding, dry hillsides, with the LA skyline in the rearview
mirror, all I thought about were the phone calls, rejection, working nights
and weekends for free, and mailing out endless tapes to find my first
job. I thought about all the early mornings in a small television market,

doing news cut-ins alone, before non-linear editing, and powering the script with a foot prompter. I thought about covering stories from raging wildfires to massive storms, the hours and days standing outside court houses and visiting the local fair and community events with mediocre equipment and limited staff.

The phone rang once. Twice. I held my breath and answered.

It was the assistant news director at KCBS Channel 2 News Los Angeles, the number two market in the US. The same station where I first saw Connie Chung on TV. The same station that would determine my entire future.

"We really enjoyed meeting you today and would like to offer you a reporter position. When can you start?" he asked.

I held back the urge to scream at the top of my lungs.

"My contract is up in a week," I replied. "I can start immediately."

After the call, hands shaking, I gripped the steering wheel for support and pulled off the Grapevine onto a side road. I wanted to celebrate with joy but something else happened instead.

I started to cry uncontrollably as the floodgates of emotion opened. I had just achieved my lifelong dream.

But my joy was clouded by anger. I was able to get the job in Los Angeles all by myself and I was proud of my determination. But I did it despite others telling me it wasn't going to work or there were no opportunities. Despite all that opposition, I made it happen.

When I finally calmed down, I felt I could breathe for the first time in months, and to be honest, it was probably the first time in years—or maybe even my entire life.

To understand how dire this moment was, let me rewind. At the time of this phone call, I had worked in Bakersfield (market number 123) for two years. I started as the early morning cut-in anchor/reporter and moved up to the weekday noon anchor/reporter. Ratings were good, I enjoyed my job, and our newsroom was like a family. My contract with them was almost up, and a month before its expiration, I was given an ultimatum: Sign on for another four years or leave.

Without a pay increase, I couldn't survive financially. I had saved for years while working as an assistant in Hollywood, but to pursue my dream of being an on-air reporter, I had taken a 50 percent pay cut. I was out of money. If I accepted Bakersfield's terms, I couldn't accept another job or move on for four years. When I asked for a shorter contract or more pay, they simply said, "No, take it or leave it."

My station saw me as valuable enough to lock me in for four more years, but not valuable enough to pay me what I was worth.

I was devastated. I gave my heart and soul to that job every day. I worked hard and never complained. The show was doing well. I was active in the community and got along with my coworkers. They hoped I would be grateful I had a job, not complain, and just take it.

I was furious and told my agent there was no way I was taking their offer.

She countered, "We don't have any other options right now, not this soon before your contract is up."

I had been interviewing at midlevel markets, thinking I wasn't yet ready for Los Angeles. But then I thought, *Why not? I have nothing to lose.*

"What about LA?" I asked.

"No, it's not possible."

"Can I at least get an interview?"

"It's hard, and there aren't any openings right now."

I read between the lines. What she was really saying was, "The stations you are interested in already have an Asian reporter. Take the Bakersfield contract!"

How many times have you been told *You can't, It's not possible,* or *There isn't room for you*? I had been underestimated before but always figured out a way. So, I did what I had to do; I networked nonstop, making calls, writing letters, and sending out tapes. I didn't sleep. I couldn't sleep. The clock was ticking. Each day, my anxiety levels rose.

Then, one week before my contract was up, I got an interview at KCBS in Los Angeles. I was floored. I did it! I got myself in the door despite my agent's pessimism.

Then I got the call. And then I got the job. I had finally made it to the "big leagues."

That longest drive of my life turned into the most life-changing drive of my career.

The morning after the LA interview, my Bakersfield news director called me into his office to talk about the contract. I immediately said, "Thank you for your offer, but my last day will be next week."

He was in shock. He started to get flustered, and with a panicked look on his face, rambled and offered me other options. I don't recall the details, but I remember feeling him backpedal when he realized I was leaving.

I replied calmly, "No, thank you. I appreciate the offer, but it's time to move on."

When I walked out of his office, I had never felt so proud of myself.

Even before receiving the offer from LA, I had already made the decision to leave Bakersfield; to bet on me and my future, even if it meant I would be out of a job. I knew they didn't respect or value me and it was time to leave, even if the job in LA hadn't come through. Luckily, it did.

The next week, I said goodbye on air, packed up a U-Haul truck, and drove to Los Angeles over the weekend. Monday came quickly, and soon it was my first day at KCBS Channel 2 News.

Now, my dad could watch *me* on the news.

I went from the verge of unemployment to working in the second-largest TV market in the country, quadrupling my salary, and achieving my lifelong dream. While this was just the beginning—and by no means the end of all my challenges, sacrifices, and triumphs—it all started by owning my opportunity.

BELIEVE YOU CAN

Not all stories of risk end in a happily ever after. My story could have turned out very differently, but I still believe we should not wait for opportunities to come to us.

Owning your opportunity isn't just saying *yes* to the opportunities in front of you; it's also showing up when others say there are no options. You don't listen to the limiting messages from society, the "You can't do this," or "You shouldn't do that." You see what is possible and believe you can achieve it.

I could have listened to my agent when she said there were no jobs for me in LA. I could have believed my only option was to stay at the station that inflexibly constrained me and offered neither a pay increase nor the ability to work anywhere else. I could have listened to all the societal voices in my head passed down from generations before me that insisted, "What you have is good enough."

I could have done any one of those things.

But I didn't.

I knew my value. I knew I was ready for the next level—or at least I wanted the chance to try. So, I chose to believe in my sense of self and went looking for the opportunity that I had always wanted.

Award-winning director Ava DuVernay spoke to a room full of reporters at the prestigious Venice Film Festival ahead of the screening of her 2023 film *Origin*. "The only way to be able to combat those ideas— 'You can't do this; they are not interested in you'—is to go out and do it!"

Origin is a narrative film written, produced, and directed by DuVernay that brings the story of Pulitzer Prize–winning writer Isabel Wilkerson to the screen. Inspired by Wilkerson's groundbreaking book *Caste: The Origins of Our Discontents*, the film explores the deep historical theories of caste systems intertwined with Wilkerson's story of her life and how she came to write the book. When asked at TEDWomen what inspired her to make this film, Ava joked, "People told me it was an unadaptable book, so the only logical thing to do was to try to adapt it."

Despite being an Oscar- and Golden Globe–nominated and Emmy-winning filmmaker behind *Selma*, *13th*, and *When They See Us*, despite being the first Black woman to win Best Director at the Sundance Film Festival, despite having a long list of awards and credits to her name (including being named one of *Time*'s Most Influential People), despite her arts and social impact collective, ARRAY, winning a Peabody Award, DuVernay still had naysayers. People told her no one would go to press conferences or screenings of *Origin*. They tried to talk her out of even applying for the festival.

DuVernay's response? "As Black filmmakers, we are told people who love films in other parts of the world do not care about our stories. I can't tell you how many times I have been told, 'Don't apply for Venice, you won't get in.' And this year, it happened."[1] In 2023, Ava DuVernay was the first Black woman in the festival's eighty-year history to have a film compete for the Golden Lion. Not only did people attend the screening, but they also gave her a standing ovation.

WHY MOST DON'T OWN THEIR OPPORTUNITY

For my whole life, I was taught to be grateful and not make a fuss. It was the built-in template of my immigrant parents. While I don't believe their behavior was the result of their culture or personality, I do believe parts of it were passed down to me. It was *their* form of a coping mechanism, and I made a conscious act to not fall victim to it.

If I had conformed to their template, I probably would have thanked my boss, accepted the subpar contract, and waited patiently for someone else to give me a green light to my future.

All of us have a set of internal rules that shape our decisions, feelings, and, ultimately, our lives. These rules can be influenced by our families, life experiences, workplaces, and communities. And sometimes, these rules can block us from our true potential.

All of us have a set of internal rules that shape our decisions, feelings, and, ultimately, our lives. These rules can be influenced by our families, life experiences, workplaces, and communities. And sometimes, these rules can block us from our true potential.

Some of us Onlys don't always own our opportunity because we simply don't think we can, or we don't think we are ready. Sometimes, we don't own our opportunities because we don't know how to make the change or are unclear on our path forward. Fear keeps us from even trying. We may have internalized societal, cultural, and generational messages that subconsciously limit us.

Tom was a successful, well-respected leader at his company. I was coaching him for a big presentation where he would be sharing his breakthrough research. Tom had never spoken at an industry conference before and told me that his team usually presented in his place. When I asked him why, he said, "It's just easier that way. I don't really like to stand out." Then he changed the subject.

After working together for a few weeks, Tom opened up to me. "I always felt a bit awkward and didn't feel like I fit in because I was short and introverted." He grew up in an Irish Catholic family, and his mother always told him not to talk too much, to stay humble, and to stay private. He recalled a faint memory of speaking up in school and being criticized, which only reinforced his mother's words.

Tom hadn't realized how much his upbringing impacted how he showed up in his life and work. For years, he had been fine to stay out of the spotlight but knew deep down that his work could help a lot of people. After all that time, he saw that he was the Only one who believed in this project and realized it was time to finally step up.

Sometimes, we Onlys don't own opportunities because the *external* environment is not working in our favor and we don't see a path ahead, so we either move on or give up. We could have the will and the confidence to forge ahead, but some opportunities may still be out of our control. If you're further along in your career or have previously seized opportunities but encountered setbacks or didn't achieve the desired impact, you might be feeling exhausted and burned out. As an Only, you sometimes face limited possibilities or even bias or discrimination, making it even more challenging to own your opportunity.

Before TV news, I had experienced working in the entertainment industry as a teen. I would only get opportunities if they were looking for a specific type—which was limited in the late '80s for an Asian girl, and I was used to being typecast. When I walked into a casting room, everyone else waiting looked like me. These were the occasions when I *wasn't* the Only in the room. Several times later in my career, I waited for a position to open, but since the "other" Asian hadn't left, I was stuck in limbo.

Things in the 2020s may be shifting a bit, but during most of my news career, scarcity in the industry was so deeply rooted that I didn't get offended by it. I played along, and to survive, I had to play it smart. I learned to accept this reality, face disappointment, and strategically create other paths. I'm sure this real, external limitation held me back from owning my opportunities. But I had to stay focused and navigate the landscape of the industry I desired, even if it wasn't the landscape I wanted.

HONORING YOUR GIFT IMPACTS OTHERS

Despite all the logical, personal, external, and probably very good reasoning as to why you didn't own your opportunity in the past, you *can* change and learn to navigate your reality with the goal of owning your opportunities in the future. You don't have to be on television or be an award-winning filmmaker. Everyone deserves to own their unique and desired opportunity, whatever it may be.

To own *your* opportunity, you must first acknowledge that some circumstances are not your fault and that you can't fix everything. Other—often uncontrollable—factors and barriers affect how you show up and whether you can own your opportunity. When you can see that situations are not always in your control but don't internalize this lack of control as a personal flaw, you can more easily access your power and move forward.

When you understand where your barriers are coming from, you can honor your past, see it as a gift, and use it as fuel for the future.

Then, you must reframe your challenges. What was once a weakness can become your greatest strength.

When you understand where your barriers are coming from, you can honor your past, see it as a gift, and use it as fuel for the future. But most importantly, you must view being an Only not as a burden, but as the most important opportunity that you own. Having the ability to navigate diverse perspectives and serve as a bridge builder is a true superpower.

You have the power. Take it. And use it for every opportunity to come.

I believe being an Only can be an honor. If you can make an impact, it is a gift. If you have a seat at the table, it's up to you to lead the way. When you're just starting out in your career, owning your opportunity is about stepping up to what is in front of you despite the circumstances or your environment. Even when you have achieved what others would call *success*, it's still important to continue to own your opportunities, not just for you but for what it can represent for others and the impact of the act itself. What we do has a ripple effect. While we may not always have control and create the impact that we envision, it is an honor and gift, even a privilege, to be able to try. I didn't always have a voice growing up, my parents didn't have a voice, and many still don't.

I believe owning our opportunity is the way forward. In the following chapters, we'll look at ways to own your opportunity.

EXERCISE

Let's start by exploring your ideas about opportunities. There are no right or wrong answers; this is only an exploration that leads to possibilities. Share what comes to you naturally, even if it's only a few words.

What are some of the opportunities you see for yourself today in different areas of your life, such as work, health, relationships, or maybe opportunities related to your family, community, or spiritual growth?

Like Tom, are you aware of any circumstances that block you from stepping into your opportunities? Consider both external and internal circumstances and write them down so you can acknowledge them.

Think of one or two things you're tolerating in your life that you could say no to, if not right now, with a little planning and foresight. Saying no to things that are no longer working is a powerful way to make room for better opportunities to take their place.

Just a few minutes of engaging with these questions before moving on can make a tangible difference. Now let's dig into the next part of the Only journey.

RECOGNIZE IT'S NOT ALL YOUR FAULT

*Remember, no one can make you feel inferior
without your consent.*

—ELEANOR ROOSEVELT

Vinh Giang, an international keynote speaker, magician, and communication coach, didn't own his opportunity for years. To step into his gift, he didn't just have to break through his personal barriers and inner voices, he had to override the expectations of his parents and community. He had been working at one of Australia's Big Four accounting firms. All his friends were accountants, lawyers, and doctors, so he followed that path; it's what was expected of him. But every day after work, he performed magic for different departments and loved it. He'd been at the firm for five years when one of the partners saw him perform and called him into his office. The partner told him, "Two things will happen in six months. One, I will fire you, or two, you can quit."

Vinh was shocked. He feared he'd been distracting the workers. That he hadn't been focused enough on his own responsibilities. He conjured up reasons for his dismissal, only to find out that none of them were true. Vinh's boss had called him into his office not to destroy Vinh's opportunity, but to help him own it. His boss recognized Vinh's unique gift because he had given up on his own decades before.

A man in his mid-seventies, Vinh's boss walked around with his left hand in his pocket but never said why. That day, for the first time, he pulled his hand out of his pocket and shared his story with Vinh.

"The biggest love of my life was piano; I gave it up at thirty-five to build this firm. I've never played piano again. I had the opportunity to travel and play with orchestras worldwide, but I gave it up, which was a mistake."

Hearing the pain and regret in his boss's voice shook Vinh to his core.

Vinh's boss had kept his hand hidden due to arthritis; a physically and emotionally painful reminder of the path not taken. He told Vinh, "You are on the wrong career path. You would make an amazing accountant but are not meant to be one."

Vinh could finally see his opportunity within reach, but he had another, potentially more challenging hurdle to conquer. He looked up and asked, "Do you mind telling my dad the same thing?"[2]

That one conversation with his boss changed the trajectory of Vinh's life. That, and when his boss went to dinner with Vinh's family to help them see something they hadn't because they'd been too afraid. *Afraid* because they didn't know another path to success.

Vinh's parents escaped Vietnam in 1979 and spent two years on Refugee Island before landing in Australia. They faced adversity and financial pressure, and they craved safety and certainty to survive. His parents supported Vinh in the end, but it took many conversations. Vinh was the only one in his community wanting to do something different from the template of doctor/lawyer/accountant. Vinh wanted to make his parents happy but couldn't fake his own happiness any longer. He finally expressed his sadness and the suffering he held deep inside. "In that moment, I realized there was so much beauty in not hiding your true emotions from your family. My parents finally realized, 'We didn't escape war to trap our son. We wanted to give our son the freedom to fly, not clip his wings.'"

As Onlys, there will be barriers that aren't our fault. Like Vinh, we need to see there's nothing wrong with us, but there may be deeper challenges to navigate. Vinh didn't just break through his own internal wall but had to chip away at a much larger cultural one. It wasn't until his boss forced his hand and advocated for Vinh that he could step into the possibility.

For some, these challenges may be cultural; you may have a language barrier or be restricted by cultural norms. Maybe you are ruled by family values or parental expectations, like Vinh. Others may face economic or social barriers that can limit access to opportunities. Systemic injustices like discrimination and gender inequality can also play a role. It's important to recognize your true value and realize that there's not always something to fix or prove.

> **It's important to recognize your true value and realize that there's not always something to fix or prove.**

Sometimes, you may feel a bit exhausted and feel like no matter how hard you try, it's not enough or there's another level to break through. It may take longer to own your opportunities than others if they don't have to overcome the same hurdles you do. These obstacles can slow you down, but you don't have to let them stop you. To own our opportunity, we first need to take a deeper look at where these external and internal barriers come from and what is ours to carry.

EXTERNAL BARRIERS EXIST

Even if we see what is possible for ourselves, people may tell us it's not. They may be well-meaning, like Vinh's parents, but others may not have our best intentions at heart. It could also be that bigger-picture systems and environmental factors make things difficult.

While explicit and systemic discrimination can't necessarily be measured, it *does* exist. A 2023 Monster poll found "an overwhelming 91% of workers said they have experienced discrimination in the workplace. Likewise, 77% said they have witnessed an act of discrimination at work. Workplace discrimination, of course, can take many forms and can stem from a number of conscious and unconscious biases related to age, race, gender, sexual orientation, even a person's physical appearance, name, or accent."[3]

According to the 2023 Women in the Workplace report by McKinsey & Company, women—especially women of color—remain underrepresented in corporate fields. Progress is even slower in middle management. In a typical company, men end up holding 60 percent of manager-level positions, while women hold just 40 percent. As a result, there are fewer women to promote to director, and the number of women decreases at every subsequent level. The data also shows that women experience more microaggressions than men and are "twice as likely to be interrupted and hear comments on their emotional state. For women with traditionally marginalized identities, these slights happen more often and are even more demeaning." This leads to more stress and can create more barriers. Women are four times more likely to almost always feel burned out and three times more likely to think about leaving their companies.[4]

It's important to be aware of potential barriers so you can navigate your environment realistically; however, you shouldn't let these statistics—or the people who perpetuate them—dominate your headspace. If you allow the negative or limited perspectives of others to control your thoughts, it can control your potential, drain your motivation, stifle your creativity, and affect your overall well-being.

OVERCOMING INTERNAL BARRIERS

Besides contending with the *external* barriers that many Onlys face, we also need to overcome many *internal* barriers that keep us from owning our opportunities. I've interviewed and coached thousands of executives, celebrities, entrepreneurs, and everyday people, and you know what I've learned?

We are not alone. Most of us struggle with the same things.

As a coach, I work with men and women of different ages, backgrounds, and industries, and while each person's experience has nuance, many of the barriers we are trying to break through are more similar than you may think. Once you peel off the masks and filters, we all have limiting beliefs and insecurities that, unfortunately, hold us back from our true potential. We are all human, and at our core, most of us are asking the same question: *Am I enough?*

However, unlike most people, being an Only means that those negative inner voices may be a bit louder, the barriers a bit harder to break through, and challenges a bit more complicated to overcome. Whether you're an obvious Only or an Only striving to break new ground, challenge the status quo, or disrupt entrenched industries or beliefs, you're likely to encounter additional obstacles. When these challenges are reinforced by stereotypes, societal norms, and media portrayals, overcoming them can be even more daunting.

I was coaching two men and one woman for their radio show, videos, and media interviews. When I listened to their show, I thought the woman (let's call her Jen) was quite good. She had a strong voice, sounded credible, and was the most relatable out of the group. One of the men

(Scott) was personable, energetic, and just wanted to be better. The older man (Michael) had a powerful voice but used a lot of business jargon and was not connecting with the audience. In Jen's presession questionnaire, she expressed that she felt like she sounded too young and was not as experienced and credible as her male counterparts.

During our group session, these barriers kept coming up for Jen. She would get nervous and apologize, saying, "Sorry, I don't sound as good." When her cohosts and I reinforced that she was doing great, she was surprised to hear it. Surprisingly enough, Jen's barrier wasn't that she was the only woman of the group; it was that she was the youngest. Where did this internal barrier that told her she was too young to be good come from?

Although awareness is the first step, we also need to think about where our beliefs come from and how they shape our actions and reactions.

After spending some time together, I discovered that Jen was not only the youngest in the company, but she was also the youngest in her family. She was reliving a pattern from her childhood. Jen had put a lot of pressure on herself to measure up to her two overachieving sisters, and she didn't realize how this pattern impacted her confidence and self-awareness as an adult at work. She was succeeding at the company yet still felt like she had to prove herself. Jen didn't need to fix anything, but she did need to recognize this self-imposed barrier and reaffirm that she already had everything necessary to be heard and respected. Like Jen, we need to take a deeper look at the source of our internal barriers.

Let's use Jen as inspiration and pause for a moment. Internal barriers can be deep and hard to reach, but they don't have to be. Take a quick look at this list of common internal barriers and see if you relate to at least one. If so, you get to claim an early win, because being able to *identify* a barrier is the only way you can start to break through it. We'll have more opportunities to reflect in exercises to come, but for now, check any of the following universal internal barriers that you relate to, at any level.

- Fear of Failure/Rejection
- Limiting Beliefs
- Procrastination
- Perfectionism
- Negative Self-Talk

Bearing in mind what you related to most, remember that we are constantly overloaded with external messages from our family, media, and society. They can be direct messages or subtle cues, and over time, some of us start to internalize them, shaping our belief system about ourselves and the world around us. If we don't override negative internal messages, they are reinforced until we don't even realize we have these barriers or know where they came from.

Stepping into the Power of the Only means not letting these barriers control you.

Not internalizing these barriers as a personal flaw.

Not letting anything stop you from breaking through what *is* in your control.

Although awareness is the first step, we also need to think about where our beliefs come from and how they shape our actions and reactions. Do they come from your family or your culture? Are they messages reinforced by societal norms, your environment, and/or the media?

When what was once invisible becomes visible, you have the power to shift these barriers rather than be controlled by them.

When you understand what you can control and what you cannot, you have more agency to access your full power and move forward. When what was once invisible becomes visible, you have the power to shift these barriers rather than be controlled by them.

LIMITING FAMILY AND CULTURAL BARRIERS

Vinh's reluctance to own his opportunity came from cultural pressure and his desire to respect his parents and honor their sacrifices, even if that meant giving up his dream. Some of Jen's limiting beliefs about being too young came from her childhood and were reinforced at work. Sometimes, these limiting external messages can lead to internal barriers that take away our power and hinder our ability to move forward and act.

Cultural and familial messages play a major role in shaping beliefs, values, and behavior. These messages are powerful because we hear them from an early age, they come from people we love and trust, and they are usually reinforced by our community. If these messages include limiting or conflicting beliefs, they can negatively affect how we view ourselves and our capabilities, instill fear of rejection, and lead to internal barriers.

LACK OF REPRESENTATION AND ROLE MODELS

As a child and young adult, I was used to not seeing myself represented anywhere. Whether it was on TV (other than Connie Chung, of course), in magazines, or my dolls, I never saw myself reflected.

I had exactly two dolls growing up. A Pretty Curls doll and a *Charlie's Angels* doll, both with blonde hair and blue eyes. I *loved* my Pretty Curls doll; she came with curlers and fake perm solution (I know, so '80s!), and I would take her everywhere. She was my best friend and my form of expression.

Even my Halloween costumes were blonde. My earliest Halloween memory was dressing up as Holly Hobbie. The plastic costume came with a face mask complete with golden locks and freckles. It's no wonder I used to daydream about having blonde hair and blue eyes; it's all I knew.

I didn't even truly realize there were other options for representation until much later. Today, there are more diverse representations in the media and even multidimensional characters who are not stereotypes and cliches, but that wasn't the case for so many of us.

We all want to be seen and heard. I know I did. But what you see affects who you want to be and how you think you're *supposed* to be, and when you don't see yourself, it can impact what you believe is possible. It's like you didn't know there was a void until you see yourself reflected and then realize what you've been missing all along. That's why we must all pay attention to how representation can affect our perceptions and shape our individual and collective experiences. The role models we see in leadership, from the workplace to our community, also send messages about what we can and cannot be and how comfortable we are in stepping into those roles.

Deepa Purushothaman, founder of the re.write, an unconventional think tank, was one of the youngest people and the first Indian American woman to make partner at Deloitte, a global consulting firm. She was also the US managing partner of WIN, the firm's renowned Women's Initiative.

"I was very young. I was an Indian woman, and I was little at 5'1". All the things that others thought what power looks like, what a partner looks like, was very different than what I was."[5] To step into her leadership opportunity, she had to overcome her own barriers and programming and others' perceptions of her.

When she first made partner at the firm, Deepa met with a new client who later asked one of Deepa's colleagues, "Why does she look at her feet when she introduces herself as a partner?" Deepa didn't realize that she had not internally transitioned to seeing herself as a leader. Becoming a partner at a firm like Deloitte was a big deal; being an owner of the company was a huge milestone. "I didn't believe it myself. I had seen all these partners in my mind; they were so senior, so wise." Deepa had to work on putting that limiting belief aside. "It's embarrassing to say, but I would have to practice looking in the mirror saying, 'I'm a partner.'" As she rose higher on the senior ladder, Deepa stepped up to the role, set the tone, and told people, "I'm the one in charge."

Growing up, Deepa felt different but still believed she could do anything. She was the only girl playing on the boys' soccer team until college, and neither her coaches nor her parents put any limitations on her. However, it still took time to override cultural and gender norms to find her voice and authority as a leader because she never saw role models who looked like her. She could believe in herself all she wanted, but internalization of those beliefs still took time. Deepa eventually embraced her leadership role, but a turning point came when she realized there wasn't a perfect example of leadership for her to follow or relate to, so she decided to create her own path. "I wrote myself an email saying this is the kind of leader I want to be. It was a conscious effort. I realized, 'I didn't have to see it to be it.' I even taped the saying to my desk and would really tell myself that."

Gina Gomez, founder and CEO of Arista Management Group, says that when growing up, she rarely saw Mexicans in the media. Gina loved singing and did musical theater in college but didn't have the nerve to audition for the big roles. "I never even gave myself the opportunity. I wonder if I had grown up seeing more representation if I would have thought differently." Even when she did finally see someone who looked like her, it was in the stereotypical role of a housekeeper. "I didn't really see a lot of representation, and I didn't even know it was a thing because we were taught through media, society, and discrimination that there was this unspoken list of so-called opportunities to choose from."[6]

Sociologist and pop culture expert Nancy Wang Yuen, PhD, immigrated to the United States at five years old, and her first cultural teacher was the television. She says that not seeing yourself represented on screen can affect your self-esteem. "Researchers surveyed a group of Black and White boys and girls in the Midwest over one year and found with every hour of television they watch, their self-esteem goes down— except with the White boys, their self-esteem actually goes up." Nancy points out that the leads and heroes living the good life on television were usually White men. "Audiences identify with the leads, and if you are not represented well or at all, you won't be able to dream. It's hard to be something you can't see."[7]

Assistant Professor Nicole Martins from Indiana University conducted the study and says, "The women's roles were limited and almost always one-dimensional and focused on the success they have because of how they look, not what they do or what they think or how they got there." She says that Black boys were often criminalized in many programs. "Young Black boys are getting the opposite message: that there are not lots of good things that you can aspire to."[8]

This research reinforced Nancy Wang Yuen's experience of not being reflected on television as a child; however, representation later in life greatly affected her. "I didn't have any Asian teachers until college. That's why I wanted to become a professor because I had a Chinese American woman as my sociology professor. It would have never crossed my mind before I saw her." To Nancy, representation in all forms matters. "As an immigrant kid who didn't speak English and then majored in English literature, then became a sociology professor that taught about the society she immigrated to and adopted as her own, [it] reflects the power of showing up."

Not just physical role models positively change perceptions; being reminded of a group's achievement can counteract the effect of negative stereotypes. Psychologists from Texas Christian University found that college women did better on a difficult math test just by reading about other women who were successful in architecture, law, medicine, and invention.[9] Exposure to positive role models can influence aspirations, confidence, and whether people own their opportunities.

HOW THESE INTERNAL BARRIERS LIMIT US

These messages and the stereotypes don't just stay in your head. These internal barriers can subconsciously cause stress, anxiety, and poor performance, sabotaging our chances to own our opportunity. Social psychologists Claude M. Steele and Joshua Aronson first defined this phenomenon as "stereotype threat," or "an individual's fear that their actions and behaviors will support negative ideas about a group to which they belong."[10] Basically, it means that being aware of a stereotype can cause you to mess up or not do as well at a task. Steele and Aronson's study was in response to the racial stereotype that Black students were "less intelligent" than White students. The study tested the idea of how Black students would perform based on what they were told about an exam. The findings confirmed this hypothesis; when the test was framed as a measure of intellectual ability, the students underperformed. However, when the test was described as nondiagnostic, the students performed just as well as their peers.[11]

Since this inaugural study, hundreds of others have revealed how stereotype threat can be the result of negative stereotyping against any aspect of identity, from ethnicity, culture, gender, age, and more.

Women are not good at math.[12]
Women are not good at negotiating.[13]
Men aren't good at social sensitivity.[14]
Men can't read nonverbal cues well.[15]
Older adults aren't as capable cognitively.[16]

Each of these stereotypes can have a lasting impact on confidence, concentration, and ability, leading to a lack of confidence, doubt, and a disengaged attitude. This negative behavior, in turn, causes a "self-fulfilling prophecy," where those trying to avoid it end up living up to the negative stereotype.[17]

Some studies reveal that being the only woman in a group can impact self-perception.[18] A study led by Johannes Keller from the University of Michigan found that performance dropped when a woman thought she was the only one in the group. This was partly because the women started to see themselves as individuals and less as part of the group. The *feeling* of being alone and standing out as the only woman can make women focus more on their individual identity and can negatively affect their performance; even if something isn't true, it can become true because of our response. When you feel like you don't belong[19] or expend mental energy worrying about your skills, talent, or capabilities, you don't have as much left to reach your full potential. That is, unless we shift our thinking and see that we are not alone in our challenges.

Gregory Walton (Yale University) and Geoffrey Cohen (Stanford University) wanted to see if they could help students overcome "belonging uncertainty," where people felt unsure about their social connections and whether they fit in. They studied a group of college students after their stressful first year and found that despite facing similar issues, Black students felt less confident about being accepted and succeeding and bad days had a bigger impact on them than White students. Sharing stories with the Black students about others' college challenges and how that doubting one's belonging was widespread and not contained to members of a particular group helped the students overcome the uncertainty of belonging.

Walton and Cohen also used stats to reinforce "with time and effort, most students come to feel they belong." Cohen said these stories and stats turned uncertainty into a "basis of connection rather than shame," and once the students saw their struggles through a different lens, they were "psychologically more ready to embrace the opportunities in school."[20] Colleges and universities have been using this "intervention" not just for minority groups, but for anyone struggling with belonging. Rather than using shared experience or precedent as a reason to turn away from opportunity, acknowledging that it's not all your fault and that you are not alone in your struggles can help you overcome inner barriers and own your opportunity.

SOMETIMES OUR INTERNAL BARRIERS ARE INHERITED

Dr. Valerie Rein, psychologist and author of *Patriarchy Stress Disorder: The Invisible Inner Barrier to Women's Happiness and Fulfillment*, says, "We need to stop thinking that there is something wrong with us." She's worked with hundreds of high-achieving women who have checked all the boxes yet keep running into an inner wall. "It's important to recognize there are invisible, unrecognized traumas in our lives. And the adaptations that developed to protect us form an invisible inner prison and can hold us back from living a full and thriving life."[21] Her work is focused on women but maintains this is a human experience. Until we start to see, understand, and befriend these protective mechanisms, or "prison guards," that keep us safe, we will keep getting stuck on the same hamster wheel.

Dr. Valerie also asserts that these traumas aren't always conventional. She explored the science of epigenetics, the study of how behaviors and environment can cause changes that affect how genes work.[22] She reviewed studies showing that trauma adaptations can be genetically transmitted across generations. "Studies found that the children of Holocaust survivors had inherited traits associated with the stress response of their parents."[23] Some experiences may be recorded and passed down through DNA, and we don't even know we are affected and holding ourselves back.

An even more fascinating experiment on mice found that subsequent generations could inherit trauma, not in response to genocide or war, but to mild electric shocks paired with the smell of cherry blossoms.[24] According to this study, the offspring became anxious and fearful when exposed to the smell. When the mice bred again and were exposed, it elicited the same anxiety in that generation, too. There is a lot of debate on this topic in the scientific community, but whatever you believe, evidence exists that previous generations can impact the next.

HOW TO BREAK THROUGH YOUR INTERNAL BARRIERS

This may seem like *a lot* of barriers to overcome, but by recognizing and understanding them, you have already reduced their impact. Just as research supports the fact that these barriers can impact you, it also supports that knowing is half the battle.[25]

Psychologists from the University of Arizona found that teaching people about "stereotype threat" can help them overcome internal barriers and perform to their potential. For example, in their study, women generally did worse than men on a math test when they believed it was a measure of their math ability. However, when they were told about stereotype threat and the anxiety it might cause, they did better than women who didn't make this connection. Those who knew about stereotype threat managed and externalized their anxiety by attributing it to external stereotypes like "women aren't good at math" rather than personal inadequacy. Researchers say this can be a practical tool for improving performance for different groups and in a variety of areas.

As I will continue to reinforce, awareness is the first step to controlling your life and harnessing your opportunity.

And *that* is your power.

Once you have acknowledged the barriers in your life—internal, external, or both—you can create your own story.

You don't have to accept what has come before. It's time to challenge the status quo and redefine power and success on your own terms.

EXERCISE

You likely owned at least one internal barrier earlier in the chapter; reflect on it/them and take some time to consider where your barriers came from and how they affect your life. Allow yourself to sit with these, as your answers will get deeper each time you return to the exercise. To start, even just a single phrase or sentence is a win.

Here are a few reflection questions to ask yourself to get things going:

- What is my negative self-talk—the most common negative messages I tell myself?
- Where do my internal barriers and negative inner voices come from?
- What voices come up for me when I'm under stress or pressure?
- Did these voices once serve me?
- Are these messages and voices still serving me?
- What can I say to myself instead?

When you recognize that you are not alone in facing barriers and struggles, know what's in your control, and have taken some time to reflect on your barriers, you are well on your way to owning your opportunities as an Only. In the next chapter, we'll explore how to *reframe* your challenges to fully own these opportunities.

REFRAME YOUR CHALLENGES AS POWER

Storms make trees take deeper roots.

—DOLLY PARTON

Farnoosh Torabi, financial expert and author of *A Healthy State of Panic*, had an overdose of fear as a child instilled by her Iranian immigrant parents. She didn't take many risks or have much fun. Despite her career success, this fear continued to shape her story, even into her thirties. As the female breadwinner, Farnoosh did well and had enough to support her family, but she stayed small. Her fear told her doing more and having more would come at a huge cost, so she cut herself off from her ambition; that is, until she realized the voices in her head weren't hers.

Then, she started to reframe her story.

Going from "'It's enough' to 'My being richer will make the world a better place' . . . [To] benefit my community, my children, my children's children. It's important."

Today, she sees fear as her superpower. Farnoosh believes fear gives you a healthy dose of adrenaline, and when it shows up, it's there to tell a story, teach you something, and help you do the hard things. "Inherited fears from the external world are not my fear, and now I have the choice to rewrite the narrative."[26] What once seemed to be challenges in her life are now her power.

> **We Onlys may have taken on barriers from society, our families, and the media; however, we have the agency to control what we take in, what we keep, and what we let go of.**

Farnoosh shared that she wasn't just an Only, but always the new girl too. Her family moved for her father's different work opportunities, and every three to five years she would have to make new friends, find ways to assimilate, and learn to read the room. While she didn't love it when she was young, she says, "It completely made me who I am. I can walk into a room and not know anybody and I can be the only woman in the room and I'm okay with it."[27]

As an Only, owning your opportunity starts with acknowledging that you may face barriers beyond your control. Then, you must reframe your challenges as power. Reframing your challenges is shifting your perspective, honoring your past, and embracing all your experiences as stepping stones to growth and empowerment. Recognizing the valuable role fear played in Farnoosh's life, instead of seeing it as something to overcome, enabled her to embrace it. Reframing her fear helped her tap into her power to shift it and fully step into current opportunities.

We Onlys may have taken on barriers from society, our families, and the media; however, we have the agency to control what we take in, what we keep, and what we let go of. To reframe your challenges as power, mine your past challenges for insights, honor your history and the challenges it presents, and embrace those challenges fully to own your opportunities and move forward with abundance and power.

MINE YOUR PAST CHALLENGES

When Emmy Award–winning TV show creator Dave Noll walks into a room to pitch, he appears to fit right into the Hollywood scene. He has created and sold more than 200 television series, including over 1,000 episodes of the *Chopped* franchise. He has shows on networks from the Food Network to Fox, has worked with dozens of celebrities, and even pitched shows on yachts in Cannes, France.

Despite all this success, Dave has felt like an Only in many ways, from his background to his creative ideas. "At VH1 and MTV, I started as an intern and worked my way up to producer, but I was the only one always pitching new shows, even though I wasn't in development." Dave jokes, "I'm a kid from Nowheresville, New Jersey. I used to joke you needed to pass thirty-eight farms and then make a left and pass twenty-four more and go over a hill to get to my town, and now I'm just a suburban dorky dad type with hit TV shows."[28] Dave grew up with limited resources and said, "My childhood was not filled with money. I remember the special coupon thing that I brought to school for free lunch. I deeply remember government cheese." Dave's simple upbringing gave him the tenacity to be successful in TV and shaped the theme of his life: persistence despite failure. To Dave, the key to owning his opportunities is doing the work and never letting go of his wonder and fire. "I think it helps because that kid is still inside me. So even on day thirty of filming on the Paramount lot, I was still like 'This is so amazing!'" The author of *The Visionary in Charge,* he believes you can bring your vision to life too.

I'll say it again: What was once your obstacle can be your greatest strength. Dave's not fitting into the norm, learning how to navigate being the Only at times, and not having much available to him shaped his creativity and tenacity, which are now the secrets to his success. We need to see these gifts in our lives, but sometimes, it takes time to fully unwrap them.

Start by identifying them in your life. Did you face a challenge as a child that, through learning to navigate it, made you stronger? Was there a challenge you faced that you wanted to wish away but have since realized was the reason for your success?

If you grew up in a low-income household or had limited resources like Dave, that likely helped you to fuel your drive and tenacity, understand the value of a dollar, and see the power of hard work. Or maybe you were the oldest sibling and felt the burden of taking care of others but now are a resourceful and caring leader. Perhaps you were forced to move around, like Farnoosh, but now are incredibly resilient and easily navigate new situations. Maybe you faced discrimination but now have deep empathy, understanding, and know how to advocate for others. You may have spent a lot of time alone, but it probably helped you foster independence, self-reliance, and creative thinking.

Once you better understand what your challenges are, you can embrace them by honoring your past. How can you reframe a challenge as a power?

Challenges	Possibilities
Moved often	Adaptable
Faced discrimination	Empathetic and open-minded
Only child	Independent
Rejection	Resilient
Financial struggles	Resourcefulness
Anxiety	Awareness and understanding

HONOR YOUR PAST

I sat in the living room of my childhood home with tears in my eyes. My parents were across from me, saying, "*Me guan xi; Me guan xi*" ("Don't worry about it") and trying to change the subject. I had just told them I was sorry. In my family, apologizing doesn't come naturally, so this was uncomfortable for all of us.

"I'm sorry for not fully seeing you and not acknowledging how smart, powerful, and brave you and Mom were when I was younger. I always felt like I had to take care of things and translate for you. I would blame you. I'm sorry if I ever made you feel less than. Thank you for everything you have done for me."

"It's okay, you didn't make us feel that way," they replied.

"I needed to tell you how much I appreciate you even if I didn't always show it," I said.

We hugged for a moment then quickly moved on from the discomfort. To some of you, this may seem like a normal conversation, but for me—born and raised Chinese—it was monumental. My family didn't talk about our feelings when I was growing up, and we *certainly* didn't hug. My parents showed love in many ways, but physical affection wasn't one of them. This was a pivotal moment in my life and a first step in honoring my past.

I was thirty years old and had just come back from my first-ever personal development weekend. I was a rising reporter in Los Angeles building a life. I thought I had it all figured out. Life was perfect.

It wasn't until my boyfriend—who is now my husband—suggested I go to the development weekend. He had a great experience when he attended, and it helped heal both himself and his family. Until then, I had never been to therapy, read any self-help books, or done anything like that. I thought he was crazy.

"I'm on TV and in the public eye," I said. "I'm not going to go talk about myself and my problems."

He convinced me to go anyway.

That weekend was the first time I realized just how *much* I had been holding on to subconsciously. I realized I had been hiding behind my exterior success and achievement. I was so busy working that I never spent time reflecting on my past and honoring what it gave me. I had spent most of my early years wanting to move far away from my simple upbringing and blaming it for any barriers in my adult life.

When I was young, I wanted to be *less* Chinese and *more* American, whatever that meant. Growing up, I was told I had a flat Asian face. I would stand in front of the mirror wishing I had bigger eyes. I'd pinch my nose and wish I had a taller nose bridge. I spoke Chinese at home but never in public. My parents spoke English, but as the eldest daughter, I still acted as their translator for important documents and the "American" way of life from a very early age. I had to explain sleepovers, Santa Claus, and other societal traditions so I could be like everyone else. I wanted my parents to be "normal."

I wanted to be "normal."

That one self-reflective weekend made me realize how selfish I was for not seeing the full spectrum of my parents and my life. Deep inside, I still held that childhood feeling of being the only one and not having a "normal" life and "normal parents." By high school, I overcame many of these internal barriers and was comfortable in my skin, but I subconsciously hid parts of myself in college and early in my career. I still felt the burden of having to take on so many things at a young age because my parents couldn't or didn't know how.

When I finally realized this inner reality, I felt ashamed.

How dare I think that way about my parents? My parents are not weak, helpless, or clueless; my background is nothing to hide. I didn't give them credit for all that they went through. Imagine moving to a new country where you didn't speak the language, leaving all your friends and family behind, and completely starting over. Even working low-paying jobs, my parents managed to raise two kids, buy a home, help put us through college, and build a good life.

That is power, strength, and resilience.

Their challenges passed down to me are my strength, and my challenges are my power. Honoring their power for the first time marked the beginning of acknowledging and reframing my own struggles. Today, I fully embrace all parts of myself: my culture, my upbringing, my past, and my challenges. Although I no longer hide, deeper layers of my authenticity continue to unfold. With age, I've gained a new perspective on the past, but it's been a journey filled with self-reflection, healing, difficult conversations, letting go, and grace.

It was one weekend that initiated my personal journey, but it takes time to peel away the layers clouding our self-perception, what we are capable of, and what is possible. We all have things in our lives that we blame instead of honor. We may carry burdens from our past, our families, and even our ancestors that don't serve us. Being limited by the past comes from a mindset of scarcity, where we cling to old stories—often not even our own—that trap us in a cycle of doubt and fear. These stories convince us that we're not enough, that what we have will never be enough, or that whatever good we experience is fleeting. This mindset blinds us to the possibilities in front of us, making it hard to see all that life offers.

Keynote speaker, technology strategist, and futurist Crystal Washington says her past is a source of strength. "When you know who you are, people can't shake you."[29] She is the keeper of her family's history and has traced it back hundreds of years to her fifth-generation grandmother. "Some of my family members founded part of this country; I come from people with grit and a tough stock of women." Crystal grew up in a predominately Black neighborhood and then moved to a very diverse area of Houston, Texas, but in her early career days, she was often the only woman and person of color. To her, honoring all parts of herself and being grounded in her history allows her to stay true to herself and own her opportunities. "To be secure in a space where you are an Only, you have to understand that you're not just an Only." While you may not know your full ancestral history like Crystal, you can still embrace all parts of your story and challenges.

Reframing our challenges is *crucial*. By shifting our perspective, we can break free from limiting beliefs of the past and start to fully embrace and appreciate the present. It allows us to recognize the gifts and opportunities we once overlooked and feel empowered to create a future filled with growth, gratitude, and abundance.

By shifting our perspective, we can break free from limiting beliefs of the past and start to fully embrace and appreciate the present.

I may have grown up with a scarcity mindset and a bit of fear, but that made me resilient and resourceful. I now believe I can figure anything out, make something out of nothing, and always find a good deal (thanks, Mom! ☺). All the things I resented or may have been ashamed of are what shaped me and are now my power. Being bilingual, translating for my parents, and navigating two cultures has given me deep empathy, awareness, and connections to those around me. I know how to navigate a room, see what others can't see, and ensure no one gets left behind.

That is my superpower.

That is why I do what I do, why I'm a communication coach, and why I want to see you shine. No one should make you feel inferior—certainly not yourself.

EMBRACE YOUR CHALLENGES

I met the founder of CAULIPOWER, who disrupted the $5 billion US pizza market with her gluten-free cauliflower pizza crust, at SXSW.

Growing up, Gail Becker felt different in every way. Her parents were divorced, which was uncommon in her community. Her parents are European but spoke a different language at home with different accents. Her mom worked when most moms stayed home. She felt compelled to explain every detail about her family, but this was made even more challenging by Gail's stuttering. For Gail, "the stuttering was probably a symptom of feeling a little out of place or a little different and not having the maturity to know that's okay."[30]

Gail navigated the worlds of journalism, politics, corporate life, and the entertainment industry, well aware of what it meant to be an Only. But when she entered the competitive food manufacturing industry as an outsider—without any food experience and as one of the few women in the field—she faced what became one of the most challenging and rewarding journeys of her life. People told her no and called her crazy so many times that she almost believed it. But instead of giving in, she reframed her challenge as a source of power, transforming obstacles into opportunities.

"It took me a little while to say, 'I'm going to use that underestimation as a superpower. I'm going to bet they are going to underestimate me, and then I'm going to go in and kill it in that category while no one thinks it's possible.' And that's basically what we did." The hypergrowth company's revenue reached more than $100 million in five years under Gail's leadership as CEO and was named one of the Top 10 World's Most Innovative Food Companies in 2022 (by *Fast Company*.) "Nobody saw us coming, nobody knew who we were, nobody knew who *I* was, and they underestimated the potential for an outsider to do something like this."

Gail redefined her barriers, transforming them from obstacles into strengths. She had felt like an outsider as a child, but as an entrepreneur, it became her competitive advantage. Instead of seeing her uniqueness as a weakness, she embraced it as a powerful asset that set her apart in the industry. Her outsider perspective allowed her to approach challenges with fresh ideas and a boldness that others lacked. By shifting her mindset,

Gail didn't just overcome her barriers, she leveraged them to carve out her own path to success, proving that what once made her feel isolated could be the very thing to propel her forward. "Sometimes being an outsider helps you think about something really differently, even though the experts told me it couldn't be done. It obviously could be done."

Although it took time to reframe her challenges as sources of strength, the turning point in Gail's career was learning to be comfortable in her own skin and celebrate every part of herself. Embracing even the smallest details, like her signature curly hair, became a symbolic act of reclaiming her power. By accepting and loving herself fully, she transformed her perceived flaws into features of confidence, allowing her to step into her true power and thrive in every aspect of her career. "I grew up straightening my hair because I wanted to be like everyone else. It wasn't until I started CAULIPOWER that I began letting my hair be its natural curly self and I never went back. Maybe there's a metaphor in there."

By embracing your challenges or what you once viewed as roadblocks, you too can step more fully into your true self. This shift not only cultivates a more positive and resilient mindset but also empowers you to own your opportunity with confidence and perseverance. The process of enduring and overcoming these challenges reveals your true capabilities, fostering a sense of self-assurance and strength. By appreciating your struggles, setbacks, and barriers, you transform them into powerful lessons that fuel your growth. This mindset allows you to continuously learn, evolve, and thrive, ensuring that you not only recognize but also fully own the opportunities that come your way. In doing so, you become the architect of your own success, turning every challenge into a stepping stone so that you can continue to own your opportunities.

HEALING THE PAST, PRESENT, AND FUTURE

I believe that what you do now affects not just your own life but also future generations. But what if this work was also for your ancestors and for your entire lineage?

Some philosophies suggest that our actions can influence up to seven generations in both directions, a concept rooted in ancient Iroquois wisdom. The Seven Generation Principle[31] involves thinking seven generations ahead and seeing how what we do today will impact the future. By reframing our challenges as sources of power, we can honor our past, heal the present, and lay the foundation for a resilient and abundant future for generations. Embracing the wisdom and strength within us— as well as that which is passed down through generations—allows us to break old cycles and forge new patterns and behaviors, creating a positive legacy for generations to come.

According to Carlfred Broderick, a marriage and family scholar at the University of Southern California, research shows that we can play a role in healing and changing patterns. Passing down negative traits from generation to generation is not inevitable, and Broderick coined the term "transitional character" to address this phenomenon. "A 'transitional character' is one who, in a single generation, changes the entire course of a lineage. . . . They break the mold. . . . Their contribution to humanity is to filter the destructiveness out of their own lineage so that the generations downstream will have a supportive foundation upon which to build productive lives."[32]

However you feel about the Iroquois philosophy or not, the impact of reframing your challenges as power can have ripple effects in the world around you. Whether your goal is to transform the world or simply to make these changes for yourself, recognizing your influence and potential on the future is crucial. Embracing this perspective empowers you to make a meaningful impact, harnessing your challenges to drive positive change and shape a more powerful future.

EXERCISE

Reframing your challenges as power involves shifting your perspective to see them in a more positive light. Here are a few strategies and reflection questions to help you.

STRATEGY 1: FIND THE SILVER LINING

First, reflect on past challenges: What are three challenges you've faced in your life? Jot down the ones that come to mind first.

Next, look for the potential benefits or opportunities that came from those challenges: What did you gain from navigating these situations? Did you learn anything new (a skill, lesson, or insight)?

STRATEGY 2: PRACTICE GRATITUDE

Start by reflecting again on a challenge you've experienced. Now, ask yourself what you are grateful for because of setbacks you've experienced.

STRATEGY 3: TRY THE OPPOSITE

Counter your habitual thoughts: What is the opposite of a negative belief or self-talk about a certain challenge you've had as an Only? Give yourself the chance to question negative thoughts and imagine the opposite is true. Does something open up and allow you to reframe things?

SEE BEING AN ONLY AS AN OPPORTUNITY, NOT A BURDEN

*I don't have a place where I belong, and that
means I belong everywhere.*

—TREVOR NOAH

I met Carla Harris, a senior client advisor at Morgan Stanley, backstage when we spoke at a conference. Her powerful, poetic words, magnetic confidence, and inspiring pearls of leadership wisdom captivated me. An international public speaker and author, Carla's had a lot of victories but also some personal missteps, and she vowed that when she reached senior management, she would help lift up others. "We are blessed so that we can be a blessing to others."[33]

Carla and I have talked about how being an Only is not a weakness but our greatest strength. When Carla hears people say, "But I'm the only one!" she tells them that it's an honor and a privilege to be the Only. "I will try to make their experience so fabulous that they will ascribe whatever that is to the next person that looks like me." Carla believes in using that leverage as your power.

Like Carla, I believe a significant part of owning your opportunity is not viewing being the Only as a burden. "If you're the only one who looks like you in the room, you're the only one who looks like you in the room!" Carla said. "It's a major asset. You don't have to vie for attention. When you speak, everybody will look, and all you have to do is deliver your excellence right into the opportunity."

Not all Onlys may want to take on this responsibility. You may be tired of trying, tired of showing up, or tired of shifting the status quo alone.

I understand.

Progress in society's efforts to make change in many areas is slow and often comes up short. That's why it's more important than ever to view being an Only not as a burden, but as a unique opportunity to create meaningful change. By embracing this perspective, we can leverage our distinct voices and experiences to affect change where it matters most.

BURDEN OR OPPORTUNITY?

For most of her life, Tricia Montalvo Timm struggled with being the Only. She is one of the few Latinas to have achieved the triple achievement of reaching the C-suite, joining the boardroom, and cracking the venture capital ceiling. She rose through the ranks of Silicon Valley and advised high-tech companies big and small, culminating in the sale of data analytics software company Looker to Google for $2.6 billion.

But early in her career, she just thought about the disadvantages of being an Only. She admits to being in victim mode, saying if someone else like her was in the room or was part of the majority, it would all be easier. Tricia saw being an Only as a burden and erased parts of herself. She would often pass as White because of her light skin and never talked about being a working mom. "Unfortunately, I was in rooms where I would hear comments and remarks that confirmed my belief people may not welcome me. So, I wouldn't talk about my family. I didn't put any attention to my difference as a Latina or as a parent."[34]

It took Tricia decades to realize how powerful it was to have a different perspective from everyone in the room. It wasn't until her late forties that she embraced her identity as a Latina woman and spoke for her company's Latinx resource group for National Hispanic Heritage Month. The day she finally told this full story and embraced her identity as an Only was a significant "Aha!" moment for her. "I literally went home that night and told my husband, 'Today, my life changed.' I had a lot of fear, the fear that I would be ostracized or kicked out of the 'club' for showing up fully, but that wasn't the case. I was not only welcomed by everybody, but more importantly, the impact that I had on the underrepresented employees at the company was something I didn't expect."

As the author of *Embrace the Power of You: Owning Your Identity at Work*, Tricia is on a mission to inspire anyone who has ever felt like an Only in the workplace to embrace their true self. She's an advocate for women and girls and serves as a mentor, advisor, and investor in female-founded companies and was selected as one of the 50 Women to Watch by 50/50 Women on Boards in 2023.

Like Tricia, you may see being an Only as a burden, or you may be burned out from being one and seeing little progress. Do you wonder why it's *your* responsibility to step up, explain yourself, and educate others? I often hear from Onlys about being disillusioned and tired of running into the same roadblocks.

The burden of belonging changed in 2020 when DEI (diversity, equity, and inclusion) initiatives became a top priority. This burden can include the additional pressure and responsibilities of being more visible; feeling like being an Only means having to represent their entire community. It can also mean downplaying aspects of identity to assimilate, facing isolation, having to teach others because peers don't understand, and more.

With the murder of George Floyd and the racial reckoning that followed, companies started investing more in people and programs. Leaders had been reassuring people that DEI efforts weren't just for show for years, but by 2023, many companies were hit with massive layoffs.

The first to be let go? Diversity professionals.

Now, with the increasing polarization and politicization of diversity issues, the original intent—to prevent discrimination and create more inclusive environments—seems to be lost. The burden has fallen back on the Onlys. However, it is not the time to stop owning our opportunities. I believe the very reasons some might view being an Only as a burden— such as not feeling like you fit in, being isolated, or facing discrimination and microaggressions—are the same reasons why it's more important than ever to own our opportunity and create change, not just for ourselves, but for others.

Once you are in a position to take a seat, share your voice, or show up, use it as an opportunity to make change possible for others.

We are at a crossroads right now. Amid divisiveness, pain, and upheaval in the world, whatever progress we've achieved in our lifetimes often seems at risk or even as if it's moving backward. True, not all Onlys have the same experiences, but it's important to recognize the impact you can make right now.

Having an Only in the room and fostering diverse perspectives are essential for effective decision-making, innovation, and preventing groupthink. *Groupthink* occurs when well-intentioned people make irrational or suboptimal decisions because they have a strong urge to conform, leading to not speaking up or raising alternative ideas, which then leads to a uniform way of thinking.[35] Diversity is not just about gender, race, and culture; it cuts across all facets of our lives and helps us survive and thrive.[36] Once you are in a position to take a seat, share your voice, or show up, use it as an opportunity to make change possible for others.

WHEN YOU ARE IN THE ROOM, YOU CAN SPEAK UP FOR YOURSELF AND OTHERS

In her book *Take Back Your Power*, Deb Liu, president and CEO of Ancestry, says, "When you are different than those around you, your point of view will often seem out of step with those of others. But that is precisely why it is so important."[37] Growing up Asian American in a small town in South Carolina, where fewer than 1 percent of people looked like her, Deb was used to being an Only. She spent her life hiding to avoid being singled out or bullied, but over the years, as she found her voice and grew as a leader, she learned that being different is a superpower.

During a fireside chat with a women's group I belong to, Deb shared stories about advocating for herself and her team and how she healed a contentious work relationship, one that she thought was unfixable.

Before becoming a CEO, Deb spent years on the leadership team at Facebook (now Meta). When her manager, one of her biggest allies, left the company, his replacement was someone who was always the "biggest voice" in the room. Deb shared, "He would speak over me, making it hard to make my voice heard. In response, I would shrink back. I found him intimidating, and he found me evasive." She avoided him whenever possible for years, but now he was going to be her new manager. Deb was on the verge of quitting when Sheryl Sandberg, Facebook COO, convinced her to talk things through. That was the pivotal moment when she finally spoke up for herself and her team. "I want you to understand that you walk into a room, and you own it. We're like little ants. You don't mean to stomp on us, but we're so small you don't see us, you don't see me. We aren't even on your radar."[38] It took many conversations, but Deb and her manager realized there had been a lot of misunderstandings. Resolving them took work. Over time, they ended up having a great working relationship, but that never would have been possible if she hadn't spoken up about how he was making her—and others—feel.

"Some may say, 'It's not fair; why do you have to do all the work to educate him and others?'" Deb said. "But in that process, I learned so much and he learned so much and actually changed for me and for all the people like me who felt the same way." Deb believes that the burden shouldn't always be put on the Onlys, but these moments can still be considered opportunities. "I'm willing to do this work because it can change the way people look at the world."

Deb believes that when you're in the room, it's important to speak up and help others understand your perspective and experience, even when it may not be easy or your responsibility. "What if we just showed up and said, 'This is what it feels like to be me,' and allowed others to respond to that? We should all be able to say, 'Have some empathy for me,' and also, 'Have empathy for others.'" It's not a level playing field for Onlys, Deb explains. Sometimes, you have to play the game to change the game, but that doesn't mean you're without power. "You may have to change certain things to be seen and heard, but you get to decide whether you do it or not."

As an Only, speaking up for yourself and others is important, but it doesn't always guarantee you'll be heard. In Deb's case, the manager not only listened but implemented changes that positively impacted the entire team. Although it was uncomfortable and difficult at first, this process led to a deeper understanding among team members, fostering empathy that strengthened their leadership, their teams, and the whole company. Speaking up can also enhance communication, prevent misunderstandings, and build stronger relationships. But even if

Deb's manager had not changed his behavior, the act of speaking up can empower you and boost your confidence and self-esteem, enabling you to continue owning your opportunities and driving change.

WHEN YOU ARE IN THE ROOM, YOU CAN OPEN THE DOOR FOR OTHERS

When Onlys take a seat at the table, then they can invite other Onlys. Shelley Zalis, CEO of The Female Quotient, says she was an "only and lonely" for most of her career and believes what will move women forward is The Power of the Pack. A pioneer for online research, she became the first female chief executive ranked in the research industry's top 25, sold her company for $80 million, and is now committed to raising the visibility of women and driving change. She says women alone have power, but collectively they have impact. "There will always be people who tell you 'No, it can't be done,' and you have to find a way, create a new pattern, and bring everyone with you."[39]

What started in 2012 with her inviting five women to CES, the Consumer Electronics Show, has now evolved into their signature Equality Lounge for the cultural events around the world and a global community of over 5.5 million across 30 industries in more than 100 countries. "At CES, there were over 150,000 people. Less than 3 percent were women. Twenty-four hours later, fifty women showed up and we walked the

It's not about maintaining the status quo and keeping others out; it's about planting seeds, bringing others in, and carving a new path to follow, until one day, there will be no more talk about being the Only.

floor together. It was like this *whoosh* moment. It was so empowering—feeling like I was surrounded by a pack of women just like me."

When Onlys join together, there is collective power. You may be "the only" right now, and the way to grow and succeed is to come from a place of abundance, not scarcity. It's not about maintaining the status quo and keeping others out; it's about planting seeds, bringing others in, and carving a new path to follow, until one day, there will be no more talk about being the Only.

WHEN YOU ARE IN THE ROOM, YOU CAN CHANGE THE ROOM

I went into news not just to be on television, but to make an impact and to have a voice. Journalism is not about my voice directly; it's about telling other people's stories. Being in the room with others who had diverse perspectives and backgrounds was invaluable, and I believed that sharing my perspective was my responsibility. My presence and ability to pitch stories and offer my perspective affected *what* was covered and *how* it was covered.

This was incredibly important.

Being the Only and drawing on my cultural background not only helped others recognize blind spots, but was essential to the stories, the communities we covered, and uncovering new angles that might have otherwise remained hidden. Our diverse voices collectively shaped the coverage, demonstrating that diversity in news and other industries goes beyond tokenism. More diverse voices in the news can challenge the status quo and lead to more inclusive and compelling stories, products, services, and innovations.[40]

During my reporting days at KNBC in Los Angeles, there was an incident in San Gabriel, a predominantly Asian community in Southern California. The assignment desk initially planned to send only a photographer to get sound bites (interviews). Unlike the rest of the team,

I recognized the challenges of potential language barriers and figured that getting the community to talk wouldn't be easy unless they could first establish trust. Moreover, I was aware of the story's nuances that had not been fully explored in the media I had seen.

I just *knew* this story needed more attention and sensitivity.

Given my personal connection to the community—my grandfather lived there—I understood what it was like and felt I needed to own that opportunity to cover this story fully. It was my responsibility to ensure the story was covered with the depth, sensitivity, and accuracy it deserved, serving both the community and our viewers. My presence and perspective were crucial in navigating this diverse community. We may never know the reach of the ripple effect from being in the room.

I was often able to add my perspective to news coverage and highlight stories that may not have been traditionally covered, such as a series on the Chinese history of Bakersfield. When I moved to this small agricultural town north of Los Angeles in the late '90s, it was predominately White. According to the 1990 census, less than 4 percent of the population was Asian, and by 2010, that number had only risen to about 6 percent, with Chinese residents making up less than 0.4 percent.[41] However, one of the roads next to the main mall was Ming Avenue. This curiosity about the street's naming origin led me to dig through the archives at the Kern County Museum and tell the story of "The Chinese History of Bakersfield." This was in 1998.

I believe it was the first time a TV news station had covered this important piece of local history. Since then, books have been written about the Chinese of Kern County and, as of 2023, researchers were collaborating with the museum to digitize and scan the archives, ensuring that this rich history is preserved and accessible worldwide.

That is our power as Onlys when we own our opportunity.

Your background, perspective, knowledge, and experience add value that can lead you to not only to empathize but also think of and create things that don't currently exist. Without your influence, many things might never come to fruition.

My perspective as an Only allowed me to see, discover, and contribute something new. Being Chinese does not define all of me, but it is a part of me, and when I show up to the table with my perspective, I add value.

That is my power.

CLAIM YOUR OPPORTUNITY

Change won't happen overnight, but you can influence how and when it does, in both small and significant ways. If you are offered a seat at the table, *take it*. If you have the chance to speak up and share your voice, *don't shy away from it*. If you can make things better or easier for others, *embrace it*. Now that I'm able to take a seat, share my voice, and show up, I am committed to use it as an opportunity to drive meaningful change for others.

EXERCISE

Reflect on the following questions to better understand your unique strengths and how to use them to fully own your opportunities.

IDENTITY AFFIRMATION
- Write down the unique aspects of your identity that you believe make you stand out.
- Reflect on how these aspects have contributed to your success and how you can leverage them further.

STORY SHARING

- Write a personal story about a time when being your unique self brought a positive change or opportunity. Share this story with your network or on social media to inspire others.
- Write down a few ideas about where you can encourage others to share their stories as well. You will help create a collective narrative about the power and impact of embracing your Only.

ADDITIONAL REFLECTION QUESTIONS

- What challenges and opportunities have I encountered because of being the Only?
- What thoughts do I have about shifting my mindset from "This is a burden" to "This is an opportunity"? (Describe what you feel is a burden, then look at your notes to explore a shift.)
- How can I use my voice and influence to create more opportunities for others?

PRINCIPLE 2

OWN YOUR POWER

PRINCIPLE 2

OWN YOUR
POWER

Chapter 2.1

OWN YOUR POWER

You cannot, you cannot use someone else's fire. You can only use your own. And in order to do that, you must first be willing to believe that you have it.

—AUDRE LORDE

"It's your job!"

It's been over twenty-five years, and I can still hear the words Alice screamed at me.

My career started as an assistant at Paramount Pictures. My duties were what you would expect: I answered phones, scheduled meetings, booked travel, and kept things organized for my boss. My days were filled with long hours, a bit of drama, and a dash of glamour. I had a front-row seat to power and politics in action. Where else could you be doing something as simple as filing when you hear the hallway abuzz because Madonna was having a meeting nearby? Or see the newest TV shows and movies being filmed and bump into Tom Cruise during your lunch break?

Despite all the Hollywood horror stories, I had a good boss; he was professional and not abusive, unlike some in the industry at the time.

Alice, on the other hand, was a lower-level executive who demanded that I do a task for her.

Immediately.

Little did she know that I was working on a key project for my boss, which he needed *immediately,* too.

I was an executive assistant, but I was also hired because I spoke Mandarin Chinese and helped my boss launch *Entertainment Tonight China.* I got to travel to China and be a part of some high-level conversations with the heads of domestic and international television. Many times, I was the only woman, the only Asian American, and the only person under twenty-five in the room. Alice didn't know this; she also didn't know that, on the weekends, I was a TV reporter in Palm Springs trying to make my way in the TV news industry.

In her mind, I was not important; therefore, what I was doing was not important. *She* was important, and *she* had the power. And I . . . was just an assistant. She placed me in a category and determined my status and power based on her preconceived beliefs and perceptions, not necessarily on what was real and true.

While Alice didn't know about my projects or my TV career, *I* knew. And that was enough.

I remember calmly holding back my anger as she screamed, ending with the words, "But it's your job!" It wasn't my job to serve her immediate needs, but explaining that to Alice wasn't worth the fight. So, I performed her task and moved on.

Afterward, I made sure my boss knew what happened and spoke up for myself. I reconfirmed my responsibilities; I was not the entire department's assistant and I would not accept being screamed at and disrespected. No incident like that ever happened again.

A few years later, I returned to Los Angeles as a TV news anchor and reporter, not as an assistant. I was with my former boss at the Paramount executive dining room, but I was no longer booking the lunch; I was having the lunch. It just so happened that Alice was also there that day.

My boss said to her, "You remember Angela. She's back and working at KCBS-TV now." Alice was friendly and said, "I've seen you on air. You made it back." We chatted for a bit before saying goodbye.

It was nice to have this internal *I showed you!* moment, but that's not really the point. Even as an assistant, my drive was fueled by my faith in myself and my goals. Although it was hard not to get swayed by how others, like Alice, treated or perceived me, I realized that my focus needed to remain on what was important to me and own my power.

Owning your power means not letting others dictate your value. You know you have everything you need inside to succeed. You are worthy *now* and not because of your title, level, awards, number of followers, or any other external metric. You don't need permission to take up space. You don't need to change who you are to access your power. You have internal status and agency. You know who you are and what you stand for, and you know you belong there.

You know you have everything you need inside to succeed.

As an Only, you've likely experienced—and will continue to experience—times when people don't see your power. Maybe your boss underestimates you and doesn't give you enough responsibility. Maybe a colleague doesn't see or understand your expertise or the critical role you play or the work you are doing. Maybe a stranger stereotypes and pigeonholes you. Regardless of the situation, sometimes you must prove your power and capabilities to them. For example, if they are the gatekeepers, you may want to understand why, build deeper relationships, advocate for yourself, take more initiative, document your achievements, reinforce your value, etc. But most of the time, those who fail to recognize your power are simply external noise and unnecessary energy that you don't need to absorb. It may be challenging, but if you stay focused on you and your objectives, their perceptions and opinions will gradually fade into the background.

You will stay centered.

What if I had spoken up and my boss didn't hear me? Or what if I did own my power and things still didn't change? This can be a harsh reality. While society is slowly evolving, factors like your industry, company, leadership team, and environment can be beyond your control. Truly owning your power is knowing who you are, owning your worth, and embracing it fully. As you read this chapter, ask yourself: *Do I know my own value, regardless of external circumstances? How can I improve my sense of self?*

> **Truly owning your power is knowing who you are, owning your worth, and embracing it fully.**

WHY DON'T PEOPLE OWN THEIR POWER?

The founder and CEO of The Inclusion Initiative spent most of her life trying to validate her worth. At three years old, Grace Yung Foster was orphaned and abandoned at the local market in South Korea and ended up in the US foster care system. "As a transracial adoptee and a foster care alum, I was often the only," Grace wrote in a LinkedIn post. "I always felt I had to prove I could contribute the most to 'earn' my place in the homes I lived in."[42]

Grace lost her confidence for years, affecting her early in her career because she was fed so many negative messages throughout her life:

You should be grateful.
You are selfish for wanting more.
You don't belong in leadership.
You don't deserve equal pay and must work harder and longer to earn it.

"I started to believe I didn't belong at those tables, in those rooms. I started to shrink and minimize myself to not feel like a 'threat' to those in power. I would assimilate into what they wanted me to be," she wrote in her post. "I kept pushing through, working harder and longer hours, thinking 'working hard' would create the opportunities. I allowed people who did not appreciate me to make me feel small as they crushed my efforts to climb the career ladder."

Like Grace in her early years, many of us struggle to own our power because we may not fully see ourselves yet. Some of us don't own our power because we cannot see it or because we've been told we don't have any. These limiting messages, whether a passing comment or consistent criticism, can affect what you believe about yourself. If others put limitations on you, you may start accepting narratives about who you are that don't serve you and keep you from stepping up.

These narratives, both external and internal, shape our self-perception. However, this self-perception is subjective and not always based on reality. As explored in the last principle, our identity can be clouded by our internal biases and insecurities and by external cultural and social influences. Internalizing these influences can impact our self-view, behavior, and ability to own our power.

FEAR OF SHOWING UP

Sometimes, Onlys may fear revealing their power because societal or cultural messages have conditioned them to believe it is wrong or unacceptable. A client of mine, Denise, grew up in a very conservative and religious family. She was always the "good girl" who followed the rules and did what everyone expected her to do. Denise looked successful from the outside, but as she got older, she had a hard time showing up and trusting her own decisions, even simple ones. She had to unlearn everything she was taught to step into her power.

Many Onlys find it easier to blend in, feeling overwhelmed and outnumbered; uniqueness can feel like a risk. It's hard enough if you think and feel differently and then *also* go against the grain. For Onlys coming from marginalized or discriminated backgrounds, the reluctance to stand out is even more pronounced.

You may not be used to owning your power. Maybe it feels uncomfortable and out of place for you. Maybe you have faced stereotypes, bias, and prejudice, which can make situations even more difficult to navigate. The sting of being *othered* stays with you subconsciously. It is like tiny scratches on your confidence that can compel you to build up your armor but also leaves you wounded and stuck. All of us want to feel accepted and safe. In a world where being different can sometimes be daunting or risky, it's understandable why many would rather choose the easier path.

Finally, some of you may not see yourself because you haven't taken the space to reflect on *who* you are, *what* you stand for, and *how* you want to show up in the world. Many of us are just too busy doing life. Who has time for reflection? I didn't really start unpacking my own story until I became a mom and had a mini breakdown. Until then, I felt like I was on autopilot, checking off boxes to reach my goals.

Each of us has our own reasons for not stepping into our own power and our own timeline for self-discovery. Yet, despite all these obstacles, fears, and limiting narratives, overcoming them is entirely possible.

RECLAIM YOUR STORY

It took time for Grace to step into her power. It started with letting go of the narratives that didn't serve her. To own her power, Grace had to shift her self-perception. When she looks in the mirror now, her inner voice has a new story. "I see wisdom, I see courage, I see power, I see joy, I see a person I am proud to be," she shared on LinkedIn. "I'm reclaiming my life. I no longer allow institutions and people who do not appreciate what I bring to the table to define my value. *I* set that bar." Grace is creating her own story of empowerment and helping others do the same. Through The

Inclusion Initiative, she is closing the professional opportunity gap that transracial adoptees and former foster youth face by building a network and community of belonging.

Like Grace, you too can discover your full power and claim it. In the next few chapters, we'll explore how you can step into it. First, you must understand that you don't need to change who you are, but you do need to discover who you are and how you want to show up in the world. Next, we'll discuss how to own your worth and recognize that it is not tied to your title, status, or others' expectations. Finally, you'll see ways to celebrate yourself and realize it's not a luxury but a necessity for stepping into your power.

How will you know you're fully owning your power?

When you can see *beyond* it.

As you progress in your career and life and earn more success and knowledge, it's important to not forget those moments when your power was challenged and you felt invisible. Remembering these moments will keep you grounded; it will give you a deeper understanding of what challenges others may face so you can help *them* come into their own power—just like Grace is doing through The Inclusion Initiative.

This is exactly what our world needs right now: people who stay true to themselves, honor their worth, *and* honor others.

EXERCISE

Reflective exercises help you to lean in on the topic of owning your power. Give yourself the gift of a few minutes to consider each question and make a few notes. You can return to these notes as you continue through the next chapters.

- How would I describe my relationship with my power right now?

- Whether in my career or personal life, how powerful would I like to feel? (Try to describe it in terms of the things you could do if you fully owned your power.)
- When I consider how I feel about power today and what I would like to feel, can I see the gap between the two? (That gap in power is the change that's available to you, that you can work to own, that can be transformed. The following chapters will help you learn more about how to do that as an Only. For now, write down your initial thoughts about the gap you've just identified.)

Chapter 2.2

DON'T CHANGE WHO YOU ARE; FIGURE OUT WHO YOU ARE

Knowing yourself is the beginning of all wisdom.

—ARISTOTLE

For most of her life, Tricia Montalvo Timm didn't publicly share her Salvadorean and Ecuadorian heritage while at work. As I shared in Chapter 1.4, Tricia saw being an Only as a burden. She didn't consciously try to hide, but subconsciously she erased parts of herself so much so that she gladly passed as White. "I'm lighter skinned. I straightened my hair. I did all the things to try to fit in," she told me. "Over time, I just blended in." Her agent even convinced her to change her name for a time to get more parts as a child actor in the '80s. "I went from Patricia Montalvo to

Patricia McLain. It was a strategy, but what does that do to a ten-year-old girl and her soul? Like my name wasn't good enough."[43]

Messages like these kept her hiding.

In her book *Embrace the Power of You: Owning Your Identity at Work*, Tricia writes about her first job after law school at an elite firm where she learned to assimilate because of her experience as an Only, getting a crash course in hiding. "I mastered the skill of looking like I belonged, but I never felt like I belonged. Despite all the success I had earned with my hard work and perseverance, I did not feel entitled to it."[44]

Owning your power isn't about changing who you are; it's about reclaiming all parts of yourself and embodying all of it.

It took a while for Tricia to find herself and her worth. She didn't talk about her background throughout her career and even hid being a working mom. "All the hiding eventually takes a toll. It's physically and emotionally exhausting." She decided she needed to make a change and, after twenty years, she started to unpack all the pain, reflect on her life, and finally figure out who she was. "There's this other piece of me that I hadn't fully embraced and I started slowly unpacking it and revealing it." Step by step, she started to show up more fully and is now on a mission to help everyone discover and bring out their full selves. For Tricia, hiding who she was had come at a cost, and the key to finally owning her power was self-acceptance and taking the time to figure out who she was and how she wanted to show up.

People often feel like they need to play a role or act a certain way to fit in, or even to hide their true selves, like Tricia. Many communication clients tell me, "I want to be more like so-and-so, or I want to be like you," to which I respond, "NO, you want to be like *you*!" Owning your power isn't about changing who you are; it's about reclaiming all parts of yourself and embodying all of it. It's not about fitting in; it's about digging deeper to discover who you are, what you value, and how you want to show up in the world. When you figure out who you are and embrace it, you no longer rely on external validation. You cultivate a sense of empowerment, authenticity, and self-respect by not changing who you are. When you are true to yourself, you can show up more fully, foster more authentic connections, and truly own your power.

When you figure out who you are and embrace it, you no longer rely on external validation.

YOU DON'T NEED TO CHANGE OR FIT IN

The bell rang and everyone rushed outside for recess. Before leaving the classroom, I took off my glasses and placed them on my desk. As I scanned the playground for my friends, things were a bit blurry, but it was fine.

Everything was fine.

While my classmates ran to the foursquare line, I started getting nervous waiting for my turn—not because of the game itself but because I couldn't really see.

What if I mess up the game? Oh well, it's better than wearing glasses and not fitting in.

Like every other kid, fitting in was all I wanted. I did whatever I could to not stand out. Since I was eight years old, I wore thick glasses and did not want to be known as "the girl with glasses." But it wasn't just about the glasses; I tried especially hard to hide my culture.

My family wasn't Buddhist, but I remember having a Buddha statue by our front door. Whenever friends came to our house, I would hide it. It was so heavy that I couldn't pick it up so I would rock it side to side across the whole house until I could get it to the backyard. It took me a long time and I'd be out of breath by the time my friends arrived. I'd also scramble to hide all the shoes by the front door. We didn't wear shoes in the house, which was different from the rest of my friends.

My mom would come home from work and ask, "Why is the Buddha in the backyard, and where are all the shoes?"

I'd shrug my shoulders and say, "I don't know."

I moved this Buddha statue back and forth every single week. It was my ritual any time my friends came over. As I got older, I became more confident but still felt compelled to hide parts of myself. Early in my TV career, I thought I needed to play a part to make it. I chopped off my hair to look older and more credible, wore boxy suits with big shoulder pads, and tried to talk with a deep anchor voice. After all this time, I finally realized how much stress, time, and energy I wasted trying to fit into a mold.

We might think we've outgrown the need to fit in or that we're no longer affected by others' perceptions of us, but the truth is that we all want to feel like we belong, and it hurts if we don't. Functional MRIs show that social pain activates the same area of the brain as physical pain.[45]

No wonder we want to belong; it actually *hurts* to be left out.

Rather than owning our true power, we try to fit in to avoid rejection, which can lead to other problems. When we try to be someone we're not, we set unrealistic expectations for ourselves, feeling like it's never enough—we're not good enough, we're not doing enough, or we don't have enough. We may also waste time seeking approval from others instead of focusing on our own path. Changing who we are can be emotionally exhausting and, for some, may even cause shame, guilt, and a loss of identity. Fitting in is supposed to make us feel more connected, but if it's not true to who we are, it can make us feel even more lonely.

What I didn't realize early in my career was that even at a young age, I already had everything I needed to succeed. I didn't have to play a part or put on a facade. While there's always room for growth, I needed to trust myself and who I already was. Success wasn't dependent on my hair, my clothes, or my voice; I just needed to embody who I was in that moment and not try to be who I thought I "should be" or what others expected me to be.

When we are clear on who we are, what we stand for, and how we want to be, we show up differently. By embracing our whole selves, we are more aligned internally with our values, beliefs, and goals, ultimately leading to less internal struggle and stress.

Ask yourself: *How can I authentically connect more with myself so I can connect more deeply with others?* When you can cultivate this power inside you, you're unstoppable.

STAYING TRUE TO WHAT YOU STAND FOR

Dr. Cleopatra Kamperveen, a scientist and tenured USC professor who pioneered the field of fertility biohacking and creating super babies, never fit the mold of what a scientist, psychologist, or professor was supposed to look and act like. "I'm a young woman, a woman of color, a woman with three children, and I have big, curly Egyptian hair." Although she went through a brutal hazing process to become a tenured professor, Cleopatra knew who she was and made up her mind that she wasn't going to change to fit in. "I could have taken the millions of cues I've received over the years and started blow-drying my hair straight and trying to be like everyone else around me, but I refuse to be anything other than I am."[46]

Cleopatra has been clear on the vision and mission of her life since she was young. "My mother was twenty-seven years old. My parents recently came to the US. We were very poor, and she didn't speak English. She died in childbirth, and it was completely preventable," she shares. "I knew I was meant to work for the world to be a healthier, happier, more loving, supportive place for women and children."

Despite the odds, knowing what she stood for helped her stay true to herself and step into her own power. She could be powerful in her own way, not just in how she looked, but in how she thought. Cleopatra created new areas of scientific inquiry, new theories, new life span and human development models, and new fertility and pregnancy protocols that hadn't existed. "If I had tried to be like everyone else or listened to my mentor who told me, 'This is the state of knowledge; don't bring these innovative ideas,' there would be hundreds of babies—and ultimately millions—who may not have ever arrived in this world, and that would have been a tragedy."

While not everyone is driven by a grand mission, being clear about who you are can help awaken your vision for yourself. This is the first step in owning your power. When you understand and embrace your values and beliefs, it gives you a strong sense of identity and purpose. This self-awareness helps you stay focused and navigate your life with confidence, enabling you to make decisions and take actions that align with your authentic self. By doing so, you tap into your power and unlock your potential, allowing you to live a life that is both meaningful and fulfilling. Recognizing and honoring your true self empowers you to pursue your goals with passion and determination, creating a path that is uniquely yours.

FINDING YOU

A client of mine, Louise, was at a huge crossroads in her life and career. After being a single mom for about ten years, she was about to remarry. Professionally, she had been successfully climbing the ranks in a male-dominated industry, but she always felt like she was trying to fit a certain type. Her company was undergoing a major transition and she was feeling a bit stuck. Louise and I started working together because she wanted to enhance her public speaking skills, as she was leading large teams and handling more client-facing events.

Before working on communication skills with my clients, we take time to create a vision for their life and career. During this first step, Louise revealed that she had never taken the time to explore *who* she was, *what* she valued, and *how* she wanted to show up in the world. Growing up in a big family with limited means, she had developed a strong work ethic but never really thought about what she wanted. As a single mom, she was just happy to have a job and provide for her son. However, as she entered a new phase in her life, Louise was ready to discover herself and redefine her identity.

After going through this self-reflection journey, Louise realized she felt stuck at work because she had been going with the flow to fit in even though it no longer aligned with her long-term goals. Recognizing this, she decided it was time to own her power and finally talk to her boss about expanding her role and seeking more growth opportunities. She left that day with a clear vision of what she wanted and how she wanted to show up, although she was still uncertain about what that meant for her job.

A few months later, I called her to follow up. Louise said that she felt confident and connected during her latest presentations, but more importantly, she felt more aligned at work. She had transitioned into a new leadership role where she felt challenged and could contribute more significantly. This new position allowed her to leverage her strengths and pursue her true aspirations, leading to greater fulfillment and career success. By embracing her authentic self, Louise had not only transformed her professional life but also empowered herself to create the future she had envisioned.

Taking the time to reflect on what matters to you, what you believe in, and why you believe in it is a powerful tool that helps you become more centered on who you are and how you want to show up. When you are clear on your values, beliefs, and priorities, you can make decisions more easily, express yourself more authentically, and stay focused on your goals or purpose. This self-awareness and clarity can help you harness your full potential and power.

When I asked these questions of myself, I started to see that everything I valued was about having a voice and speaking up. Watching my parents sometimes lose their voice and feel unseen or less than drove me to want to create a different path for myself and others. Being a reporter wasn't just about being on television; it was about helping others tell their stories so *they* could be seen and heard. Empowering others to own their power and voice is the core of what I do now.

This is what drives me.

At this realization, I started to ask myself what truly mattered to me and how I wanted to show up in the world. Answering these questions gave me the foundation to own my power. With newfound clarity, I created my company, infusing it with all my strengths, passion, and mission.

Once you take the time to understand your strengths, values, and boundaries, you too can navigate your life with more clarity and intention. Doing this also helps you live in alignment with your *true self* rather than being influenced by external pressure, expectations, or the need for validation. Finding yourself doesn't usually happen overnight, but you can start the conversation today. Or, if you've had this conversation before, now is the time to revisit it.

THE NEVER-ENDING SELF-DISCOVERY JOURNEY

Peeling back the layers to get to your true self is a personal journey, and what it looks like is entirely up to you. There is no specific timeline or right way to navigate the process. You get to decide when and how you embark on this path of self-discovery.

That is owning your power.

Over the years, I have learned to embrace all parts of myself and my journey, but it's been an evolution. Who I am now, as an entrepreneur and mother of two teenagers, is not who I was as a rookie reporter just trying to make it, nor is it the young girl hiding a Buddha statue and shoes. I'm not even the same person I was last year. I continue to grow and evolve every day, and you do too. Every few years, take the time to rediscover yourself. Now I'm in yet another transition, midlife (that journey is enough for another full book!).

But this is how we continue to grow—through awareness, small shifts, and practice.

Sometimes, we can't see how far we've come until we take a deeper look back. Change happens when you take time to reflect and then make shifts over and over until they become part of who you are and you don't even realize it. When your true self is embodied and part of who you are, *that* is owning your power.

Sometimes, we can't see how far we've come until we take a deeper look back. Change happens when you take time to reflect and then make shifts over and over until they become part of who you are and you don't even realize it.

EXERCISE

To reflect on what matters to you, what you believe in, and therefore who you are, consider these questions. You can write down the answers or just close your eyes and feel what comes as you spend some time with each.

- **What I value.** What's important to me? What makes me mad and why?
- **What I believe in.** In the wider world, what guides my life?
- **What I stand for.** What and who do I support?
- **Why I do what I do.** What motivates me to pursue my goals and interests?
- **How I want to show up.** How do I want to be perceived by others?
- **How I want others to describe me.** What words would I like others to use when describing my personality?

If your answer to these questions is "I have no idea" or "I don't know," it's okay. You don't have to answer each of these immediately; the questions are just to help get you started. Answer what you can now, even if it just means saying "I'm not sure," and/or you can come back to them later. Going through the process and thinking about these questions will help you start to understand who you are and step into your power.

Chapter 2.3

OWN YOUR WORTH

You alone are enough. You have nothing to prove to anyone.

—MAYA ANGELOU

One of the most beautiful milestones in my life—motherhood—also became one of my lowest points. I had been waking up at 2:30 a.m. for the morning shift as long as I could remember and I went through my pregnancy on air.

It was well past time for a break.

After working nonstop in TV and news for thirteen years, I left my full-time morning anchor job in San Diego. I still loved my job, but I was ready for a different pace. I wanted to be present for my newborn and start exploring other paths.

Before building my speaking and coaching business, I turned to blogging. This was in 2008 when "mom blogs" were just gaining momentum. I started my blog and spent all my time writing and creating videos for other sites while juggling motherhood. I'd "mom" all day, then stay up late, overextending myself. This worked for a while, until it didn't.

I burned out.

Staring blankly at my computer late at night eventually turned into sitting frozen on my couch. Many times, I would cry or feel numb. This went on for *months*—and no one knew. I made it look like I had it all figured out. I never asked for help.

I wasn't consciously overworking. Driven by old rules of success (and my ego), I was being my type A self: Get an idea, set a goal, focus your mind on it, do whatever it takes, and push through. I had left the news business to create space in my life, but I just replaced the nonstop intensity with something else. I had spent most of my life sharing others' stories; my words had an impact, and *I* made a difference.

Once I didn't have the big-time TV job, the title . . . then what?

I wanted to matter.

After losing the external status and validation I had enjoyed for years, I was trying to make up for it. Eventually, at a retreat, I realized that I had been trying to work within my old framework of success. It had been six years since the first transformative personal development weekend leading to healing my past self and my relationship with my parents. I had been at the peak of my career and felt so *full* after that first weekend. But I wasn't the same person anymore. I was a new mom. I had left the career I dreamed about as a little girl. I had been chasing external status when what I really needed was to lean on my internal status.

> **Owning your worth and internal status is knowing you are enough. It's about seeing and honoring who you are *right now*, even if others don't.**

Owning your worth and internal status is knowing you are enough. It's about seeing and honoring who you are *right now*, even if others don't. It's knowing you are more than a title, position, label, or whatever category others may want to place you in. It's about developing strong internal status—seeing all your strengths, knowing and trusting your value, and understanding what you bring to the table. It's about remembering who you are, even when facing challenges or transitions. Your internal status follows you no matter where you go, no matter what happens around you. You stop comparing yourself to others. You realize it's not about doing more to be worthy or defining yourself based on your achievements or others' rules and standards.

Although, doing so *is* easier said than done . . .

CHASING EXTERNAL STATUS

Julie had never experienced a break in her career. Recruited right out of college, she dutifully and diligently followed the traditional path, climbing the ranks in every company she joined. She prided herself in being "the best" and doing things "right," and she was rewarded for her efforts. Her résumé shines with a college pedigree and a list of achievements and titles.

When we started working together, Julie had just been laid off. She was devastated. Her industry was going through a downturn, but she was blindsided by the extent of it, which affected her. She *said* she was excited to have time to work with me finally and was looking forward to other opportunities, but deep down, I could sense she was hiding her pain. Her objective in our coaching sessions was to enhance her communication and speaking skills, aiming to emerge more confident and prepared for whatever opportunities lay ahead.

As we started creating a vision for Julie's life before starting on her communication, she realized she didn't have one. Julie was so focused on reaching the next career level that she never thought about what *she* wanted and why. She started to cry and confessed that, without a job, she didn't know who she was. She wasn't in a relationship, hadn't made time for any hobbies, and felt lost.

Like Julie, most of us spend our lives chasing external status. Some of us are focused on achievement and love checking off boxes. Some strive to fit in or meet others' expectations. We chase society's standards, feeling the pressure to be "the best" or at least "good"—good employees, good partners, good parents—instead of defining success on our terms. We all want to feel validated, rewarded, and seen; however, this external validation is only temporary. When you rely on external factors to validate your self-worth, your value becomes out of your control. Jobs can change or end, people may leave, and situations can shift at any moment.

True worth comes from being in alignment with yourself.

As Julie and I continued to work on her communication over the next few months, she gained more clarity about her life. The forced time off allowed her to figure out who she was beyond her job title. Julie realized that she needed to appreciate all that she had already accomplished, and for the first time, she was also focusing on her social life. Soon, Julie had a few job offers but was also exploring starting her own consulting business. Getting clear on what she wanted and valued—who she truly was—and honoring her strengths and skills beyond titles and past accomplishments allowed Julie to discover her internal status.

> **_True_ worth comes from being in alignment with yourself.**

SEE YOURSELF EVEN WHEN OTHERS DON'T

In the TV news industry, working in top markets like New York or Los Angeles automatically carries a certain weight. These markets are *very* competitive and to get (and stay) there, a lot of dedication and effort is involved. As in any industry, specific titles and accolades validate your credibility.

You've *earned* that status.

For most of my career, especially in the early years when I was "just an assistant" or "paying my dues" and when others didn't recognize my worth because I lacked the right title or was working in smaller markets, relying on my internal status kept me motivated. As a young reporter, I didn't know when I would make it back to Los Angeles. There were so many variables, but the only one I could control was myself: my knowledge, my experience, my work, and how well I knew my craft.

The first step was to put in the work, then be good, listen, and learn. While there was always more to learn, once I felt confident in my experience and believed in my work, I refused to let my value and worth be dictated by others or by market size. Even when I transitioned from news to being an entrepreneur and what some would call "just a mom," I needed to call on my internal status to own my worth.

Creating internal status means having faith in yourself and trusting your path based on your choices. It isn't dictated by what looks good, what you think you need, or what others tell you. Instead, it's driven by the vision you consciously create, strive for, and want to bring to life.

I know, I know . . . as Onlys, it can be challenging to maintain a strong inner status because others may automatically assign us value based on external measures, like titles and appearances. You may feel unseen, undervalued, and even spoken over or ignored at times. It may be hard for others to see through the labels that society puts on us. This is especially true for neurodivergent Onlys like Jonathan Mooney.

Writer and speaker Jonathan Mooney faced low expectations from others growing up. He was told he wouldn't be able to finish high school or find a good job and would end up in jail. On his website, he explains that he didn't learn to read until he was twelve years old.[47] He was diagnosed with dyslexia in fourth grade. Limiting beliefs from others took a toll on his mental health and well-being until he realized *he* wasn't the problem.

In his book *Normal Sucks*, Jonathan says it was society's concept of "normal" that kept him trapped in an environment that labeled and shamed him. Shifting his perspective and owning his worth saved his life and helped him step into his power, and the predictions didn't come true. He graduated from Brown University with honors and a degree in

English literature; instead of ending up in jail, he wrote books and became an advocate, creating organizations and initiatives that help people who get the short end of the stick. He is on a mission to reorient how we think about diversity, abilities, and disabilities.

KNOW YOU ARE ENOUGH

Krishanti Vignarajah was pregnant, exhausted, and out of breath in the last few minutes of a cycling class. She looked up from the back of the room and heard the instructor say, "You got this, you're enough!" The instructor's words stuck with her, and she repeated them to herself as she walked out of class. "Maybe it was the way she said it, maybe I was delirious, but it felt like she was looking right at me and this message was for me. When I first said it, it was kind of quizzical, like 'Am I enough?' And then I realized, 'You got this, you're enough.' I think many times we—especially women—feel like we're never good enough. This is why sometimes, even if it doesn't feel natural, you have to go for it."[48]

Krishanti and her family escaped the civil war in Sri Lanka and immigrated to the US when she was just nine months old. She was lucky and always driven by the responsibility to pay it forward; she did just that as president and CEO of Global Refuge. But before leading one of the largest immigration organizations in the world, Krishanti ran for governor of Maryland in 2018.

The only woman, against eight men.

Despite having all the credentials and support behind her, she still felt a bit uncertain at first. After her role as Michelle Obama's policy director and being pregnant with her first child, Krishanti was confident, accomplished, and knew her worth. Yet even she needed the simple reminder "You are enough" to truly step into her power.

Although Krishanti didn't win the race for governor, she redefined what leadership should look like by owning her worth and showing up fully. "I ran despite being a woman, but in part *because* of being a woman." Her first campaign ad featured images of breastfeeding her daughter and embracing her whole self. "It was really important for me to run as myself. To embrace womanhood as a strength, and motherhood as strength."

Even when we've met all the external markers set by ourselves and others, we might still experience doubts or need reminders. When we define ourselves through external status, it can affect our self-esteem, as these factors—titles, financial success, and social recognition—are beyond our control and can change at any time. As we explored in Principle 1, we also face societal stereotypes, pressures, and cultural expectations. These expectations are often unrealistic and can leave us feeling inadequate.

To combat society's limitations and our own negative thoughts, such as perfectionism and our inner critic, we must reinforce our self-worth. By shifting the focus from external validation to internal self-worth, we can cultivate a more stable and enduring sense of being enough. We do this through developing more self-compassion, practicing gratitude, setting healthy boundaries to protect our time and energy, and creating a support system of people who value our true worth.

Jennifer McCollum is president and CEO of Catalyst, a global nonprofit that drives gender equity from the front line to the C-suite, and author of *In Her Own Voice: A Woman's Rise to CEO*. Despite these credentials, even Jennifer has questioned across her career whether she was enough. Before she led Catalyst, Jennifer was the "first and only" female CEO of Linkage. When she was first approached for the job, her inner critic went crazy:

> *You can't be the kind of mom you want to be with a big job.*
> *You're not ready to be CEO.*
> *You haven't been properly groomed.*

It was two men in her network who intervened and helped her see how her own thoughts were preventing her from her aspirations. They said, "If we think we're ready for a private equity–backed CEO job, why don't you think you're ready?" Jennifer says our inner voice is often more critical of ourselves than others and can prevent us from taking action and following our dreams. With the reminder from her peers, she was able to quiet her voice and step into her power. "I have succeeded before when I was the 'only,' so I'm going to embrace it. My only other option is to turn down my light, and I love the idea of this job, and I'm going to step into this challenge."

Even if you have conquered your inner critic, it can still manage to creep back in. This is especially true when stepping into something new and bold or going through a transition like Jennifer. So, I'm here to remind you:

You are enough!

When you know you are enough, you can recognize and embrace your unique value and fully own your worth.

NAVIGATING INTERNAL STATUS DURING TRANSITIONS

It was late at night and the house was finally quiet. I sat staring at my computer screen in my messy makeshift office, one that I had pieced together with a desk in the corner hallway. The room I used to work in at home was now the baby's room. I had piled up files of ideas, to-dos, and hidden bills in one corner, random baby things were strewn across the floor, and I had a breastfeeding pillow strapped around my waist.

I had *so much* to do, yet I didn't feel like doing any of it.

I just sat there. I was a new mom, simultaneously filled with awe and joy over my newborn son yet struggling to do everything. To be "perfect." I had worked my way through the hierarchy of the journalism industry, but when I became a mom and pivoted to professional speaking and coaching, I had to find my way through an entirely different maze.

When you're learning something new, doing something unfamiliar, or transitioning careers like I was, your brain can become a major obstacle, causing you to forget who you *really* are. The human brain is wired for negativity: It's a survival mechanism. We have a "negativity bias" where we tend to overlook our successes and fixate on what we haven't achieved. Giving more weight to negative information can undermine our self-belief, casting doubt on our competence, abilities, and worth.[49]

Other cognitive biases can also get in the way of our self-perceptions. For instance, when you're good at something and it comes naturally, you might assume that it's easy for everyone. The Dunning–Kruger effect is often used to describe when a person's lack of knowledge and skill in a particular area causes them to overestimate their competence. However, it can also lead those who are highly skilled to underestimate their abilities, mistakenly believing that their expertise is effortless for others as well.[50]

Each of your experiences is cumulative, contributing to your power and internal status. Yet, when you're shifting, pivoting, and exploring something new—whether in your career or your life—it can feel like you are starting from zero. This could trigger discomfort, manifesting as fear, self-doubt, or the belief that you're "not ready" or "not good enough." While these responses are a natural part of the growth journey, they can be disorientating and destabilize your internal status.

You need to see and understand that you are not starting over when you are doing something new or challenging the status quo. Everything you've done, learned, and experienced doesn't disappear, even if your cognitive mind can't see it right away. That's why we must bring it to your brain's attention. When you do, it naturally boosts your self-worth.[51]

It is crucial to recognize your strengths and your zone of genius. Understanding and showcasing these qualities not only helps you appreciate them but also allows you to leverage them effectively, boosting your sense of self-worth. Owning your worth and developing a strong inner status, especially during transitions, requires trusting that you *are* on the right path—the path you've chosen for yourself.

TRUST YOUR PATH

Ali Brown, founder and CEO of The Trust, a modern, premier community for seven- and eight-figure women entrepreneurs, always felt like an Only. From feeling lonely in high school to being one of the few women speaking on large entrepreneurial stages in the early internet marketing days, Ali consistently stood out.

As one of the world's most recognized coaches for higher-end women entrepreneurs, she now advises leaders to challenge the status quo. Ali shared that the key to stepping into her power has been unwavering trust in her own path. "You will feel lonely because there will be times in your life when no one will understand your decisions but you. It's important to remember that, especially today when you're surrounded by social media and hordes of people all doing certain things, the same things, and you decide to make a sharp right turn."[52]

Ali started her entrepreneurial journey at twenty-eight and never looked back. "I found it really exciting to go off and be the only. I had no one to look to, so I got to figure it out and choose what I wanted." We all want to fit in and be liked, and when Ali was the only woman speaking to predominately male audiences, many questioned her credibility. She had to learn quickly how to navigate the negativity. "I knew I was here for a reason; I would just pick and choose the events I went to, the people I would work with, and kept my nose down and worked hard. I chose to focus on being respected rather than liked."

While she was confident, Ali also needed some reminders to truly own her worth. At one of her first big speaking engagements, she felt a bit nervous until a woman handed her a note that read, *Thank you for doing this for all the women in the audience.* "When I read that, I realized this wasn't even about me or all the naysayers. It was and still is about owning my worth. I think about what is the power [that] I have in this moment, what is within my control, what am I creating, and then I get back on purpose."

Throughout your life and career, you will face people who advance more quickly than you and underestimate and judge you—and not necessarily accurately or fairly. This can happen in any group dynamic: at networking events, parties, or conferences; anytime you meet someone new or are in a new environment, industry, or community; or anytime you're trying to do something that challenges the status quo. People often try to assess hierarchy, status, and roles and may box you into a category that simplifies their understanding, whether it's intentional or not.

Trust your path and protect your energy.

It is about them, not you.

Remember, you are not defined by titles or however someone categorizes you. Trust your path and protect your energy. If others haven't taken the time to know who you are, what you offer, what you stand for, it's their loss. Continue on your path with your priorities. Who are the people that have taken the time to know who you are and what you stand for? How can you surround yourself with others who support you?

In Principle 3, we'll explore ways to own your voice and use it, but for now, consider a few reflections to help you own your worth.

EXERCISE

- What is a good quality, strength, or something I appreciate about myself? (Close your eyes and reflect on how that makes you feel. Embody this energy and enjoy it.)
- How do I define success for myself, independent of societal expectations? If I could wave a magic wand and have the life I want without seeking anyone's approval, how would it look?
- (Think for a moment about a few achievements you're proud of—whatever comes to mind first.) What steps can I take to acknowledge these more fully internally and externally?

Chapter 2.4

CELEBRATE YOUR WINS

Becoming proud of yourself is the best gift you can give yourself.

—MARGO VADER

Dave Noll walked onto the Paramount Studios lot in Hollywood like a kid in a candy store: filled with wonder and awe. "I remember saying to myself, 'Take lots of photos, enjoy every moment. Every moment of this is a win.'" It was the first day of production of *Face the Truth*, a show he created with his partner Cleve Keller for CBS and hosted by Vivica Fox. Dave captured every moment, from photos with the host to inside the soundstage, outside the soundstage, the famous water tower, and even shots with Dr. Phil.

You might assume this was Dave's first visit to a studio lot, but as a veteran TV show creator and executive producer with over 200 shows to his name, Dave (introduced in Principle 1) was no stranger to Hollywood. Despite his extensive experience, Dave understands that pitching frequently and embracing rejection are crucial to his success. Celebrating even the smallest victories is essential for him to truly own his power. "You realize that you have to celebrate every moment. When we pitch, we know twenty-nine times out of thirty we're going to get turned down, but you have to think, 'We just pitched Netflix, and we did a great job!' Or an executive from NBC says, 'They've never seen anything like that before.'

> **Celebration is not a luxury—it has the power to rewire your brain and change how you feel and perform.**

We constantly take the win, no matter what the win is. In TV, you think you're waiting for this big moment, but once you've been in the business a while, you realize there's not *one* moment. It's every moment."[53]

As explored in the previous chapter, we often fail to own our power because we overlook and undervalue our achievements. Celebrating both major and minor victories is crucial; it helps us reconnect with our power and fuels our drive, as it does for Dave. It's what keeps his fire alive.

Celebration is not a luxury—it has the power to rewire your brain and change how you feel and perform. In this chapter, you'll learn how to tap into this positive cycle of celebration, discover what is holding you back from celebrating your wins, rewrite your celebration patterns, and incorporate celebration into your daily routine to fully own your power.

THE POSITIVE CYCLE OF CELEBRATION

Research shows that celebrating isn't just beneficial for your well-being; it also has the potential to restructure your brain and positively influence both your emotions and performance.

Celebration can lower your cortisol level, reduce stress, and increase all the "feel-good" chemicals (dopamine, serotonin, and endorphins) in your brain—the neurotransmitters that also act as hormones to keep you happy and motivated. Dopamine gives you a sense of pleasure and is part of your reward system. Serotonin regulates mood and makes you feel more focused and calmer. Endorphins relieve pain, reduce stress, and give you the feeling of being on top of the world.[54] Research from the Center for Healthy Minds at the University of Wisconsin–Madison shows how celebration activates a part of the brain's reward center (ventral striatum). The more we savor these moments, even briefly, the more they can enhance psychological well-being. This practice can help sustain that positive feeling longer and help us remember it.[55]

It's easy to forget or dismiss our power unless we take the time to savor our wins. Celebrating them helps move the wins from our short-term to our long-term memory so that we don't lose them. Celebration helps you to not only recognize your wins but also feel them and remember them. When you savor something, it triggers all those feel-good chemicals in your brain. When you feel good, what happens? You achieve more and you're more productive.

Celebration helps you to not only recognize your wins but also feel them and remember them.

That is the cycle of celebration.

But not everyone can easily tap into this cycle of celebration. Depending on your upbringing and the environment around you, celebrating your wins and drawing attention to yourself may not come naturally for you; it didn't for me.

YOUR UPBRINGING AFFECTS YOUR CAPACITY TO CELEBRATE

I sat at the dinner table in a new dress waiting for my parents' out-of-town friends to arrive. Just before they walked in, my mom said, "Hey, don't tell them it's your birthday; I don't want them to make a fuss." I'd turned eleven years old and sat there quietly, not knowing how to feel.

It's my birthday; why can't we celebrate?

I was quiet during the whole dinner. It wasn't that my parents didn't want to celebrate my birthday, but it was that their friends had come into town at the last minute, and in my Chinese home, it was all about reciprocation. Mom didn't want to make them feel unprepared or obligated to give me a gift or money. My parents wanted to keep the dinner simple and not mention my birthday. I now understand the Asian values behind this moment, but as an eleven-year-old girl growing up in a Western world, it was painful.

My family always made things less when I was growing up; it went along with being humble or not rocking the boat. While we did celebrate major occasions like graduations and holidays with food and family, we tended to minimize things verbally. I remember when I won the Miss California National Teenager scholarship pageant at fifteen. I knew my parents were proud of my win, but their reaction was more like, "Oh, I didn't think you would win." To be honest, I didn't think I would win either. I was in shock. However, the parents of *other* girls were holding up big posters in the stands and cheering their names. This tendency to downplay success kept me grounded but also made it hard for me to truly savor my accomplishments. Even today, when I try to celebrate my parents or plan something special for them, they often respond uncomfortably with, "It's no big deal," or "We don't want to make a fuss."

Each of us come from different upbringings, values, and cultures, and these things can affect how we celebrate our accomplishments. My client Chris, for instance, had a childhood vastly different from mine. Always the center of his family's attention, he was very shy, and now as an adult, he shrinks away from the spotlight and struggles to embrace recognition. Pam, the oldest sister in the family, carried a heavy sense of responsibility, constantly busy with tasks and checklists, often forgetting to pause and celebrate her achievements even though she intellectually understood the importance.

Your personal experiences have uniquely shaped your perception of what you deserve and how you celebrate your wins. For some, celebrating may not be a priority, but once reminded to celebrate your wins, it may come more easily for you. Others still may not be able to see or feel it at all; it may be a subconscious mental block. Whether or not you adhere to the values you were raised with, they can still influence your mindset unless you actively recognize and rewrite these patterns for yourself.

REWRITING OUR CELEBRATION PATTERNS

During a group video call, Tamela said, "Thanks, but I didn't see it as a big deal because that's what I am supposed to do." I was leading a communication workshop with a sales team that was feeling a bit overwhelmed and burned out and the year had only just started. Before we could get to the communication training part, I needed them to feel more engaged, motivated, and resilient. During the call, we had a *Woo Hoo!* check-in (explained at the end of the chapter). Each person celebrated some amazing moments, ranging from recent project successes and surpassing annual sales goals to winning prestigious awards and creating impactful internal video training. They also marked significant personal milestones, including the birth of a first child and major life transitions like moving to a new home.

When it was Tamela's turn, she shared that it had been a good year and she was proud of her team for meeting their sales goals, but there wasn't anything specific she wanted to highlight about herself. Her manager chimed in to mention several wins for Tamela, including being recognized by the CEO and speaking on stage at a recent conference. Tamela immediately downplayed these accomplishments. "Oh, yeah, that was nice. I forgot because I was just doing my job. I didn't want to make a big deal about it."

I asked her how it felt to be recognized by the CEO and then be reminded of it by her manager. I then repeated back her wins. I wanted Tamela to *feel* the win. Doing well, reaching the goal, and receiving recognition are great, but what makes the difference is if we feel and internalize the win. She began to smile and admitted, "That was a big win. I guess I should do a better job at seeing it for myself."

Sometimes you need to rewire yourself not only to appreciate celebrations but to genuinely feel you deserve them. Do you struggle with recognizing your wins and celebrating yourself? Do you accomplish something and then move on to the next thing? Do you forget your wins? Gloss over them? Like Tamela, you might see reaching goals or milestones as just part of the job, as something that is just supposed to . . . happen.

But this is not true; it happened because of Tamela's hard work, and it happened because of you. You make an impact. Celebrating that impact—whether it's big or small, at work or in your daily life—can make you feel good, help you achieve even more than you thought possible, and allow you to fully own your power.

MAKE CELEBRATING YOU A DAILY HABIT

While celebrating major achievements and milestones is important, it's equally vital to recognize everyday wins. These small celebrations bring joy and support your overall growth and well-being. It doesn't have to be elaborate, but how you choose to celebrate should be intentional and meaningful. You don't have to wait for that next "big" thing; making celebration a daily habit can fulfill your emotional needs in the present. Celebration isn't a luxury—it's a vital practice for nurturing yourself and recognizing your ongoing progress.

It's been a process for me, but I try to savor the little things: buying myself flowers, treating myself to lunch, or even taking mini moments with my kids, like watching the sunset. I make them pause for twenty seconds to savor the beauty. Although my teenagers complain, they still indulge in these celebrations. It's important to savor these moments—not just your wins from today, but all that you are right now. It can be hard to see just how far you've come because you're too busy moving on to the next thing. So, let's savor the *Woo Hoo!* moments in your life and step into your power!

EXERCISE

Woo Hoo! **Check-In.** List anything you'd like to celebrate, acknowledge, appreciate, or savor from your work or personal life, no matter how big or small. Whatever makes you feel like shouting *Woo Hoo!* You can list something specific, or if you're feeling a bit stuck, here's a list of small wins to consider (inspired by TinyBuddha.com[56]).

SMALL WINS TO CELEBRATE

Strength and Commitment	Love and Kindness
• Finishing a task • Making progress toward a personal or professional goal • Receiving recognition or positive feedback • Overcoming a challenge • Honoring your boundaries	• Listening to someone • Forgiving yourself and letting go of your past • Helping others

Health	Purpose
• Taking care of yourself • Practicing mindfulness • Making positive choices • Exercising	• Life milestones • Creating something • Supporting a cause that matters

Once you have the wins you want to celebrate, rewire your celebration patterns:

- **Reflect and savor:** Take time to acknowledge the win or appreciate the moment. Reflect on your journey that led to the win and savor the feeling of accomplishment. Recognizing and being thankful for your win amplifies its positive impact. How does it feel in your body?
- **Share:** Share your win with friends, family, or colleagues. Celebrating with others amplifies joy and strengthens social connections and your sense of achievement.
- **Reward yourself:** Treat yourself to something you love. This reinforces the positive behavior and makes the win more significant.
- **Celebrate with others:** Joining together with others can make the win more special.
- **Plan for the future:** Use your win as a stepping stone to other goals. Planning your next steps can keep the momentum going.

PRINCIPLE 3

OWN YOUR VOICE

Chapter 3.1

OWN YOUR VOICE

You can't move mountains by whispering at them.

—PINK

Candice sat at her desk, reluctant to reply to her boss's email. She had been struggling with how to respond for the past week but finally sent her *Yes*. The next morning, she called me.

Candice had agreed to represent her company and speak at a leadership event but needed my support. "I feel like an impostor. I always tell others to take risks, yet I'm still hiding. I couldn't keep saying no." Candice was one of the only women on the leadership team at her company. She was fine with speaking up in meetings, but she usually preferred being behind the scenes and avoiding the spotlight. This time was different. It was for an extremely high-profile event, and sharing her story would help many women in her traditionally male-dominated industry. Despite feeling nervous and "not good enough," Candice felt the tug to make a bigger impact and knew it was time to own her voice.

It's important to own your opportunity and know your worth. As an Only, you can make an impact in the room. But unless you speak up and use your voice, nothing will change. To leverage the Power of the

Only, you also need to own your voice. Owning your voice isn't about just speaking up. It's knowing that what you have to say matters and can make a difference. And it isn't just about what you say to others; what you say to *yourself* matters too. It means finally realizing you don't have to find your voice—you already have it. It is already with you. Now it's time to own it and use it. You don't need permission; you have the power of agency.

Owning your voice isn't about just speaking up. It's knowing what you have to say matters. You don't have to find your voice—you already have it.

WHY YOU DON'T OWN YOUR VOICE

Maybe, like Candice, you've broken through barriers, owned your opportunity, and made your way into the room. You know your worth, yet you are *still* reluctant to speak up—whether it's sharing your thoughts and opinions in a meeting, presenting your ideas to a group that matters to you (like a special task force, a nonprofit, a networking group, or a PTA meeting), or addressing an audience at a public event.

Speaking up is hard for many people. We're afraid of what others will think about us. We fear showing up, being seen, and not being good enough. As an Only, it may be even more difficult to do these things. Some might feel the burden of representing an entire group or may not speak up in fear of standing out or "rocking the boat." For whatever reason, it doesn't feel safe.

You could be in an environment where conformity is valued, and feel pressure to fit in. Or, there are power dynamics at play, and you don't feel you're in a position of authority.

You may be scared that others won't listen.

You've had experiences where you were ignored, criticized, or rejected.

You might let perfectionism, overthinking, or even comparison hold you back.

You don't feel ready and need more experience.

You're someone who once confidently spoke up but now needs to reclaim that voice.

Whatever your reason, overcoming these barriers is essential for making an impact and owning your voice.

Candice was reluctant to step into the spotlight but not necessarily defining this reluctance as "fear." It wasn't until she actively embraced this challenge that she discovered a fear of being seen. During our sessions, she began to recognize and unravel subconscious blocks that were holding her back more than she knew. The idea of showing up more visibly brought up a lot of uncomfortable emotions for Candice—ones that weren't always related to work.

Candice realized that many of the voices in her head that kept her hiding weren't her own. She recalled a specific conversation early in her career during a family holiday dinner. With everyone gathered around the table, she proudly shared, "I just got the opportunity to represent my division at a national meeting." Her older brother chimed in, "Who, *you*? You're so awkward in public." Everyone laughed. His words and her family's reaction drained the joy from her. As she revisited this memory with me, she started to get emotional, admitting, "They made me feel so self-conscious, like a kid again, and really hurt my feelings."

Candice struggled to fit in while growing up and was often labeled "off-beat." Though never formally diagnosed, she considers herself neurodivergent. She revealed that she hadn't *honestly* thought about the impact of her brother's words before but saw how these painful memories affected her willingness to show up. She thought about all the times she said no to opportunities at her company. How she wasn't close with her brother and never spoke up when he was rude. Candice finally understood where her reluctance was coming from and could start to override it. This breakthrough opened her up to owning her voice more fully. Instead of feeling "not ready" or "not enough," she was looking forward to speaking.

After the presentation, Candice texted me. "The event was a hit. I'm so excited. Dozens of women came to me for advice afterward and to thank me for sharing my story. For the first time, I really felt the impact of my work. Thank you!" She told me her boss also asked her to speak at more events and lead a program for emerging leaders. From that day forward, Candice harnessed her newfound momentum and confidence, chipping away at her fears and paving the way to even more opportunities. Since then, she has earned an expanded and more visible role at her company and has even started healing her relationship with her brother.

RECLAIMING YOUR VOICE

Melinda French Gates might seem like the last person who would need to learn how to own her voice, but even she's had to face a journey of rediscovery. Despite her high profile, she admitted to losing her voice while married to Bill Gates. In an interview with *CBS Mornings* she said, "When I realized I wanted to step out on reproductive rights in 2012, it took a lot of courage because I had lost my voice. The girl I was in high school and even in college where I just spoke my mind all the time, somehow, I had lost that over time."[57]

Joining the Microsoft team in 1987, Melinda was the youngest recruit and only woman among ten new employees with business degrees. Starting as a marketing manager, she played a pivotal role in developing multimedia products, from Microsoft Word to Expedia.com. She was later promoted to general manager of information products and held that position until she left Microsoft in 1996 to focus on raising her expanding family with Microsoft cofounder and CEO Bill Gates.[58]

When asked how someone as confident, intelligent, and talented as herself could lose her voice, Melinda replied, "I didn't know everybody thought I was smart and talented. Women come up against 10,000 paper cuts. They're told they are not enough, you don't know enough, somebody speaks over you, somebody speaks for you. And so, I started to lose it." Despite building the Gates Foundation from the ground up, providing funding to fight poverty, disease, and inequity around the world starting in 2000 with Bill Gates, people still looked to him first.

"I think the external world, when we would walk into a room—initially with a prime minister or president, and it was usually a *him*—they would look to Bill because he was the leader of his industry. They didn't know that I had a lot of expertise and that I was traveling more in philanthropy than Bill was because he was busy with the company. I think over time I became less of myself, and I didn't like myself." Despite all of this, Melinda learned to interrupt those conversations and reclaim her voice. "They wouldn't actually sometimes make room. I had to interrupt and speak, and then the person would say, 'Oh, she knows what she's talking about.'"

In June 2024, Melinda left the Gates Foundation. Although the work she and Bill started continues, she focuses all her energy on Pivotal Ventures, which she started in 2015. She has $12.5 billion from the foundation to donate. Melinda wants to create social change and now has full decision-making control. Already, $1 billion is being directed to groups supporting women and children around world, including initiatives for reproductive rights in the US. In a guest essay for *The New York Times*, she explained why.

> As a young woman, I could never have imagined that one day I would be part of an effort like this. Because I have been given this extraordinary opportunity, I am determined to do everything I can to seize it and to set an agenda that helps other women and girls set theirs, too.[59]

REPROGRAMMING YOUR BRAIN TO OWN YOUR VOICE

Owning your voice starts with unraveling everything that makes you feel like you don't have one. Where did these feelings, voices, and blocks come from? How do they serve you? How do they protect you? How do they hold you back and stop you? How can you start to reframe them?

Recent studies show that our brains may take mental shortcuts daily, such as pattern recognition, filtering information, intuition, and more to save time and keep us focused. These processes are primarily unconscious and automatic.[60] Think of your mind as a computer. While there is debate in the scientific community about whether this analogy is accurate,[61] I believe it's a simple way to explain how the brain works. Your conscious mind acts like a keyboard and monitor: information goes in and you see it on the screen. The preconscious is like your recent files folder, holding day-to-day habits and thoughts we can quickly access. The subconscious, or unconscious, mind is more like a hard drive, storing your long-term memories and programming.

Sometimes though, the programming isn't your own.

As we explored in earlier chapters, your programming can come from your childhood, the criticisms you heard growing up, and other social and cultural influences from family, friends, education, and even the media. This programming affects what shows up on your screen and what shows up in your life. Thankfully, if you are aware, you can start reprogramming your brain.

To do so, start by reconsidering the messages it sends you daily. Psychologists estimate that we talk to ourselves ten to twenty times faster than we speak. A study by Dr. R. J. Korba says the rate of our inner speech is more than 4,000 words per minute.[62] Unfortunately, much of that inner talk is negative. So, what are our inner voices telling us every day? What do they tell you in moments of stress and uncertainty?

I'm not ready.

They are better than me.

I feel like an impostor.

I'm not achieving enough.

I'm scared I'll fail.

I'm being judged.

Am I good enough?

Am I getting this right?

Why does this always happen to me?

For me, it used to be *Am I getting this right?* It's like I was asking for permission or felt the need to have everything perfect and to make sure I controlled the things around me. If I constantly second-guess myself and ask, "Am I getting it right?" do I genuinely own my voice and trust myself? And what happens if I don't, in fact, get it right? Am I a failure? After a "Date with Destiny" event with Tony Robbins early in my coaching career, I realized that this is what my inner voice was constantly asking me.

Many of us have these negative inner voices, but Robbins introduced the concept of a "primary question."[63] This is a question that we ask ourselves over and over; it can become part of our identity and shape what we do, why we do it, and what we expect out of life. When we ask this question, our brains come up with answers and evidence to support our beliefs. If the question is negative, it can lead to pain and hold us back.

Your primary question likely formed in childhood as a survival instinct. Our brains are not designed to make us happy; they are designed to protect us and identify potential threats. The primary question serves as a safeguard, helping us avoid emotions and situations we fear, like failure, criticism, feeling like we don't belong, or being uncomfortable. This question often surfaces when we are most upset or stressed, aiming to keep us safe but potentially limiting our growth and happiness. Understanding and reshaping this question can lead to personal transformation.

Unpacking my primary question over the years, I realized it stemmed from my experiences as the older sister growing up in an immigrant family. I had a lot of responsibility and always felt I had to do everything right. I prided myself on achievements and doing well. However, life doesn't always allow for perfection. Asking myself *Am I getting this right?* reinforced my strengths, like being dependable and going above and beyond to troubleshoot and ensure everything was taken care of. But this mindset can be exhausting. What happens if I *don't* get everything right? If it's not perfect? Up until my kids were toddlers, I often struggled with perfectionism, trying to meet unrealistic standards, and feeling anxious when I fell short.

It has taken *years* of inner work (and a few breakdowns in early motherhood) to realize being perfect wasn't a badge of honor or something to strive for. Over the years, I've learned to lighten up, be more flexible, and let things go. It's not a big issue for me anymore. Still, it does creep up when I get stressed, especially around parenting my teenagers, and when I'm trying to do everything *and* anticipate *and* troubleshoot any problems. This can create a lot of unnecessary stress. Now, when the question of *Am I getting it right?* pops into my head, I tell myself, "Angela, you got this! How can you trust yourself even more right now?"

Once you discover your primary question, you gain the power to create a new one. While the process to change and grow isn't always easy, it is worthwhile to develop a thriving mindset for your future. It starts by understanding the fears that hold you back and keep you stuck. Next, you must change how you talk to yourself *about* yourself.

In the next two chapters, I show you how to own your voice by reframing your fears and identifying the messages or questions that conflict with what you are trying to achieve. We also explore the power of words, how labels can keep you trapped, and how to break free of them.

YOUR WORDS MATTER

In the 1990s, Japanese scientist Masaru Emoto performed fascinating experiments on the effect that words have on energy. Emoto's experiments and photos, detailed in his book *The Hidden Messages in Water*, demonstrated that energy and emotions generated by positive or negative words can change the physical structure of an object.[64] Using high-speed photography, Emoto found that crystals formed in frozen water that had been exposed to loving words showed beautiful, complex, and colorful snowflake patterns. Those exposed to negative thoughts formed incomplete, distorted patterns with dull colors. Although some in the scientific community are still skeptical of Emoto's research, his work with water remains a testament to the power of our voice's impact on ourselves and the world around us.

Your voice matters, your words matter, and the energy around them matters. How you use your voice is up to you.

We are made of about 70 percent water, so it feels right that the words we say to others impact the world and our ability to own our voices. Your voice doesn't have to be the loudest or boldest to have an impact; it just has to be yours. What you say—and whether you say it—affects the world in big, little, and even invisible ways. Remember: Your voice matters, your words matter, and the energy around them matters. How you use your voice is up to you.

EXERCISE

Take a few moments to review and reflect on the following warm-up questions about your relationship to your voice. If a question resonates deeply, invest just a few minutes to jot down your answers.

- How do I feel about my voice at this moment in my life?
- To what degree do I feel I fully own my voice?
- What are my initial ideas about why I'm not owning my voice as much as I could be?
- What could progress look like if I was to improve my relationship with my voice?

Chapter 3.2

BREAK THROUGH YOUR FEAR

*Use your fear; it can take you to the place
where you store your courage.*

—AMELIA EARHART

My client, functional medicine physician Dr. Ann Shippy, had a thriving practice and was a renowned expert in healing from toxic mold exposure, frequently contributing to various print publications. She was offered many opportunities to appear in videos and do interviews, but she kept turning them down because she had a fear of being on camera. "I was petrified. I'm the girl with twenty-six years of education who never raised her hand in class. I don't even like having my picture taken."[65] Her apprehension was holding her back from further expanding her influence and reaching a broader audience.

Ann healed herself from several autoimmune disorders and even mold toxicity. She understood intimately the challenges her patients were going through. She realized that if she wanted to help others heal and make a bigger impact, she needed to share her story as an Only and break through her fears. We started working together to help her step into the spotlight.

Breaking through her fear was challenging for Ann. Her natural shyness and anxiety about being the center of attention were significant barriers; however, by focusing on her larger purpose and message, she was able to reframe her fear. Helping people heal and prevent suffering became more important to her than feeling scared or unprepared. "It was a compulsion, like I can't be quiet anymore. There are so many people who need the information that I have. I learned so much every day that it was getting to the point where it felt irresponsible not to share what I'm learning."

Her first live video got more than 12,000 views, and taking that first step—breaking through the fear of being seen—unlocked even more opportunities and ways to make an impact. Since that first video, Ann has become a TEDx speaker, is regularly featured on television and several top podcasts, and has launched her own podcast. Most importantly, the moment expanded her ability to help others, amplifying her impact in ways she never imagined.

Maybe, like Ann, you feel confident speaking up one-on-one but are afraid of the spotlight—whether it's speaking up at a large meeting, giving a presentation for your department, participating on an industry panel, or being in front of the camera for social media promotion or a news interview. Maybe you get nervous and stiff, and your energy shifts. Your heart starts racing, you begin to sweat, or you feel tightness in your stomach or chest. Perhaps, for you, the fear of speaking up in public—regardless of the size of the audience—manifests differently. So, how can you make this fear go away?

You shouldn't necessarily want it to go away; instead, you need to *reframe* it. You want to understand where it comes from and why you need it. You need to learn how to use your fear as your partner. Shift your focus away from yourself to your message, purpose, and/or mission, and develop tools to calm your fear through practice and preparation. Embrace fear as a catalyst for growth, and let it drive you to deliver your message with greater clarity and impact.

THE FEAR OF SPEAKING UP

How many times have you heard that people fear public speaking more than death? This notion comes from the 1973 R. H. Bruskin Associates' study on American fears that appeared in *The Sunday Times*. While public speaking is indeed a top fear for many, a 2012 study, "Is Public Speaking Really More Feared Than Death?" found that people didn't actually fear public speaking more than death.[66] But while giving a presentation at work or giving a talk in front of a big crowd isn't life-threatening, it can feel that way for many because it activates the amygdala, the brain's emotional center that activates the "fight or flight" response.

The amygdala is your protector, but it can sometimes overreact, creating a fear response in situations that aren't truly dangerous. Evolutionary scientists suggest that we are prone to interpret being watched as a potentially dangerous situation, a remnant of our ancestors' survival instincts.[67] This may explain why Ann was initially triggered by being on camera. Additionally, the risk of rejection comes from the ancient fear of being rejected by your group, which could have meant facing predators alone—a potential death sentence.[68]

Feeling like all eyes are on you can be overwhelming, especially if you're an Only in the room. In these situations, it's natural to become hyperaware of your differences and to wonder how others perceive you. This heightened awareness can magnify the feeling of being scrutinized. You might feel pressure to be a certain way to avoid being judged negatively based on stereotypes or bias. If you've faced rejection before, you might fear it happening again. Not having others like you in the room can make you feel like you have no support or validation and make it harder to show up.

The fear you feel as an Only is *real*.

For many Onlys, speaking up has been—and continues to be—a very real life-threatening experience. Activists and advocates for underrepresented groups often face risks to their lives and livelihoods when challenging the status quo and defending marginalized communities.

In everyday work situations and beyond, the sensation of being observed and potentially rejected can trigger a primal response, making us feel as though we are facing real danger. While being in the spotlight—whether it's giving a talk or appearing on video—does not usually threaten our survival, our brains may react as if it does. To overcome this, we need to shift our perception of fear.

SHIFT FROM FEAR TO POWER

Understanding where your fear comes from allows you to appreciate it as a means of protection and support. That may be difficult when everything in your body is telling you otherwise, but it's important to remember that your brain is doing exactly what it is supposed to do. The good news is that your brain is adaptable. The amygdala is learning and shifting based on each experience. The key is to reframe your mindset from fear to power.

What if I told you that feeling wasn't fear but just energy?

What if I told you that feeling wasn't fear but just energy?

This energy is natural when you are about to do something *big*. It's your engine revving up for greatness. Speaking up and sharing your message demands a lot of energy, and that's exactly what your body is preparing for.

You *need* that energy.

When you're in front of an audience, whether it's a crowd, a camera, or a virtual platform, energy comes toward you. You need to hold that energy and project it back. Instead of labeling that physical response you get before speaking as "fear" and reinforcing your preprogrammed responses, like "I'm not ready" or "I don't know what to say" or "I'm going to die," think of this energy as your power. It's something that works *for* you, not against you. Reframing this energy from fear to power retrains your brain. Below are four ways to help you break through fear.

REFRAME FEAR AS YOUR PARTNER

Lin was gaining visibility in his company and was invited to represent his firm as a financial expert on a local TV show. Although he was confident in his expertise and comfortable with presentations, he had never been on television before and was scared that he would "make a fool" of himself. "Every time I even think about it, I start to sweat." When working with clients like Lin on media appearances, we start with mock interviews and discuss potential interview questions and key messages. For Lin, though, our first step was to address and reframe his fear. I wanted him to understand that having just the right amount of fear is not a bad thing.

According to psychologists Robert Yerkes and John Dodson, everyone needs some fear, stress, or arousal to reach peak level of performance.[69] With too little stress, there is no motivation, energy, or incentive. With too much fear, you can become overwhelmed and lose focus. At that point, the energy starts to work against you and keeps you from your full potential. Their ideas were so influential that the concept was named the Yerkes–Dodson Law.

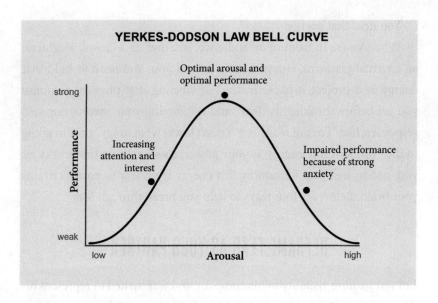

The key to reframing and making fear your partner is to ensure you have the optimal level of arousal. "Optimal" is when fear works for you: your brain and body are energized and you feel a sense of clarity and focus. To know whether an upcoming task—like delivering a presentation—will provide you with the optimal level of arousal (just enough to be energized into action but not paralyzed), you need to know how complex it is. If you're doing a simple task, a broader range of arousal levels can achieve the optimal level. However, if it's more complex or challenging, you may be more affected by higher arousal levels.

In those situations, the following five steps can help you handle your fear or stress to bring it down to an optimal level.

1. **Acknowledge it.** Why is this happening? Remind yourself that fear is a natural response.
2. **Understand it.** Is the fear real or imagined? Try to get to its root cause.
3. **Assess the risk.** Is the fear rational or exaggerated? Ask yourself, *What's the worst thing that could happen?*

4. **Challenge it.** What is another perspective? Question the negative thoughts that lead to fear.
5. **Reduce it.** How do you make it stop? Take small steps to build confidence and reduce fear over time.

With Lin, we began by acknowledging his fear, reinforcing that a bit of nervousness is okay; the energy will drive his performance on camera. Next, we needed to understand where his fear was coming from. During our time together, we discovered that his fear was rooted in a need to be perfect. Raised with high expectations and no room for error, Lin had internalized an "all-or-nothing" mindset that made him exceedingly hard on himself. Recognizing this pattern, Lin began to understand the source of his anxiety and worked on developing a more flexible mindset.

We then assessed what was at stake. What would happen if he *did* mess up? Lin realized that even if he made a mistake or two, the consequences would be minimal. His job security was solid, and while the appearance would boost his visibility, it wasn't a high-stakes situation and he likely wouldn't face significant scrutiny. This realization eased his anxiety. Lin saw this as a valuable opportunity to practice before more critical national appearances.

Then, we challenged his fear. Lin mentioned being afraid that his "voice didn't sound strong or credible enough." I offered another perspective: He didn't need to sound a certain way to be credible. He just needed to be clear, stay on point, and confidently share his expertise.

This is how you step into your voice and build credibility.

Finally, after a few rounds of mock interviews, Lin felt more prepared and confident, significantly reducing his fear.

By reframing and using fear as his partner—through acknowledgment, understanding, assessment, challenge, and reduction—Lin was able to complete the media interview. He used his fear of "making a fool" of himself to help drive his motivation, ensure he was prepared, showcase his expertise, and maintain his energy.

It turned out *great*.

While he found a few things he'd like to improve for the next time, it wasn't nearly as stressful as Lin had imagined. Most importantly, he was ready for the next opportunity. Although owning your voice can initially feel uncomfortable, starting and then taking action is crucial. The more you practice, the more natural and effortless it becomes.

SHIFT YOUR INNER TALK

Just moments before taking on the balance beam at the 2024 Paris Olympics, Simone Biles whispered to herself, "You got this!" As the most decorated US Olympic gymnast, Biles has used her platform to emphasize the power of intentional inner talk. In a CNBC interview, she shared, "Most of the time before I take the mat, I just tell myself, 'Confidence' and 'You have this.'" This mental strategy contributed to Biles's and Team USA's gold medal win in the women's gymnastics team all-around final.[70] Achieving peak performance at this top level takes *years* of commitment and determination, but it all begins with speaking intentionally to yourself.

The best part? You don't have to be an Olympic athlete to use this strategy!

In the previous chapter, we explored reprogramming your brain to own your voice. Instead of doubting myself with thoughts like "Am I getting this right?" during stressful moments, I now tell myself, "Angela, you got this!" By shifting my inner talk, I am reminded to *snap out of it*.

Studies show that talking to yourself in the second or third person—that is, using "you" or your own name instead of "I" or "me"—boosts clarity, confidence, and performance;[71] it flips a switch in the brain. Psychologist Ethan Kross, director of the Emotion and Self-Control Lab at the University of Michigan, says "distanced self-talk" is a psychological hack. By detaching from your thoughts, you can focus, consider them more objectively, and reframe your fear more easily.

In this study, Kross and his team gave volunteers only five minutes to prepare for a five-minute speech, instructing them not to take notes. Before the presentations, Kross's team had the participants reflect on their fears and anxieties. One group used the first-person pronoun "I" to talk about themselves, while the other half used "you" and their own name. After this reflection, they had to deliver their speeches in front of a panel of judges.

As predicted, the group who used distanced self-talk—referring to themselves as "you" and their own names—reported that they "experienced less shame and embarrassment" and "ruminated about their performance less afterward." Even the judges who reviewed the speeches indicated that "people in the distanced self-talk group performed better on the task as well." They not only experienced less stress and fear before *and* after speaking, but doing this also improved their performance.[72] Essentially, treating ourselves as other people can change how we think, feel, and behave. And most of the time, we are a lot nicer to and more objective about others, allowing us to reframe our fears more effectively.

So, the next time you are trying to reframe your fear, try to talk to yourself in the third person or address yourself by your first name. Instead of saying, "I got this!" say, "You got this!" or "Jim, you got this." Instead of saying, "I can do it!" say, "You can do it!" or "Stacy, you can do it!"

STOP FOCUSING ON YOURSELF

Most of us have some complicated feelings regarding our voice—not just how we sound, but how we come across and show up. We all have built-in templates of what we should and shouldn't sound like, and when reality doesn't quite match our expectation, it can make us uncomfortable and insecure. Most people dislike how they sound because it's not what they expect. This phenomenon is known as "voice confrontation."[73]

Remember when you first heard your voice on a recording? When you hear your voice through your body, it resonates differently. When it's not filtered, you hear more nuances, which may make you uncomfortable. If we believe our voice doesn't "sound right" or isn't "good enough," it can hinder our ability to speak up, keep us feeling small, keep us from fully owning our voice, and bring up all our fears.

I don't like the way I sound!
It feels weird.
I'm too stiff.
I don't feel natural.
I don't like my energy.
It doesn't feel like me.
I don't feel comfortable.
I hate my voice.

But are we good judges of our own voice? Not really.

Psychologists have found that people tend to focus on the negative quality of their voice recordings, magnifying imperfections that might go unnoticed by others. Studies show we usually view our own performance worse than others view it, yet we can see the performance of others more accurately.[74] This means how we see ourselves is often much more complicated, and only sometimes is it an accurate reflection of reality and our skill or performance. So, of course we judge ourselves more harshly. Our high standards, feelings of inadequacy, comparisons with others, and external pressures can all contribute to harsher self-judgment.

One way to break through your fear is to realize people aren't noticing you as much as you think. They are more concerned with themselves. This phenomenon, known as the "spotlight effect," was identified by researchers Thomas Gilovich, Victoria Husted Medvec, and Kenneth Savitsky. In their study published in the *Journal of Personality and Social*

Psychology, they discovered that people often believe the social spotlight shines more brightly on them than it actually does.[75]

In one experiment, Gilovich, Medvec, and Savitsky had college students wear an embarrassing T-shirt to class and asked the students to predict how many of their peers would notice. "While 50% of the students suggested that their fellow students would notice, only about 25% actually reported noticing the shirts."[76]

In another experiment of the same study, participants wore a T-shirt featuring a famous person they admired. "Even when participants wore T-shirts that they were not embarrassed to wear, they substantially overestimated the number of those present who could identify the celebrities depicted on them." Participants in the study predicted about 45 percent of their fellow students would notice their T-shirt; however, less than 10 percent of the students could identify the shirt. If you realize no one is paying attention to you that closely, you may be able to stop worrying and break through your fear.

Unfortunately, for many Onlys, breaking through fear isn't always so easy.

There may be instances where people are more critical *because* you are an Only; your unique identity might subject you to increased scrutiny or criticism. Those who have faced criticism based on their accent or perceived differences might understandably feel heightened anxiety about how they are perceived.

It's important not to let these experiences cloud your current reality, affect your performance, or undermine your belief in yourself. The key to breaking through your fear is to *stop focusing on yourself.* When you intentionally shift your focus to others, it helps alleviate the pressure you place on yourself and counters the "illusion of transparency"—the mistaken belief that others can see your nervousness as clearly as you feel it.[77]

Your fear is not as noticeable as you may think.

Now that you understand that how you view yourself isn't necessarily reality, you may be asking, "Well if I don't focus on myself, what *do* I focus on?" To continue to shift from fear to power, you need to focus on your message and mission.

FOCUS ON YOUR MESSAGE AND MISSION

Another way to break through your fear is to stay focused on your message and your higher purpose. What you have to offer—your stories, your insights, your wisdom, or your perspective in an everyday interaction—is a *gift*. Your voice matters, and what you can contribute to the world is bigger than your fear. What you want to say matters more than your fear.

To help you stay focused on your message and shift from fear to power, ask yourself:

1. What are the benefits and positive impacts of sharing my message?
2. What will happen if I don't share my mission or speak up?
3. What makes my message unique or valuable?
4. What "Only" expertise or experience do I bring?

> **Your voice matters, and what you can contribute to the world is bigger than your fear.**

Focusing on her impact is what enabled Ann to break through her fear of being seen. It was no longer about her; she had expertise and information that could help a lot of people. The potential consequences of *not* sharing her gift finally outweighed the fear holding her back. Similarly, Candice (from the previous chapter) was able to overcome her fear of speaking and embrace her awkwardness because she wanted to have an impact on women in her industry. She recognized her chance to share her journey, help younger women feel seen in a male-dominated field, and assure those struggling with invisible barriers that their voices matter too.

Research shows that focusing on others and what you are contributing can reduce the impact of stress in your life.[78] By concentrating on your message and your mission, you'll be able to reframe your fears, see your value, and fully own your voice.

CLAIM YOUR VOICE

Once you've made fear your partner and shifted your focus from yourself to your message and purpose, there's still one step left to own your voice: believing you deserve to be heard. It's important to recognize and value your voice, and to expect that others will listen and respect what you have to say. This belief affects your self-worth, confidence, and how your message lands with those around you.

When I first started as a reporter in Los Angeles at age twenty-seven, I wanted to sound more credible by having a deeper voice. I was referred to a celebrity voice coach and decided to invest in myself—a big step since I had just started making real money. I learned some voice exercises and strengthened my vocal cords, but the *real* lesson was about slowing down and claiming my voice.

I've always been a fast talker, which is great for getting things done, but not for establishing a strong presence. I learned not to fear taking up space or airtime. I learned to center myself on the core of who I am. After a few sessions, I did sound more credible, but it wasn't because of how deep my voice sounded. It came from how deeply I believed in myself and knew that I deserved to be heard. When I stopped needing permission

When I stopped needing permission and realized that I had a voice all along and claimed it, everything shifted.

and realized that I had a voice all along and claimed it, everything shifted. And that's how it can shift for you, too.

EXERCISE

One of the most important steps in using fear as your partner is learning how to reduce it; that is, to lower or calm your fears if they ever exceed the optimal level of arousal needed to effectively speak up. The following exercises can help.

BREATHING TECHNIQUES

Consciously slowing down your breath can help you relax and reframe your fear. According to the Cleveland Clinic, "The normal respiratory rate for an adult at rest is twelve to eighteen breaths per minute,"[79] which means most of us breathe too fast or shallow, especially when stressed. Navy SEALS use this "box breathing" strategy to stay calm before and after highly stressful situations:

1. Inhale for 4 seconds.
2. Hold your breath for 4 seconds.
3. Exhale for 4 seconds.
4. Hold your out breath for 4 seconds.
5. Repeat.

Continue this cycle of inhaling, holding, exhaling, and holding for at least four to five minutes or until you feel more relaxed and centered. There are more advanced techniques you can access at www.AngelaChee.com/poweroftheonly. But this will give you a simple start.

SHAKING TO RELEASE TENSION

According to recent studies, shaking prevents you from going into fight or flight mode, releases muscle tension, burns off excess adrenaline, and calms the nervous system. Animals do this naturally. When they get scared, they shake or shiver. It's their natural automatic response to fear or overexcitement. Shaking dissipates that energy.[80] But humans tend to hold on to it and power through stress. Shaking relieves that tension and tells your brain to calm down. To reduce your fears, do a systematic full-body shake.

1. Shake your right hand and arm, then your left hand and arm
2. Shake your right leg then left leg
3. Shake your hips
4. Shake your whole body

Or you can turn on your favorite song, let loose, and just shake.

HUMMING

I usually hum to warm up my vocal cords and increase my voice resonance before a speech. But humming is also a great stress reliever. Research shows it can decrease the heart rate and calm you down, but it increases your heart rate variability—an important metric displaying how well you deal with and recover from stress. It also improves attention and sleep quality.[81] To hum, breathe in through your nose, and then breathe out on a hum (*hmmm*) with your lips closed. You should feel the vibration on your lips and your face. Have fun changing the tune or volume and moving the vibration around your face, nose, and throat.

Chapter 3.3

REFRAME HOW YOU TALK TO YOURSELF ABOUT YOURSELF

When you start to rewrite the story of not-mattering, you start to find a new center. You remove yourself from other people's mirrors and begin speaking more fully from your own experience, your own knowing place. You become better able to attach to your pride and more readily step over all the despites.

—MICHELLE OBAMA

I was attending a panel at The Female Quotient's Equality Lounge at SXSW when founder Shelley Zalis asked, "Who in the room has impostor syndrome?" I looked around the room and noticed that almost everyone raised their hands—even some men. I felt this invisible pressure to fit in, like I was *supposed* to join the communal self-criticism to bond with others. But I stayed the course even though I felt a tinge of discomfort. Shelley's work on women's equality and closing the gender gap resonates with me. She is someone at the forefront of shifting cultural perspectives, so I was surprised when she asked that question. I thought, *Here we go again with the "How do you overcome impostor syndrome" questions.*

After everyone put their hands down, Shelley made a powerful declaration: "We need to stop putting these labels on ourselves!" Shelley and I were on the same page after all. She explained the importance of flipping the script, urging us to shift our internal dialogue and tell ourselves, "I'm not aggressive, I'm *assertive*. I'm not bossy, I'm *confident*."

When an audience member asked, "What do you say when someone says, 'You're too emotional?'" one of the panelists, Laura McElhinney from SXM Media, responded brilliantly with, "You're welcome."

Everyone laughed.

Most of us like labels. It's easier to relate to things when we can define them with a universal term. Unfortunately, the problem with labels is that they are *not* universal and can limit us in many ways. Using specific labels to describe certain behaviors can unintentionally create barriers that weren't there before. For example, labels can also lead to stereotyping, enforce rigid social expectations, and encourage binary thinking—favoring group identity over individuality, overgeneralizations, internalized bias, inflexibility, limited perspectives, and even discrimination. We often use labels to define ourselves:

I am Asian American.

I'm a recovering overachiever.

I'm a mother.

I'm a firstborn.

I'm an ambivert (a mix of introvert/extrovert).

Labels like these can give us a sense of identity and community. However, depending on the label and its use, they can also be very reductive. What may have been used to connect and allow us to share common experiences can also overshadow our individuality. Instead of making us feel seen, certain labels can trap us in our own limiting jail, restricting our growth and potential. Just the *use* of the language and a specific word can keep us stuck. We all apply different labels to ourselves that might not serve our best interests.

I'm not likable.

I'm invisible.

I'm not strong enough.

I'm a perfectionist.

I'm too much.

Words have power. It's time to change the language we use with ourselves.

It's time to reframe how you talk to yourself about yourself! How can you do that? Start by taking a closer look at how you interpret the labels others assign to you, as well as those you give yourself. We often internalize the words used to describe ourselves or our experiences, impacting our self-perception, emotions, and behavior. You need to reframe these labels so they empower you rather than limit your potential, ensuring they reflect your true identity. You must challenge your negative self-talk, self-limiting language, self-criticism, and assumptions. Understand where these labels come from, their history, the context in which they came to be, and how they are evolving today.

Once you see how some labels describe parts of yourself that don't need fixing or overcoming, you can leverage them positively and see them as a strength rather than an obstacle. You may even realize that these labels no longer define you at all.

In this chapter, we focus on three concepts that heavily rely on labels and disproportionately affect Onlys in the workforce: impostor syndrome, executive presence, and code-switching. We'll explore where they came from, why they lead us to talk about ourselves in ways that aren't always beneficial, and what we can do to reframe our self-talk.

Words have power. It's time to change the language we use with ourselves.

REFRAMING IMPOSTOR SYNDROME

Impostor syndrome is defined as "a psychological condition that is characterized by persistent doubt concerning one's abilities or accomplishments accompanied by the fear of being exposed as a fraud despite evidence of one's ongoing success."[82] Researchers estimate that around 70 percent of people will experience impostor syndrome at least once in their lives.[83] Despite its prevalence in the general population, it is usually associated more with women. I've worked with hundreds of clients and interviewed people of all genders and at various levels; many come to me when they feel unprepared or are ready to step into something bigger. Many confide their insecurities and fears, including the fear that they are impostors. For Onlys, these feelings are often magnified.

Not feeling "good enough" at times is a human experience, but is it really a *syndrome*?

These feelings of insecurity weren't always described as such. In 1978, professors Pauline Clance and Suzanne Imes published "The Impostor Phenomenon in High-Achieving Women: Dynamics and Therapeutic Intervention" in the journal *Psychotherapy: Theory, Research, and Practice*. After five years of interviewing and observing 150 high-achieving women in academia and professional fields, they coined the term "impostor phenomenon" to describe the pervasive feeling of being an impostor among their accomplished peers.[84]

Leslie Jamison's article "The Dubious Rise of Impostor Syndrome" in *The New Yorker* notes that Clance and Imes's paper spread widely, gaining traction over decades. In 1985, Clance published a book, *The Impostor Phenomenon*, and introduced an official "I. P. scale" for researchers. However, it wasn't until the rise of social media that the concept, now rebranded as "impostor syndrome," truly exploded. Imes has remarked that the popularization of the term as a syndrome distorted its original intent. Clance clarified that their goal was always to *normalize* the experience, not pathologize it.[85]

The original study not only validated the experiences of the women involved but also fostered a sense of connection and camaraderie. Tricia Montalvo Timm, author of *Embrace the Power of You*, shared with me that learning about the doubts and insecurities of older, more accomplished women was encouraging. "Hearing others talk about impostor syndrome helped me overcome my fears and made me feel that I wasn't alone."[86] However, for many of us, this label can be limiting and may reinforce the notion that something is inherently wrong.

After my keynotes, I frequently heard from many, especially young women who grappled with impostor syndrome and sought advice on overcoming it. Initially, I used the term in my coaching and training, but as I delved deeper into its implications, I realized how it can be disempowering. I've come to believe that when individuals strongly identify with impostor syndrome to fit in or perceive it as a personal flaw, they risk reinforcing the very problem it represents—feelings of inadequacy and being "not enough." Instead of challenging the status quo and asserting their own power, they may inadvertently perpetuate their own sense of being "out of place."

The term has recently faced public scrutiny, with experts questioning its usefulness and relevance. In the 2021 *Harvard Business Review* article "Stop Telling Women They Have Impostor Syndrome," Ruchika Tulshyan and Jodi-Ann Burey criticized the label for overlooking the systemic barriers and inequality faced by professional women, particularly women of color. "Impostor syndrome directs our view toward fixing women at work instead of fixing the places where women work."[87]

What actions can you take to shift the status quo? Stop telling yourself you have a syndrome!

Feeling like you are not good enough, especially when trying something new, carving a different path, or being an Only in any given environment *is* a natural emotion. We need to stop calling it a "syndrome" and pathologizing it.

Feeling like you are not good enough, especially when trying something new, carving a different path, or being an Only in any given environment *is* a natural emotion. We need to stop calling it a "syndrome" and pathologizing it.

There is nothing wrong or abnormal about you, and *you don't need to be fixed*.

Instead, we need to reframe these feelings as the growing pains that come from being unique, challenging ourselves, trying something new, and/or showing up differently. That feeling of wanting to be better is what keeps us going. We wouldn't grow or evolve as much if we felt we already had it all figured out.

Founder, CEO, and chair of The Garcia Companies and owner of the United Football League Dany Garcia stands as the only woman in the US to carry a majority ownership of a large sports franchise. Born in New Jersey to Cuban immigrants, she grew up watching her father support three children by managing an auto body shop. She started working at age twelve and had huge aspirations.

Despite her goals, Dany always carried around the "you're not enough" burden. At the 2024 Makers Conference, she shared that despite reaching leadership positions, she still battles her inner critic, and this gap fuels her drive. "You get to a position of leadership, and I'm so grateful to be in them, but almost everyone forgets that your insecurities, your doubts—

they actually come with you. They don't take away the spot, they make you better, they make you show up with clarity and they make sure you do all the work and maybe extra work. So, something that was a detriment to confidence became a superpower when it came to execution."[88]

Next time you feel insecure, don't tell yourself you are an impostor. Instead, tell yourself that your feelings of nervousness and insecurities are a healthy sign that you are embarking on a growth opportunity.

REFRAMING CODE-SWITCHING

Keynote speaker and former college director Frank Kitchen was talking to a group of students on campus when an introverted Black student asked him for advice. "How do you get along with everyone? I just saw you talking to a group of White students, then you started speaking Spanish to the Latinx group, and now you're with us at the Black Student Union and have no problem talking to all of us. How do you do that?" Frank, who is Black, responded, "I try to find what we have in common versus what separates us. What is our uniqueness? Let's connect about that."[89]

For Frank, how he connects is a sign of respect. "When I speak to a group where I know they speak a different language, I try to say 'Hello' in that language; if I go to an Asian house, I may take off my shoes, when I travel, I want to be part of the culture. For me, it's not conforming. We're showing how to better value people."

Born into a military family in West Germany, Frank moved to Japan before eventually settling in various locations across the US. Throughout his life, he often was the Only in many settings, initially making it difficult for him to form relationships and contributing to his introverted nature. However, he now views these challenges as his superpower. "I can connect with people because of these experiences, and it has set me up for success as a speaker because I'm constantly [talking to and] with different groups."

Code-switching, initially documented by sociologists like John J. Gumperz, referred to the practice of alternating between two different languages within a single conversation.[90] For example, I grew up switching between Mandarin Chinese with my parents and English with my friends. But code-switching also has a broader meaning: it involves individuals from underrepresented groups adjusting their language, behavior, appearance, etc. to align with the dominant culture. It means that you change the way you speak based on who you are talking to or the context of a situation.

This broader definition of code-switching often carries a negative connotation, especially when it implies losing one's identity to "fit in." Some view code-switching as phony or inauthentic, believing it to be a form of self-betrayal. In many contexts, code-switching can be both exhausting and detrimental, imposing significant psychological costs and leading to burnout. For some, the constant need to shift between different linguistic and cultural codes to align with the dominant group may feel like an unfair burden. This ongoing adjustment can be stressful and emotionally draining, preventing individuals from showing up authentically. The pressure to self-monitor and the fear of judgment can induce anxiety, social pressure to conform, and deep-seated identity conflicts.

Despite this potential mental toll, and unless code-switching is involuntary and you feel compelled to conform to others' standards and expectations under threat of dire consequences, labeling it as a negative behavior can be limiting. Internalizing the concept of code-switching as something inherently bad creates a conflict between your authentic self and external norms. However, when viewed through the lens of "connecting," code-switching can be a powerful and beneficial skill for Onlys.

Instead of perceiving the ability to navigate between languages, cultures, and social groups as a form of self-neglect or compromise, recognize it as a form of connection, as Frank does. This flexibility allows you to engage more effectively and authentically with diverse environments without diminishing your true identity. Reframe code-switching not as a survival tactic to fit in, but as a superpower that taps into your multidimensional nature and enhances your capacity to bridge different worlds.

As an Only, I've faced the challenge of navigating environments where I didn't fit in. However, instead of seeing this as a weakness, I prefer to see it as a *skill* I've cultivated. Like Frank, I choose to see code-switching as a tool, one that allows me to relate and connect with diverse groups—whether speaking to my Chinese relatives, addressing a room full of male executives, or engaging a group of children. In each interaction, I might shift *how* I relate to them or speak to them, but I won't change *who* I am.

> **Reframe code-switching not as a survival tactic to fit in, but as a superpower that taps into your multidimensional nature and enhances your capacity to bridge different worlds.**

I believe that effective communication is about understanding my audience without compromising my authenticity. In this sense, code-switching is not about masking who you are but about confidently owning your voice and connecting with others on a deeper level.

Tony Chatman is a keynote speaker, author, and organizational culture expert. He told me, "Effective communication is measured not by what you said but by what was heard. If you want to be an authentic communicator and be good at it, then you have to be able to adjust your wording so that the receiver can receive it."[91] He added, "There's a narrative about the Black community that if I'm assertive, authoritative, or even competent in a certain way I can be viewed as a threat. So, figuring out how to be confident, competent, and likable is a gift and skill every Only needs to figure out."

According to Tony, we are *all* complex individuals, and that needs to be honored. "I should be able to communicate in a complex way that reflects different facets of who I am and I'm not being fake or conforming. There's a part of me that is corporate, so for me to communicate in a corporate way, that's part of who I am. There's also a part of me that hangs out with the boys, and that's also part of who I am. And for me not to be both and shift back and forth, I feel like it would be less authentic for me. For some people, I'm not Black enough; for other people, I'm too Black, and I can't let it affect me. I know how to navigate that, and I know how to deal with it, and I know how to connect."

I'm not telling you whether you should code-switch; rather, I encourage you to critically examine the label when it's applied to you—especially the negative connotation, and particularly when you apply it to yourself. Does the label affect your self-perception and make you feel like you are always out of place or disconnected? You shouldn't feel forced to code-switch; you get to *choose* when you use this power and what to label it.

I understand that not all environments offer this freedom, and that it's important to acknowledge that you may still feel a sense of anxiety and pressure about code-switching. But by questioning and reframing it, we can start to create new norms that help us own our voices even more.

REFRAMING EXECUTIVE PRESENCE

Elaine was a manager at a male-dominated tech company, preparing for her first-ever conference as a panel moderator. Despite her success and expertise, she was overwhelmed with nervousness and self-doubt. This anxiety wasn't new; earlier in her career, she had been the sole woman on a software engineering team. Despite her technical prowess, high-quality work, and dedication as a team player, she was consistently overlooked for promotions. When she finally sought feedback, her manager bluntly told her she lacked "executive presence." Elaine shared, "I was devastated.

I thought my work should have spoken for itself but it became clear that wasn't enough." Although she eventually found a better fit at her current company and has received the promotions she deserved, those words lingered with her. As we worked together, Elaine kept telling me that she didn't deserve to be on stage.

Executive presence is the "it" quality that leaders are expected to have and that can either make or break a leader's career trajectory. Economist and author Sylvia Ann Hewlett, who first coined the term "executive presence," tried to crack the code in 2012. Her research shows that confidence, decisiveness, superior speaking skills, ability to command the room, and being polished were the most important traits and skills for executive presence. Her second round of research in 2022 shows that what people expect from a leader is continuing to evolve.[92] But while people often use the term, it still doesn't have a universal definition.

Research by Tracom Group revealed that 51 percent of HR practitioners found it challenging to define executive presence clearly. This quality isn't based on concrete performance metrics but rather on how others perceive you. This makes it difficult to quantify or assess; however, 81 percent of people believe that executive presence is easy to identify. It "continues to be an '*I know it when I see it*,' concept—identifiable but undefinable."[93]

Research reveals that the lack of a clear definition for executive presence opens the door to stereotypes, biases, and assumptions, leading to unfair criteria for evaluating leadership and potential. It can exclude people and perpetuate stereotypes of what makes a good leader—which in our male-dominant culture historically has been defined as having traits typically attributed to male leaders: assertiveness, aggressiveness, decisiveness, and a commanding presence. As a result, those who are perceived as not having these traits are presumed to lack executive presence and not be leadership material. In pursuit of executive presence, people try to shape themselves into a traditional leadership mold instead of allowing their individual strengths to shine.

What makes the vague "executive presence" label so dangerous to Onlys is that it can be internalized and create self-doubt. The lack of a clear definition allows the imposition of biased, stereotypical expectations that can unfairly marginalize those who don't conform to traditional leadership molds. Some Onlys may already feel like outsiders or face unique challenges, exacerbating feelings of inadequacy and perpetuating a sense of never measuring up. The pressure to fit an undefined—and often exclusive—standard can cause immense stress and hinder growth. This not only affects confidence but can also limit career advancement opportunities.

You might not be able to control how others perceive you, but you have the power to reshape your own perception.

For instance, Elaine (despite her success and the respect she's earned in her current role) was haunted by a previous employer's vague criticism of her executive presence. Like Elaine, many of you might preemptively rule out opportunities or second-guess your capabilities because you have internalized an elusive standard of executive presence that seems out of reach. This internal conflict and fear of failure can ultimately stifle your potential and impede your progress.

Jennifer McCollum, the CEO of Catalyst, vividly illustrates the dilemma many women and Onlys face. Early in her career, she was labeled "a cupcake with a razor blade inside," a description that showcases the conflicting expectations placed on female leaders. Research shows that when women take charge, they are viewed as competent but disliked; however, when they are nurturing and emotional, they are liked but viewed as less competent.[94] "I was supposed to be this cupcake: soft, kind, and collaborative, but if I'm also competitive and driven, it wasn't okay. I realized decades later that a man would never [have] been described that way."

This is why it's important to reframe the labels for yourself.

You might not be able to control how others perceive you, but you have the power to reshape your own perception. Actively reject the stereotypes and biases associated with traditional labels of executive presence and leadership. Instead, focus on your unique strengths and the distinct value you bring to the table.

In her twenties, Jennifer didn't view the label of "a cupcake with a razor blade inside" as a compliment. However, she has since embraced it, understanding that both the razor blade and the cupcake are integral parts of her authentic self. "As I got more comfortable in my position as CEO [at Linkage], I could more readily balance the two and encourage people across gender—especially the men—to demonstrate their cupcake qualities that are traditionally associated with women. We can all be this beautiful blend, and the expectation shouldn't only be that women have to toggle between these things."[95]

Reframing the "executive presence" label for Elaine allowed her to see it through a broader lens; one that embraced her strengths as a good listener and her ability to make others feel seen and valued. By redefining this label, she overcame her fears and took the stage with newfound confidence. As a panel moderator, Elaine asked thoughtful, insightful questions that drew on her expertise as a software engineer and delivered a performance that exceeded even her own expectations.

While public speaking isn't her natural strength, Elaine understands that she can cultivate a form of "executive presence" that aligns with her authentic self. She's learned to focus on a leadership style that reflects her values—being knowledgeable, collaborative, and inclusive. I believe it's essential to develop your presence and continually refine how you show up as a leader but ensure you don't let the narrow definition of "executive presence" hold you back. Embrace your own unique leadership style and use it to propel yourself forward.

CULTURAL SHIFTS START WITH YOU

I've personally stopped using the phrases "impostor syndrome" and "executive presence." While I've always believed in the power of words, the heavily label-reliant concepts of "impostor syndrome," "code-switching," and "executive presence" didn't bother me for years. It wasn't until 2021 that I started to see how they are misused and overused. I began questioning them. My reporter brain led me down the rabbit hole of research to discover how they started and how they often are internalized negatively. Then I started to question other labels. Once you are aware of something, you can't unsee it. It starts to show up *everywhere*.

It may seem subtle, but pausing to reflect on how words and labels can hold us back and intentionally choosing not to use them anymore can start to shift conversations and cultural narratives that create inequities and unfairness. Change happens over time through acknowledgment and small actions.

My first step was to internally validate that I no longer believed in these labels. By not using them and continuing to change the narrative around them, I may start to change the actual use of the word itself in society. One person at a time. Others may not notice immediately, but I know that if we change the words, we can change the collective mindset. It will take time, but that is how it starts.

It begins with you.

If you relate to a label that has been assigned to you or that you have adopted—and you don't mind—by all means, continue using it. But first, ask yourself *Is the label serving me, or is it telling me something that I need to fix about myself to meet someone else's standards? Is it limiting my view of myself and my ability to own my voice?* If the answer is yes, ditch them.

EXERCISE

This chapter focused on words and ideas and how they can either support or undermine you. The exciting part is that it often takes only a moment to recognize how you speak to yourself and to reframe it positively. The following reflection questions are designed to help you do that.

- What labels (words, phrases, or descriptions) have others put on me in the past?
- How have people labeled me in ways that do not necessarily reflect who I am or what I am capable of?
- What labels have I put on myself, now or in the past?
- What labels have I put on others that I could consider reframing?

Write the labels you've been given or put on yourself in Column A. In Column B, write a new, empowering word or description to replace it.

Column A   Column B

_____   _____

_____   _____

_____   _____

_____   _____

PRINCIPLE 4

OWN YOUR COMMUNICATION

Chapter 4.1

OWN YOUR COMMUNICATION

Every act of communication is a miracle of translation.

—KEN LIU

My eyes were barely open as the sound of hissing hot oil and the smell of fragrant frying dough filled the house. Most weekends, I woke up to my dad cooking Chinese food in the kitchen. This time, it was *cong, you bing*. Green onion pancakes.

He would make the dough and roll it out by hand, transforming the kitchen into a whirlwind of flour. I'd stand next to him and watch silently as he flattened the dough, covered it with oil, and layered it with diced green onions and salt. He'd then roll it up, twist it like a cinnamon roll, and then roll it out and flatten it again. Labor-intensive work.

Each pancake was filled with swirled layers of dough and pieces of green onion and fried to a golden crisp. He'd lay them flat on paper towels to soak up the excess oil before cutting them up like a pizza, making it easier to pass out to my neighbors up and down the block.

"Hurry, they have to be hot!" he prompted me in Mandarin Chinese to deliver them fast. Then, switching to English, he exclaimed, "Chinese pizza!"

"That's *not* pizza!" I retorted in Chinglish—Mandarin with English words thrown in—because the word pizza didn't have a translation.

"I know," he said. "But they don't know *cong, you bing*; pizza is something they can relate to."

To my dad, sharing our culture through food was a nice community gesture, one of connection. But for a seven-year-old girl who just wanted to fit into an all-White neighborhood, it was potential for rejection.

I reluctantly dressed, packed up the food on paper plates, and went to my friend's house next door. Keri's mom greeted me with a smile.

"What is this?" she asked me.

"Chinese pizza! My dad made it for you." I watched as Keri took a bite.

"Yum, Chinese pizza. Thanks!"

Seeing that she liked it, I felt a sense of relief. "You're welcome," I said and ran to the next house.

Sharing our culture through food became a weekend tradition in our family. Who knew Chinese pizza had so much power? In the 1970s, Chinese food wasn't as accessible as it is now. Even though we lived in Los Angeles, we were in the suburbs, so we had to drive about forty minutes to Chinatown every weekend to find Asian groceries and ingredients. Most of my neighbors didn't know anything about us or Chinese food. But they quickly learned they liked Chinese pizza, and that was one seed planted in their cultural awareness.

My dad used food as a way to connect.

As a communication coach, my work goes deeper than just how to speak or deliver a presentation. Most of my clients first come to me because they are preparing for something specific—a big event or meeting, a TV interview, a product launch, etc. They're often so caught up in how they look, how they sound, or how their slides appear that they forget to focus on what *really* matters: the audience and the impact of their words. They often miss what my dad understood years ago with his Chinese pizza—connecting with the audience and framing the communication in ways that will resonate with them.

In this way, my dad owned his communication.

Owning your communication means you know how to communicate so that others will hear you, allowing you to navigate any environment—whether you're leading a team, pitching an idea, advocating for change, or even negotiating with your partner or children. It's about more than just what you say; it's about how you engage with your audience to create meaningful impact and drive change. It means being heard and felt. It means that in our interconnected and digital world, you have the tools to be clear, confident, connected, and ready for any opportunity.

It also means that, as the Only, you can see your gift of being a bridge builder and know that *you* have the power to plant seeds of understanding, amplify the voices of others, and foster inclusive conversations.

Owning your communication is vital to harnessing the Power of the Only.

By owning your communication, you not only overcome your own barriers and step fully into your potential but also pave the way for other Onlys to do the same.

You can thrive in any environment when you can connect and communicate effectively. Projecting clarity, confidence, and presence reinforces your power. It builds trust and credibility, enhances your leadership and influence, and positions you to effect change and empower others.

Whether communicating in person, on video, or from the stage, doing so authentically and powerfully is crucial. It will prepare you for any situation and amplify your impact. By owning your communication, you not only overcome your own barriers and step fully into your potential but also pave the way for other Onlys to do the same.

COMMUNICATION IS A LEARNED SKILL

Anne Chow is a transformative business leader, author of *Lead Bigger*, and the first woman of color CEO in AT&T's 140-plus year history. Leading AT&T Business—a $35 billion global unit with 35,000 employees—Anne is celebrated for her authentic leadership and talent in fostering meaningful relationships while delivering extraordinary results through high-performance teams. Despite this record, communication was the skill Anne struggled with the most. "I was shy. I fancy myself as an introverted engineer. I was stereotypically great at math and science but wasn't a good communicator." She told me she struggles with anxiety in the spotlight, but over the years, she learned to manage her fears and stepped into her leadership role. "I realized to get anything done, you have to work to understand relationships and build connections."[96]

As an engineer, Anne was used to solving problems on her own. It wasn't until she attended business school that she focused on collaboration and learned how to communicate in groups. Early in her career, Anne also worked with a public speaking coach and media trainer. "Their first job was to record you, which is horrifying." And she continued to look for opportunities to grow. "I worked at it. It was super hard and very, very uncomfortable, but I knew I had to do it. The more you practice, the better you get." As her teams grew, Anne continued to challenge herself. Communication may seem to come naturally for successful leaders, but for many like Anne, it's a learned skill cultivated over time.

Do you believe communication skills are innate? If so, you may not see any point in working on them. Why invest your energy into something you're never going to be good at, right? Or maybe you haven't experienced the critical role it plays in your personal and professional success. Like many, you may underestimate the importance of communication and connection, so you don't focus on it or make the time to improve.

Most people believe they are at least decent communicators and often rely on instinct and improvisation. While this approach may work for those who are natural communicators, for many, it only reinforces poor habits and leads to ineffective communication. Some people are overconfident in their skills, others are oblivious to their audience—whether it's an audience of one, or ten, or one hundred. They fail to accurately read the room and fail to connect with it. Some people struggle with both overconfidence and a lack of awareness, further complicating their communication efforts.

One of my clients, Jonathan, was a brilliant scientist. Outside his tight-knit scientific team, Jonathan struggled to connect with people. He spent most of his career in the lab, so he felt no need to put in the effort. However, when he moved into a leadership role at a biotech company and needed to interact with other departments and the public, Jonathan found it incredibly challenging. Despite his obvious passion and intelligence, he used a lot of jargon and didn't know how to explain things well. He didn't even realize when he was talking over people's heads. He believed the science spoke for itself. Jonathan was more focused on the facts and proving his expertise than sharing information that resonated with others.

While we would like to believe we are effective communicators, most of the time we are thinking about what to say and how we come across to others. True communication goes beyond speaking; active listening, an understanding of the audience's needs, and the ability to pick up on subtle cues like facial expressions and body language play vital roles. Sometimes, we are so focused on speaking itself that we don't take the time to consider the audience's perspective, listen to their feedback, or focus on the overall purpose and outcome of the interaction.

To truly own your communication, you need to focus on connection and making sure your audience feels both seen *and* heard. When you don't, it may damage your personal and professional relationships or lead to significant misunderstandings; at best, it might result in a missed chance to make an impact and can hinder your growth. If you manage to enter the room but fail to engage your audience, you forfeit the opportunity to share your ideas, showcase your leadership, and inspire others. Visibility and recognition are crucial for professional growth. If your voice isn't heard, your contributions may go unnoticed, and your stories may remain untold.

Anne admits that she still gets butterflies in her stomach when she speaks, but she continues to hone her craft. Ultimately, she realized that the journey to own your communication isn't just about public speaking and being confident in front of thousands. "It means the ability to authentically connect one-on-one, one-to-many in different settings, in a way that's true to you and resonates with others and ideally inspires others." Mastering communication requires intention and purpose; it's a skill that you can and must cultivate.

COMMUNICATION IS VITAL FOR THE FUTURE

The microphone was pointed at me, and for a split second, I froze. My mind went completely blank. I didn't know what to do or say.

I was at a conference when the host interviewed me for an event recap video. I had just left the news business and started to blog/vlog. I don't remember her exact question or what I said, but I *do* remember not feeling ready. And I didn't like it.

How could someone like me, who had been on TV, not be ready?

Throughout my career, I was accustomed to being on camera and interviewing others, but being interviewed myself was a whole new challenge. I knew how to connect with an audience, but I didn't know how to articulate my own beliefs and share my story as I transitioned to this new phase of my life. I hadn't taken the time to really think about it.

This was a new skill set I had to learn, and you can too.

Unfortunately, most people lack access to formal communication training. Organizations don't offer enough opportunities for people to develop their skills or only offer them to those on a management track. When training is available, it often focuses on public speaking, but there's more to owning your communication—such as showing empathy, listening, understanding body language, and connecting with others. In our interconnected world, mastering communication across various mediums and audiences is essential. It is vital to go beyond just public speaking; we must cultivate a comprehensive set of communication skills.

After my experience being interviewed, I developed a framework to help me gain clarity on who I am and how I wanted to own my communication. I wanted to be prepared for any opportunity that came my way.

In the next few chapters, I will show you how to use this framework— the YOU, Amplified!® Connection Framework—to help you become a clear, confident, and connected communicator in any situation, whether on stage, leading an important meeting, having a one-on-one conversation, recording videos, or being interviewed by the media. I'll also explore how you can create the change you want in the world, have the difficult conversations you need to have, and manage it all without burning out.

As Onlys, we have spent much of our lives navigating environments where we didn't always fit in. This unique experience has given us a powerful edge—a communication superpower. Through these challenges, we have developed an exceptional ability to be in tune with our audience, showing heightened empathy, adaptability, and flexibility.

We've learned to understand and articulate diverse viewpoints, often more deeply than those who have never had to contend with such differences. This skill is crucial in today's polarized and disconnected world, where effective communication can bridge divides and bring people together. When you embrace and own your communication, you harness this ability to foster collaboration and unity that others might struggle to achieve.

Your unique perspective allows you to connect with others in ways that promote understanding and cooperation. Societal and professional landscapes are increasingly fragmented, but we can be bridge builders. Leveraging our communication superpowers, we can lead conversations that inspire change, build consensus, and create a more connected and inclusive future.

EXERCISE

Before diving into the possibilities of becoming more assertive and owning your communication, consider some self-reflection. This will help identify areas in your communication that are ripest for improvement and make it easier for you to gain new skills.

- The last time I communicated something powerfully, what exactly did I do well, and what makes me proud of that moment?
- In the past year or so, when have I wished I had communicated something more effectively at work? What was missing that led to this less-than-ideal communication?
- If I can learn to own my communication (covered starting with the next chapter), what are the possible rewards?

Chapter 4.2

CONNECT WITH YOUR AUDIENCE

Communication is not about saying what we think.
Communication is about ensuring others hear what we mean.

—SIMON SINEK

Susan walked into the boardroom clutching a towering stack of papers, looking frazzled, and hastily setting up her computer. With a sigh, she said, "I'm sorry, I stayed up all night trying to finish the presentation, which was just approved." She handed me a massive set of printed slides and started reviewing her PowerPoint presentation.

Slide after slide was crammed with bullet points and dense information. At times, she barely glanced at me, absorbed in reading from the slides. Despite her extensive presentation, I still struggled to grasp the main takeaway and its relevance to the audience.

Susan was one of several leaders I coached to prepare for speaking at an industry conference. Many of them, like Susan, spent all their energy on the wrong aspects. They became so absorbed in perfecting their slides and ensuring every detail was approved that they lost sight of the audience's needs, the essence of their message, and the true purpose of their presentation. Many executives I've worked with (especially in traditional corporate industries) focus intensely on refining data and slides but often neglect what truly matters—connecting with the audience.

Connecting with your audience is vital to owning your communication. It builds trust, enhances engagement, and makes your message more relevant and effective. When people feel understood, seen, and valued, they are more likely to hear you, allowing you to make an impact and move people to action.

When I work with leaders like Susan, I employ a proven process that I've honed through years of experience—and one that I personally use before every event or appearance. This process is designed to help clarify the message, organize thoughts, and forge a meaningful connection with any audience. The **YOU, Amplified! Connection Framework** consists of seven steps.

Combined, all these steps lead to one destination—a successful connection with your audience. Whether you are preparing to have a one-on-one conversation, lead a meeting, give a talk, shoot a video, or make a media appearance, whether in person or virtually, with the YOU, Amplified! Connection Framework, you have the tools to feel clear, confident, and connected for every opportunity. A worksheet at the end of the chapter provides a space for notes as we break down each step.

> **When people feel understood, seen, and valued, they are more likely to hear you, allowing you to make an impact and move people to action.**

YOU, Amplified! Connection Framework

A UDIENCE Know your audience. Who are you speaking to? What do you want them to walk away with?

M ESSAGE Be clear with your message: What is it? What do you want to share with others? Why do you believe what you believe and do what you do?

P URPOSE Know your objective. What is YOUR purpose for this appearance? What are YOU hoping to achieve?

L EAD Decide how you will show up. How are you going to lead? How will others see you?

I M A G E Visualize your image. What image do you want to convey? This may be through wardrobe, makeup, style, brand colors, or video background if applicable.

F EELING Embody the energy you want. How do you want to feel? What feeling do you want your audience to have?

Y OU, Amplified! It's all about you. Step into your amplified self.

KNOW YOUR A̲UDIENCE

Who are you talking to?

This question may seem straightforward, but it's often overlooked. Many people like Susan become so consumed with their presentation—how they look, how they sound, or how polished their slides are—that they lose sight of the audience's needs. Ask yourself:

Who's sitting in the audience?
Who's receiving my message?
Who is at the meeting?

Who is watching the video?

But more importantly, what do they care about?

What do they need?

How am I going to connect with them and serve them?

What's in it for them?

Focusing on the audience helps you with two things: it helps put you at ease and connect at a deeper level. When you shift attention away from yourself and concentrate on addressing the audience's needs and concerns, it reduces the pressure you feel. It's about what *they* will walk away with. What gift are you leaving *them* with?

When you understand what the audience needs and what the world looks like from their perspective, you can create a better rapport—establishing understanding and trust. Effective communication can lead to shared brain activity, what neuroscientists call "neural coupling." Research shows that when you deeply connect with your audience, their neural activity aligns with yours, leading to even deeper comprehension and emotional connection.[97]

The first step in the process is to understand your audience's specific and unique needs. For example, if you're speaking to a group of corporate executives, their expectations and interests will differ significantly from those of small business owners or high school students. Similarly, the way you communicate in a team meeting might vary from how you pitch to investors. When making a media appearance, the approach for a business-focused segment on CNBC will differ from that of a local morning show.

Even in a one-on-one conversation, understanding your audience is crucial. While the core content of your message may remain the same, your method of delivery, the stories you choose to share, and the perspectives you emphasize should be tailored to resonate with your audience.

Ask yourself: *Why are they listening to me? What challenges are they facing? What can I do for them?*

Now that you understand your audience's needs, ensure you address them right at the start. Don't wait until the end to highlight the key points. In journalism, we say, "Don't bury the lede," which means don't obscure the most important part of the story with less relevant information. Start with the lede instead. For example, Susan didn't explain why the information she was about to present mattered to her audience or how it could solve their problems until the end of her presentation. She could have led with that insight to capture the audience's interest and then supported it with research and slides. This is how Susan initially started her presentation:

> Hi, I'm Susan. Today I'm sharing our latest product that has X, Y, and Z, and here's all the research. In summary (forty minutes later), I hope this new program will save you and your company time and money by reducing costly processing mistakes that you have told us are your number one problem. And by being here, you will be the first group to have access to the program before your competitors.

Compare that with what she said when she put her audience first:

> We know that processing mistakes is your number one problem right now. Imagine if there was something that could help you reduce these mistakes, save you time and money, and get you more customers. We just released the program. You've heard about our research for years, but today, we are launching the app. Right now, we will show you how it works and give you early, exclusive access.

If you can tell the difference between these examples, you can make the same kind of shift.

To practice, choose an upcoming event, meeting, or appearance and visualize the audience. Then ask yourself the following questions and write down your thoughts if you are ready to dive in.

- **Who am I speaking to?** (Demographics, background, interests.)
- **What do *they* want to walk away with?** (Their needs and expectations.)
- **What do we have in common?** (Shared experiences, values, and interests.)
- **What are they struggling with? What challenges do they face?** (Pain points.)
- **At what level are they?** (Tailor the message so it's not too basic or too complicated.)
- **What do I want them to walk away with?** (Takeaways.)

BE CLEAR WITH YOUR MESSAGE

What is the message you are trying to convey?

Whether you are leading a meeting or speaking at a large event, being clear about the message you want to convey helps you stay focused on what you want to achieve or express. Clarity in your message provides a framework to organize your thoughts and pinpoint exactly what and how you want to say it. It prevents the discussion, presentation, or speech from being too broad. It helps you to keep it simple, allowing your audience to understand, retain, and hopefully act on what you are sharing. A clear message helps you respect your audience's time and attention.

Being clear is as simple as listing your top three talking points or the main idea you want to convey. Presenting information this way follows the "rule of three" that is widely used in storytelling, public speaking, advertising, comedy, and more. This principle suggests that ideas presented in threes are more effective, memorable, and satisfying because they leverage the brain's natural pattern recognition. Three is the minimum number needed for our brains to create a pattern, enabling the audience to easily remember and process information.[98] Of course, you can have as many talking points as you need; the point is that streamlining and simplifying your message avoids overloading your audience with information.

If you want to build an even deeper connection with your audience, consider sharing a personal story that captures your message, what you believe, and why you believe it. Understanding your story and the "why" behind your conversation or speech helps draw people to your message and work. Stories move people.

I was working with a group of executives in the mortgage industry and Vanessa, one of the up-and-coming leaders, stood out. She was already an accomplished speaker with an authentic presence and didn't need much coaching on delivery. However, she was about to receive an industry award and wanted some support for her acceptance speech. She knew her messaging and how to connect with her audience but hadn't shared her personal story.

When I walked her through the YOU, Amplified! Connection Framework, I asked her, "Why do you do what you do and believe what you believe?"

As Vanessa reflected on her life, she became emotional and shared that her family couldn't afford a home when she was growing up. Despite her parents working nonstop, they struggled financially, and she was homeless for a while. That's why she is so passionate about helping people find and afford their first home. She doesn't want them to endure the hardship and uncertainty she experienced.

When I asked whether she'd shared that story publicly, she admitted she hadn't on a large stage. Vanessa was so busy working and sharing her company's goals that she never thought about her personal story. Receiving the award made her think more about the long-term impact of her work. Over the next several sessions, we explored her story and her deeper message, working to tell it in a way that connected with both the audience and her industry.

You don't always need to share deeply personal details of your life to connect with your audience, but Vanessa's story was relevant to her work and her message. In such a context, telling your story can feel vulnerable, but choosing to share it helps others relate, building trust and credibility. When your audience can relate to you, they feel a stronger connection. Your stories can empower others, raise your visibility, and help you step into your thought leadership.

Your stories can empower others, raise your visibility, and help you step into your thought leadership.

To connect with your audience, be clear in your message. Keep it simple and relevant and share your story in a way that serves them and meets your goals. Here is some space to help you get clear with your message. Write down the top three points you want to convey in your next presentation or speaking engagement.

1.

2.

3.

To make your message more relatable, consider whether you can share a personal story. Answer the following questions to help you uncover your story, understand your underlying motivations, and reflect on your deeper message:

- **What are my core values?** Identify what guides your decisions.
- **What motivates me?** Reflect on what drives you.
- **What do I believe, and why? What do I do, and why?** Explore the deeper purpose behind your beliefs and actions.
- **What were some defining experiences in my life?** Reflect on the defining moments that shaped you.

KNOW YOUR PURPOSE

What is your *objective and/or goal with your next communication?*

We've covered audience and message so far and that's *Woo Hoo!* worthy. Now it's time to talk about purpose.

Your purpose is the reason behind the appearance, event, or conversation you are preparing for. What are *you* hoping to achieve from it? Are you trying to impress your boss at a meeting, network with your peers at an industry conference, sell something to clients, or build up your brand and expertise?

Understanding your purpose and mentally noting your personal objectives creates a powerful alignment of energy where your thoughts, actions, and emotions work together to propel you toward your broader goals. This clarity of purpose acts as a guiding compass, helping you make decisions consistent with your values and aspirations. When you are clear on your purpose, you are more likely to stay focused and motivated, even when facing challenges or distractions.

> **Understanding your purpose and mentally noting your personal objectives creates a powerful alignment of energy where your thoughts, actions, and emotions work together to propel you toward your broader goals.**

For example, Susan was presenting at the conference to share her expertise, research, and a new app to serve her clients. She was also up for a promotion and knew that key players from her company would be at the event. While the content of her presentation remained focused on serving the audience and providing valuable information, awareness of her broader goals added a layer of engagement and passion to her delivery.

Knowing your purpose will also help you stay focused and achieve your specific goals while connecting with your audience. One of my media clients, a health coach named Lisa, was excited after she successfully booked her first local TV interview. Her goals for the interview were to establish herself as an expert in the community and create a relationship with the station. She was clear and concise, provided value to the audience, and did so well that she succeeded—the station asked her back.

Next time, her purpose may be to promote her book. She will still serve the audience with her health expertise and provide value first, but because her purpose evolved, she'll share more stories and examples and find ways to naturally seed (briefly mention) her book during the interview. Lisa's purpose shifted from simply impressing the producers and establishing an ongoing relationship to promoting her book. Although the core content remains similar and her connection with the audience as an expert remains a priority, being clear about her purpose will keep her focused on promoting herself and her book authentically. By aligning her objective with her delivery, Lisa can strategically showcase her expertise while advancing her career goals.

Knowing your purpose can also help you pivot your topic when necessary. David is a financial expert who frequently participates in various weekly engagements. For one event, his primary objective might be to sell services and acquire clients. At another, he could be part of an industry panel where the focus is on giving back and networking. He may also have an internal meeting where his goal is to raise his visibility within the company. His topic might not change for each talk, but his purpose shifts with each new context.

When you take time to know *your* purpose, it becomes easier to tailor your content while still serving the audience and their needs.

To become clear on your purpose and personal objectives before any event, meeting, or conversation, think about *why* you are there and *what* you want to get out of it:

- What is the purpose of this communication?
- What do I want to walk away with?
- What does this presentation/conversation mean for a future goal or action?
- How does knowing my purpose keep me focused and aligned?

TAKE THE LEAD

Who are you going to be? Who are you going to step into?

Connecting with others starts with knowing who you are, what you stand for, and how you want to be seen. How do you think you come across, and how do others see you compared to how you would like to be? Do you even know? Many of my clients haven't taken the time to think about this, yet it is essential.

Edward had been at his company for over ten years. He was a dedicated and respected manager, ready to step further into leadership. He was ready to develop some presentation skills, but after working together, he had a breakthrough.

Edward told me he was so busy working and taking care of his family that he never thought about how he was showing up. He realized that who he thought he was and how others saw him were not consistent with how he wanted to show up. The adjectives he chose to describe himself at first were: *thoughtful, hardworking, supportive*, and *resilient*. All great attributes, but he wanted to show up as *strategic, innovative, passionate*, and *strong*.

If you were to visualize these two leaders Edward described, what would you see?

For the first set of adjectives, I'd picture a hardworking manager who puts others first and may be a bit burned out. For the second set, I'd picture a visionary leader who is ready to make an impact with his team and industry. It's not that Edward shouldn't be thoughtful and hardworking;

he can still embody these traits while stepping into being a more strategic and innovative leader in his field—you can feel the power in the second set of traits.

How you see yourself matters, and taking the time to purposefully choose and visualize the person you want to become is empowering. When you are self-aware, you understand your values and identity, break through your barriers, show up clear and confident, and interact more authentically, enhancing your ability to connect and take the lead.

To understand how you want to show up and who you want to embody, ask yourself: *How would others describe me? If I could list four adjectives to describe myself currently, what would they be?* Now ask yourself, *What four adjectives describe what I want to embody?* Here is a list of adjectives you can draw from.

YOU, AMPLIFIED! ADJECTIVES

Adaptable	Decisive	Hardworking
Accepting	Dedicated	Honest
Accountable	Detail-oriented	Humble
Ambitious	Dignified	Independent
Appreciative	Diligent	Innovative
Approachable	Diplomatic	Intelligent
Assertive	Disciplined	Inspiring
Attentive	Driven	Inviting
Authentic	Dynamic	Kind
Calm	Empathetic	Knowledgeable
Caring	Empowered	Likable
Charismatic	Encouraging	Logical
Clever	Engaging	Memorable
Collaborative	Enthusiastic	Mindful
Compassionate	Entrepreneurial	Observant
Competent	Ethical	Open-minded

Composed	Fair	Optimistic
Confident	Flexible	Organized
Conscientious	Forward-thinking	Passionate
Creative	Friendly	Personable
Curious	Fun	Persuasive
Customer-centric	Grounded	Positive
Principled	Sensible	Transparent
Progressive	Sincere	Trusting
Receptive	Smart	Truthful
Reliable	Strategic	Upstanding
Resilient	Supportive	Welcoming
Respectful	Tenacious	
Results-driven	Thoughtful	

How you show up now.

1.

2.

3.

4.

How you want to show up.

1.

2.

3.

4.

If the list of adjectives is the same for both questions, then you're already in alignment with your YOU, Amplified! self. However, it's more common for the adjectives in your lists to differ. Typically, your YOU, Amplified! self, how you want to show up, is a bit more powerful and represents qualities you aspire to embody. Listing the adjectives side by side allows you to see the gap between how you *are* showing up and how you'd *like* to show up—then it's up to you to do something about it.

What in your life would you have to shift to align the two columns? What habits would you have to let go of or take on?

Visualizing your ideal self lets you start to step into it mentally, then you can create your reality. Once you know how you want to show up, you can step into it anytime; you are taking the lead and becoming YOU, Amplified!

VISUALIZE AND ALIGN WITH YOUR IMAGE

What do you want your image to convey? What would other people's first impression be of you?

Owning your communication is an important part of becoming a powerful Only. Even your image can contribute in sometimes surprising ways.

First impressions are important. Research shows it takes as little as one-tenth of a second to make a first impression.[99] To connect with your audience, make the most of that time. Decide what you want your image to convey

Visualizing your ideal self lets you start to step into it mentally, then you can create your reality.

and then visualize how you would express that through your clothing, brand colors, makeup, video background, body language, etc. Knowing and visualizing your image will help you gain clarity on how you want to present yourself. This preparation boosts your confidence.

When your external image aligns with your internal intentions, you feel more at ease and centered. This enhances your connection with the audience, creating more interest and engagement. Ensure your look reflects you and your brand, makes you feel comfortable, and leaves you stage- and camera-ready.

Christina, a parenting expert, had previously worked with me to prepare for several morning show interviews, and she was aligned with her image. However, when the pandemic hit and everything shifted online, producers asked her to do interviews from home instead of the studio. She called me in a panic, unsure of where to start. Like many of us, she had to quickly create a makeshift backdrop and camera setup for video meetings. While some could get away with using kitchen tables or cluttered home offices, as a go-to expert who had appeared on television before, Christina needed to convey a more polished image.

She already knew she wanted to appear credible but accessible, so she dressed professionally without being too formal. She understood that solid colors and avoiding patterns worked best for TV. Now, at home, she needed to visualize and align with the image she wanted to project. Christina initially wanted to sit at her desk, but the background was just a white wall. So we moved her to a corner of her office near a window with excellent natural light for her face and that had a bookshelf and a plant behind her. She organized her bookshelf to match her brand colors and removed clutter to create an inviting look.

Some of you may already have an established part of your home that is camera-ready—your go-to spot for video meetings and interviews. Or this may be the first time you are thinking about the image you want to convey through video. If you haven't considered it before, now is your chance to explore it. However, your image isn't just about setting up your background for meetings; it's about knowing how you want to be seen, both on camera and off.

Taking the time to visualize your image before any meeting or event is crucial because it helps you feel more aligned and prepared. You'll know what you want to convey and how to embody it, ultimately enhancing your connection with your audience.

Body language can also impact how others perceive you and the image you project. How you enter the room, your posture, and whether your words match your physical movements and energy can affect how the audience connects with you and your message. It also influences whether your audience listens to your message and whether they like or trust you. Posture, energy, and congruency matter. Do you ever nod in agreement, smile when expressing happiness, or lean forward while listening? Maybe you consciously try to keep your arms open to allow more connection. These are all part of the image you can convey as an Only. When your gestures align with your words and emotions, you will be perceived as *congruent*. This enhances trustworthiness. Incongruent body language can create doubt and suspicion; for example, crossing your arms while saying you are open and flexible, having a sad or emotionless expression while expressing excitement, or turning away while expressing interest. It all adds up.

If you are speaking at a meeting, on stage, or on camera, it's important to own your space. In a meeting, this means making eye contact and not rushing through what you are saying. On stage, it means making sure you pause and land your entrance before speaking. Don't start speaking as you are walking. Walk with confidence. Pause, make eye contact with the audience, then speak once you arrive on stage. Avoid swaying or fidgeting. This can be distracting, signal nervousness, and make you appear less competent and secure.

To visualize and align with your image, practice your body language either in front of a mirror or by recording yourself. Consider how you come across and feel when:

- **Standing and sitting up straight.** Watch yourself with your normal resting posture. Then pull your shoulders back and stand up or sit up straight. *Does that make me look and feel more like the powerful Only I am?*

- **Owning your space.** Walk into the frame of the camera or mirror and start speaking. *Did I stop and take up space before I started speaking or did I rush to start? Did I start swaying and fidgeting or were my feet firmly planted? What else did I notice?*

- **Using congruent body language.** As you continue practicing your speech or conversation, experiment with your gestures. For example, open your arms when talking openly, smile when expressing happiness. *Do my gestures feel natural and align with my words?*

Ask yourself the following questions to help prepare your external image:

- If I was to speak on stage or lead an important meeting tomorrow, what clothing would reflect me, be comfortable, and make me feel confident?

- If I was to do an on-camera media interview tomorrow, what would be my camera-ready outfit? Do I feel comfortable sitting in it? (Some interviews may use a wide-camera angle, so you want to know what you look like sitting down, just in case.)

- If I'm shooting videos or conducting virtual meetings/interviews, where would I set up in my house or office? What would that background convey about me and my brand? Is it just a blank corner of my office, or is there anything I can add behind me that reflects me, my business, or my brand? (For free resources on how to prepare for virtual meetings, interviews, and events, go to www.AngelaChee.com/poweroftheonly.)

With all the inner work you're doing to own your communication as an Only, enjoy the external parts of owning your image. When you embrace being an Only both inside and out, your power will become more obvious and magnetic.

IDENTIFY THE FEELINGS AND ENERGY YOU WANT TO ELICIT

How do you want to feel? How do you want your audience to feel?

We are almost at the end of the YOU, Amplified! Framework; as you own your communication, these final steps are essential.

Considering these questions is the most important step in preparing for your meeting, presentation, appearance, event, or conversation, yet it's often overlooked. Your energy sets the tone before you even open your mouth, enter the room, step on stage, or join a videoconference. Taking the time to think about how you want to feel and how you want others to feel as they listen to you can make all the difference.

Think about the emotional impact you wish to create—whether it's inspiring confidence, sparking enthusiasm, or fostering a sense of calm and reassurance. Aligning your energy with these intentions can profoundly influence your delivery and how your message is received. Focusing on your energy not only enhances your own performance but also leaves a lasting impression that resonates with your audience long after the interaction ends.

Do you want to feel calm, centered, and/or energized? Do you want your audience to feel inspired, intrigued, surprised, and/or supported? People remember your energy and how you make them feel. Reflect on how you want to feel and how you want the audience to feel and think.

1. What kind of energy do I want to project?
2. How can I ensure my body language, tone, and facial expressions align with that energy?
3. What do I want the audience to feel and take away during my next presentation or communication?

Before every appearance—in addition to reminding myself of the other steps of the framework—I do a set of warm-ups for my body and voice to activate the vagus nerve[100] that activates my parasympathetic nervous system. If you do something similar, you'll find that even in high-stakes meetings where your voice is the sole messenger of a crucial point, these warm-ups help you relax, shift your energy, and positively influence how you feel.

Here are a few simple things you can choose from to practice quickly relieving stress or shifting your energy for your body and your voice. These exercises aren't as easy to do in public, but you can often find a quiet space backstage or just plan ahead.

- **Jumping jacks.** The rhythmic nature of the exercise increases heart rate and circulation, releasing endorphins and helping you feel good.[101]
- **Dance around the room.** Dance has double benefits; the music stimulates the reward center of the brain and activates sensory and motor circuits *and* can improve brain health.[102]
- **Stretch out your jaw.** Take your index finger and your thumb and make a V. Then put the V on the bottom of your chin and pull your jaw down gently. There is a link between anxiety and jaw tension;[103] stretching your jaw releases your facial muscles and reduces stress. Curious about a more advanced move? Stick out your tongue and release a deep breath and/or sigh. Feel free to make noise. Do this several times until you feel relaxed.
- **Singing.** Sing in the shower, the car, wherever you can. Is there a go-to song you like to sing? Singing activates your deep breathing and vibrates your vocal cords. It also lowers your cortisol,[104] reducing stress, stimulating your immune system,[105] and improving the tonality of your voice.

Now you have a way to bring your body into an amplified state and are ready to own your communication as an Only.

VISUALIZE YOUR YOU, AMPLIFIED! SELF

What do you look like when you own your communication in an amplified way, when you're being YOU, Amplified!?

Once you understand the previous six steps, you can put them all together and visualize your YOU, Amplified! self. Before most of my talks, video calls, and meetings, I close my eyes. I visualize myself standing on the stage or in a virtual meeting and imagine the room or background. I create my own virtual pop-up video or canvas in my mind. Then I mentally go through each of the previous six steps:

- **Audience.** How many people? Who are they? What do they look like? What is their energy? What do they want? What would keep their attention? ("High-level tech leaders, both men and women, at a digital marketing industry conference. They want to learn about the latest trends and products so they can get an edge on their competition.")

- **Message.** What am I there to talk about? Do I focus on my main point or three talking points? Or am I telling my deeper story? ("I am presenting the latest research, innovations, and products in the field. I am there to offer as much new information and insights as possible. My message is my company, and its products are leading the way.")

- **Purpose.** What do I want to achieve for myself with this event? ("My purpose is to make my company look good, showcase its product to potential customers, and raise my visibility as an expert in the space.")

- **Lead.** How do I want to show up? What qualities do I want to embody? ("I want to show up as knowledgeable, innovative, connected, and inspirational.")

- **Image.** How do I want to come across externally? What am I wearing—what color? If I'm at home, what does my backdrop look like? ("I want to come across as relaxed and friendly. I will wear an elevated or dressier version of the 'tech casual' outfit.")

- **Feeling.** How do I want to feel while delivering the talk and after it? How does my audience feel? What reaction can I see and feel on their faces? ("I want to feel prepared and energetic. I want the audience to be intrigued and engaged.")

The vision of who you are and who you want to be are aligned. You understand your audience and what serves their needs. You are clear on what you will share and why you are sharing it. You know the purpose of this interaction and how it will move your goals forward. You can convey and express yourself through your image and body language. You can visualize and step into a new mindset and energy and embody your amplified self.

CONNECTION IS VITAL TO COMMUNICATION

I'm sitting at the airport waiting for a flight. I'll admit that many times I find myself absorbed in my phone, catching up on email, checking social media. But today, I just sit, look around, and observe.

I see the tops of people's heads with the glow of their phones shining in the distance. I spot a frustrated mother with a toddler in a stroller holding an iPad, then see a teen in a hoodie sitting hunched over playing a game, another girl in the corner making selfie faces. Behind me, a long line of people wait for a bagel while scrolling through their phones, and next to me, a businesswoman frantically types on her computer. Everyone is distracted, in their own bubbles.

It makes me sad.

But then I hear a group laughing. I see them talking to each other face-to-face, sharing a story, making eye contact, and listening. I see joy, connection, and fun. In this moment, my faith in humanity is restored.

With technology advancing at lightning speed and new AI breakthroughs, real human connection is more important than ever.

That's why my work is so important to me. That's why knowing how to connect with your audience should be important to *you*.

Connection enables you to command attention, motivate and inspire people, strengthen relationships, and share your vision. Most importantly, it enables you to connect to others one-on-one in everyday life. Owning your communication is a vital skill and the key to our humanity. But for Onlys, it's not just a skill; it's also a powerful tool for empowerment, representation, and change.

When you know how to communicate and connect with your audience, you're able to navigate any environment, ensure your voice is heard, and advocate for yourself, your ideas, and others. You'll be ready for any opportunity and can impact change. You've owned your opportunity, your power, and your voice; with communication, you'll create a path to the future.

EXERCISE

You can use the YOU, Amplified! Connection Framework any time, any place; when you must prepare for a work presentation, a challenging one-on-one conversation, or an appearance at a conference, big meeting, or media interview. With practice, it can become a natural part of your communication preparation. If you would like to download the full worksheet (see the preview on the next page) and find more YOU, Amplified! resources, go to: www.AngelaChee.com/poweroftheonly.

YOU, AMPLIFIED! CONNECTION FRAMEWORK

7 steps to confidence, clarity, and connection

AUDIENCE
Know your audience. Who are you speaking to?

_____

MESSAGE
Be clear with your message; what is your message?

_____

PURPOSE
Know YOUR purpose. What are YOU hoping to achieve?

_____

LEAD
Take the lead. How will you show up?

_____

IMAGE
Visualize and align with your image. What image
do you want to convey?

_____

FEELING
Identify the feelings and energy you want to elicit.
How do you want to feel? How do you want your
audience to feel?

_____

YOU
Be YOU! YOU, Amplified!

_____

Chapter 4.3

BE THE BRIDGE BUILDER

*Bridges are built by those who are brave enough to
reach out, and strong enough to hold on.*

—CHIMAMANDA NGOZI ADICHIE

The smell of turkey roasting in the oven wafted through the house as we ran up and down the stairs at my cousin's house. I loved going to Jeremy's house, especially during Thanksgiving—the turkey, mashed potatoes, stuffing, and pumpkin pie dinner was a welcome change from the usual Chinese food at my house. A few years younger and more "Americanized" than me, Jeremy was also Chinese American. His family lived in a two-story house in a more affluent suburb and spoke English at home. During dinner, I'd translate and convince him to eat some of the Chinese food my mom brought. I'd switch between speaking Chinese and English.

Several years later, my six- and eight-year-old cousins from Taiwan moved to California and joined us for their first Thanksgiving. This time, I was prompting them to try the traditional turkey and stuffing, again switching between speaking English and Chinese. Our family is a tapestry of cultures, levels of assimilation, and generations. Some cousins live in Taipei, others immigrated to the US as toddlers, and some arrived as teens. Some of my cousins were born in the US and don't speak Chinese, others are mixed-race and could pass as White. When they visit, I translate between cultures, much as I did for my parents.

Even if you aren't a child of immigrants, you probably have experiences of translating for someone in some way, maybe on the school playground or for a friend trying to understand a new topic. I was a translator for my parents. They spoke English but still needed support for certain things, whether reading official documents or learning about certain cultural nuances. I was born on the East Coast but raised in Southern California, and although Mandarin Chinese was my first language, I assimilated quickly. Like so many who have grown up with multiple influences, there's more than one version of me that makes me who I am.

Onlys are the bridge builders of the future, shaped by the unique experiences and challenges of being the only one in a room.

I'm *very* Chinese, but also *very* Southern Californian.

What started as survival skills—translating for my parents and cousins and taking on adult responsibilities at a young age—grew an important set of skills. It enabled me to see and understand what others don't, help others communicate with each other, and protect and speak for those who couldn't.

That is my ability to be a bridge builder.

Onlys are the bridge builders of the future, shaped by the unique experiences and challenges of being the only one in a room. These experiences foster a deep understanding and strength in connecting with diverse people and seeing perspectives others might miss.

Christina Blacken, speaker and founder of The New Quo, a leadership development and behavior change training company, exemplifies this. Growing up Black in predominantly White, Mormon, and Republican Utah, she often felt like an "extreme minority"—not fitting in racially, religiously, or politically. Despite facing racism and misunderstanding, Christina learned to find common ground with others. "It taught me to cherish the similarities that bind us while celebrating the differences that define us."[106] Though gaps in understanding remained, Christina believes her ability to connect with others on a meaningful level is a powerful gift, one that has served her well in life.

In these polarizing and divided times, being a bridge builder is more important than ever. As you rise and show up more, especially in leadership, part of owning your communication is understanding how to navigate diverse environments, connect with different individuals, and recognize this power. From this strength, you can create opportunities for yourself and others and be an agent of positive change.

BUILDING BRIDGES IS NOT "ACCOMMODATING"

Being a bridge builder isn't easy, and at times, it felt like a burden while I was growing up. When you translate something, you bridge the gap between groups and between what people know and what they don't. This can be an immense responsibility.

To bridge gaps and build connections, you need to truly understand where people are coming from, embracing deep empathy, patience, and understanding.

These are your superpowers.

However, it's understandable if you're feeling exhausted from constantly wielding these strengths. While everyone desires meaningful connections, it's often the dominant culture or group that may not fully grasp or share these unique superpowers.

For some Onlys, you may feel like you spent your whole life in this role. Building bridges may feel like accommodating, but it is *not*. What may have once been a survival skill probably actually taught you the skill of how to connect. Christina says of learning to navigate her homogenous environment, "As I got older, I realized how to stand my ground and respect myself while also being able to have deeper conversations with people who are not like me just so I can build connection and understanding."

Leadership and diversity speaker Jess Pettitt had to do just that in her early activism days for LGBTQ rights. Once, Fred Phelps—a notorious antigay activist known for his homophobic views and protesting gay weddings—was demonstrating outside the opening of an LGBTQ high school in Manhattan. Amid the tension, Jess asked her college students at New York University, where she was a program director, what they believed was the most important action they could take in response to his protest. "The best thing we could do is give them a positive experience of LGBTQ people because maybe they never had one." Instead of spreading more hate, they chose kindness. "I showed up with donuts for all the protestors. The joke here is that Fred Phelps got a rainbow sprinkles donut," Jess told me. "It's easy to connect when someone is like you or thinks like you, but how you communicate and connect with someone completely different, and maybe even against you, matters most."[107]

Like Jess and Christina, we can stay true to ourselves, create connections, and not view bridge building as making ourselves less than, disregarding the truth within us, or ignoring the reality around us.

That is the difference between accommodating and bridge building.

Having this power to build bridges is an asset. Bridge building is finding a mutual understanding, creating connections, and creating networks of support. It's a collaborative effort that benefits everyone.

STAY CURIOUS AND REMEMBER YOUR HUMANITY

It's easy to own your communication when you're on the same page with others, but what about when being a bridge builder takes more time, effort, and emotional investment to be effective? Like when people aren't aligned and you're forced to have difficult conversations with bias, opinions, and stereotypes getting in the way?

For Christina, the key to connection in those cases is to stay curious. She remembers a time when she told a first-grade student that she was not Mormon, an anomaly in their home state of Utah.

"You're going to hell!" the girl shouted at her.

Christina was shocked. "How would you know? Are you a higher power? Like, do you dictate who goes to hell?"

"No?" The girl replied with a confused look on her face.

"So how would you know?"

As they continued sharing, Christina started to understand. "The girl was afraid for people because she had been taught a specific thing and wanted to save their souls." At first, Christina was mad, but as she got to know other kids in similar circumstances, she realized their intentions weren't bad. "That doesn't mean what they did wasn't harmful, but I think every once in a while, it's good to understand the context of where someone's bad behavior comes from . . . I learned how to be an ethnographer, like understanding someone else's culture to see where they are coming from and where they have gaps in knowledge."[108]

Being curious helps build bridges by learning about another's perspective and background to cultivate more understanding. But it can also help others become more self-aware. Christina says most people have binary thinking, and asking others open-ended questions instead of rushing to judgment or attacking can bridge the gap without making someone feel wrong. "They start to consider and unpack their own beliefs and where their opinions come from."

Similarly, Jess emphasizes that her role involves understanding the perspectives of those who may not share her views. "I would rather have an informed opinion about what my opposition really thinks versus what I *think* I know about what the opposition is thinking." Recognizing that people enter conversations with their own biases, she challenges us to set aside our preconceptions: What would happen if we let that go and got curious instead?

Jess understands that people don't always agree, but treating people like they are wise is important. "If you have a story that Todd has nothing to offer you, you're not going to listen to Todd as if he has something to offer you. That's on you." She suggests maybe we avoid certain topics but find a commonality in others. "Imagine what it would do to Todd's story about you. If you listened to Todd as if he had the answer or something you could learn from. How would you show up to that conversation? Because it's not how you typically show up."[109] This approach has helped Jess find a lot of commonality and connection with people who are wildly different from her.

Through music, Jess found common ground with Fred Phelps. Both had a shared appreciation for Johnny Cash. Despite Phelps persistently protesting her work, Jess recognized that she wouldn't change his views on homophobia. Instead, they began exchanging Johnny Cash cover songs. This simple gesture—finding a shared interest—served as a bridge, allowing Jess to model a different approach for her students. By focusing on what connects us, we can foster empathy and respect in our interactions. Yet, in a world where disconnection is common, achieving such understanding can be challenging, often leading some to stop communicating altogether.

"Most people are waiting for others to extend a hand, and sometimes we must go first." Jess recounted a parable from her grandfather (attributed to many faiths and cultures): People are seated at a long table with a giant vat of soup and spoons too long and heavy for them to feed themselves. They struggled and were on the verge of starvation until one discovered that they could use the spoons to serve each other across the table. This act of cooperation ensured everyone was nourished, illustrating the essence of bridge building. "The long spoons are a metaphor for bridge building because you are reaching across something and role modeling instead of just focusing on yourself." By remembering our humanity, we can bridge gaps, reduce stereotypes, and facilitate more understanding and collaboration across groups.

Riaz Patel, a two-time Emmy-nominated TV director/producer recognizes the destructive nature of division in our world. He has dedicated himself to bridging gaps between deeply divided individuals, aiming to find common ground and restore meaningful dialogue. Having experienced feelings of alienation himself, Riaz emphasizes the importance of reconnecting with our shared humanity to heal and unify. "In the Muslim world, I was the gay one. In the American world, I was the Muslim or the immigrant. In the Pakistani world, I was the American. In the gay world, I am the minority one. There is nowhere I can go where I am the majority one. I have always been the 'other.'"[110]

Riaz traveled the world, putting himself at the heart of debates—from guns and politics to gender and racial discrimination and more—to learn how to help people connect profoundly, so rather than being forced to have "hard conversations," the bonding over their shared humanity allows conversations to become much more open and relaxed, even enjoyable. He created the ConnectEffect, an interactive dynamic experience for schools, businesses, and groups that facilitates complex conversations among divided people to transform their views of each other, themselves, and what they believe. It changes the way they see the real world and the "screen world." Riaz says when "people self-discover the common ground between them, trade their false assumptions and biases for openness to what they don't know, and when they see the other person as human," everything shifts.

Riaz's EPIC model builds bridges through four steps. Take a moment to think about someone with whom you have conflict, disagreements, or even irreconcilable differences. Visualize taking the four steps of the EPIC model as if you were sitting with them. The goal is to work up to doing the four steps in real life.

1. **Equalization.** Take a moment to talk about what you both know.
2. **Personification.** Take turns to talk about what only you know.
3. **Information gathering.** While one person is personalizing, the other is listening and learning what they don't know.
4. **Collaboration.** Finally, talk about what neither of you know.

Riaz hopes the intervention will combat the growing global problem of isolation and polarization. Essentia Health ran the data on the effectiveness of the EPIC model and of a sample of 283 people, 97 percent said it was useful to bridge divides, 96 percent felt more hopeful going through it, and 99 percent recommended it.[111] Now you can use this model to create connection—even across divides on your journey as a powerful Only.

BRIDGE BUILDERS CREATE POSITIVE CHANGE

Marcia Davies, COO of the Mortgage Bankers Association, has worked in the industry for more than thirty years and believes that while there has been progress, more is needed. "For the majority of the first part of my career, I was the only woman in the room, and it was shocking to me that even a few years ago, there were times I was still the Only."[112] So, she founded mPower, Mortgage Bankers Association's networking platform designed to unite women and Onlys in the mortgage finance industry.

What began in 2015 as a modest luncheon for connecting women leaders has blossomed under Marcia's leadership into a vibrant community of over 24,000 members. She shared with me that her goal was to build the supportive network she wished she'd had early in her career. "It has grown bigger than I ever imagined and has given back to me tenfold."

Owning her communication allowed Marcia to advocate for herself and give back to others. "I've always spoken my mind—for better or for worse—and I was able to deal with conflict in a constructive way and not be afraid of it." Despite her innate confidence, there were times early in her career where Marcia felt stuck and in need of other bridge builders' support. "Even with my accomplishments, there was this voice inside my head that asked, 'Am I worthy? Am I up for the next challenge?'" Eventually, her male boss encouraged, advocated, and promoted her at a pivotal moment in her career despite her questioning her own qualifications.

Feeling another's experience, understanding where they come from, and seeing their worldview can help you navigate almost any environment.

Feeling another's experience, understanding where they come from, and seeing their worldview can help you navigate almost any environment. Having the tools to connect and knowing how to communicate in ways so others can hear you doesn't just help you to communicate; it can also help *others* communicate with each other. You can use your tools to protect others and advocate for those who don't have a voice. Marcia says this way of leading is vital for the future. "Many times, we try to be interesting, and what we need to do is be *interested*. We need to be good listeners and really understand and appreciate the other voices and experiences that are around the table so we can come up with the best solutions and the best way to lead."

Being a bridge builder is a valuable gift, but it can also be draining; it's important to acknowledge when the responsibility is too much. Maybe you recognize translating a certain case is not for you, or you simply can't take it on. Christina Blacken recommends bridge building when you have the capacity and energy, and recognizing when to walk away. "It's really important to have a balance and know when you need to disengage from certain situations and when you can come back."

In a world divided by differences and where we seem to live in our own information silos and one-sided realities, you can be a conduit for a new world. You can be the Only that shifts it all, paving the way for a more inclusive, compassionate, and united future. A world in which one day society catches up with us and there will be no more talk about "the Only."

In a world divided by differences and where we seem to live in our own information silos and one-sided realities, you can be a conduit for a new world.

EXERCISE

Asking yourself the following questions will help you deepen your understanding of how to effectively own your communication and be a bridge builder. This self-reflection not only sharpens your skills but also helps you stay aligned with your values, ensuring that your efforts to connect with others are both purposeful and sustainable.

- What is my relationship to being a bridge builder or translator? Have my experiences impacted me positively, negatively, or both?
- Empathy, patience, and understanding are superpowers in bridge building. Have I ever felt drained by these superpowers? How do I/would I recharge?
- How can I use position and influence to support and advocate for others?

PRINCIPLE 5

OWN YOUR FUTURE

Chapter 5.1

OWN YOUR FUTURE: FOCUS ON THRIVING, NOT SURVIVING

*While we are living in the present, we must celebrate life
every day, knowing that we are becoming history with
every work, every action, every deed.*

—MATTIE STEPANEK

I sat freezing in an air-conditioned office, my suit wet, itchy, and clinging to my body. I could feel the damp pantyhose on my legs, and my toes squishing in my '90s pumps when I moved. I sat there trying not to look bothered and hoping I didn't ruin the chair as I finished my work for the day. I was a summer intern at BBDO, an advertising agency in New York City, and the VP came by.

"You sure you don't want to go home early?"

"No, I'm fine," I said with a smile.

Just moments before, I was sent out to get coffee for a team meeting and was caught in a sudden torrential rainstorm. Flash flooding in the street. Everyone running to the nearest cover.

As a California girl, I'd never seen anything like it.

In a matter of minutes, I was trapped in Midtown Manhattan, holding a tray full of coffee, trying to strategize how to get back to the office without getting soaked. I didn't have an umbrella—and there were no umbrella vendors in sight—and running from awning to awning wasn't helping. As the water filled the gutters, the only way to cross the street was to step into calf-deep water.

I wasn't just a "bit" wet. I was *drenched*.

My hair was a mess, my brand-new black Jones New York suit was soaked, and makeup was running down my face. I returned with the coffee safe, but I was completely wet and thoroughly embarrassed.

It was my first week. I was *not* going home early. I didn't want to make this situation a bigger deal than it was, so I just dealt with it. I was determined to prove that I was tough and stick it out, even if I was really uncomfortable.

As an Only, I was used to taking on anything and everything with the goal of success. It's what I was taught, used to, and rewarded for. To my young, striver self, leaving would have meant failure, weakness, and an inability to handle setbacks. So, I stayed.

Maybe you can relate?

Looking back, I love that young girl for her work ethic, but I'm sure the job wouldn't have held it against me if I went home.

That wasn't the only time in my life I'd put on the smiling "It's okay, I'm fine" face when, in truth, I really wasn't. I did it in my morning news reporter days, working late or seven days a week and sleeping only a few hours a night, and I did it again during the sleep deprivation of the new parent phase, often not asking for help.

No, I'm fine.

And I kept this up during the transition of starting a business, working late nights/early mornings to build something to prove myself, feeling burned out or tired.

No, I'm fine.

Through the years, I continued to push myself past my limits or put everything and everyone else first, as if my burnout were a badge of honor.

Hard work and sacrifices are part of the job, especially early in our careers and when we start something new. But who does it serve when this behavior is self-imposed and unnecessary? When it's an unconscious pattern and a burden we put on ourselves rather than a required part of the journey? What if you're not an intern anymore and it's not your first week? Are you still pushing yourself to the limit and not really serving anyone?

Leveraging the power of being an Only means that when something doesn't serve you, you change it. It means YOU own your future. The foundation of owning your future is focusing on thriving, not just surviving. Thriving requires recognizing that the mindset, habits, and skills that brought you this far may not be sustainable or enough to propel you forward. Instead of clinging to outdated models of success, you create your own path. You acknowledge the influences of societal norms and past experiences but choose to break free from limiting patterns. By holistically caring for your body, mind, and soul, you preserve your energy and well-being. You discern between external barriers and self-imposed limits, and you prioritize your health and growth above all else.

Cultivating a mindset of abundance rather than scarcity is key to owning your future.

Cultivating a mindset of abundance rather than scarcity is key to owning your future. When you shift your focus from merely surviving to actively thriving, you break free from outdated patterns, societal conditioning, and others' expectations. Instead, you create a future defined by what *you* desire and design for yourself.

From this and previous chapters, you've gained the tools to own your opportunities, your power, your voice, and your communication. You are now poised to own your future. It's time to envision, create, and contribute to the world you want to build for yourself and others.

THE EXTERNAL AND INTERNAL PRESSURES THAT KEEP US IN SURVIVAL MODE

I've always had an urgency inside and put everything else first: the story, the job, the station, my ambition. Now, as a mom, I often put my children first. In my rookie reporter days, I even risked my life to get a story. Maybe it was just blind youth, but I often put my job and career ambition above my well-being. I believed that's what made me good—I was dedicated, tenacious, and a hard worker. Even as an intern in the '90s, I learned very quickly that whoever sacrificed the most or stayed the latest won. I remember coworkers doing what I call "sacrifice bragging."

"Oh, I stayed until nine this whole week!"

"I didn't even have time for lunch."

In my early career days, the seed was planted. *This is what you do: you pay your dues and you sacrifice; if you don't, someone else will.*

The rationale was all fine and good when I was twenty. I was there to work and learn. I didn't mind staying late. But I couldn't help but wonder about the SVP with a corner office. *Why is she still here? Doesn't she have a life or a family?*

Many of us are stuck in survival mode rather than truly thriving and appreciating our present selves and circumstances, largely because our society places a high value on productivity and achievement. We absorb these messages so deeply that they become woven into the very fabric of our identities.

What do people usually say when you ask them how they are doing? "Good, busy, stressed."

This mentality has become a normal mode of operation for many, especially in the US. For whatever reason, people have gotten it into their heads that if they aren't stressed, what are they? Lazy? Boring?

In our culture, overwork is not just socially acceptable but often rewarded, leaving many of us feeling anxious about taking time to rest. A 2023 Pew Research Center study revealed that nearly half of all US workers don't use all their allocated vacation days, citing excessive workloads and fear of falling behind.[113] Often, we don't realize we're pushing ourselves beyond our limits until we experience a breakdown.

But for many, even a physical breakdown may not be enough to stop them. Psychologist Dr. Valerie Rein shared in Chapter 1.2 about the origins of some of our internal barriers. Despite living what many would consider a dream life—two graduate degrees in psychology, a cherished family, and a thriving private practice and coaching business—her body was telling her a different story; her "dream life" was too much.

"One day, I was on the phone with a client, and the left side of my face and body went numb," she shared with me. "I finished my call and drove myself to the ER with my right arm. They scanned me up and down, and thankfully, although I was having symptoms of a stroke, it wasn't one. It was just stress."[114]

Instead of resting when she got the news, she looked at the clock and realized she could still make her evening appointments. She changed out of her hospital gown, drove to the office, and saw her clients like nothing happened.

"That moment was an awakening for me because my stress diagnosis didn't make sense to me. I did not *feel* stressed. My life was just normal. I was busy, I was doing work I loved, I was taking care of my family," she said. "And that's what I see—over and over—with my clients; that we don't stop. We are on this hamster wheel of doing more and more. Then, if there is a breakdown, we realize 'I'm not as happy and fulfilled as I look on paper.' Then we get on another hamster wheel of trying to fix it, and we are constantly rinsing our achievements and that it's never enough."

In my life, the notion that you don't stop and must be productive all the time—that stopping or letting your guard down is dangerous, even—stems from childhood.

Work hard.
Don't stop.
Can't stop.
It's not safe!

This is a pattern I learned from my parents. My father, who worked in the restaurant industry, was rarely home during the week. He'd leave shortly after I went to school, work through lunch, rest briefly in his car, then continue through the dinner shift, only to come home around midnight. His job took him to a more affluent city about an hour away where he could earn better tips. Sometimes, the sound of the garage door would briefly wake me. Knowing he was home, I would then fall back asleep.

Meanwhile, my mother worked a traditional office job at a bank and always pursued entrepreneurial opportunities in her free time. She would drop me off at school in the morning, but I was usually on my own until she got home after five. With my father's demanding schedule, my mom shouldered most of the responsibilities at home. I don't recall ever seeing her truly relax or take a break—there was always *something* that needed her attention.

Even now, I don't think my mom ever sits down. When my parents come over for the holidays or family gatherings, she's always helping or cleaning. If there is nothing to do, she will find *something* to do.

She may pause briefly when I encourage her to sit down and take a break, but then she gets back up to clean the kitchen. It used to frustrate me because I felt she was missing out on the moment, but I've come to accept this part of who she is. It's not our place to dictate or judge others' habits. For my mom, staying busy and helping others brings joy, purpose, and a sense of worth. She has associated acts of service and constant activity with love and necessity. I've recognized similar patterns in myself and have consciously worked to shift them over the years. I strive to forge a different path but still find myself getting caught up in old habits occasionally.

You may feel trapped by similar pressures, too. That's because many of us don't notice or take the time to break through old patterns and create a new vision of what is possible. We are stuck with the status quo, saying, "That's just the way it is," rather than proactively creating a new path for ourselves.

A MINDSET OF SCARCITY KEEPS US FROM THRIVING

When I worked in the news, I always sensed a feeling of scarcity; if I didn't pursue a story or take on something extra, someone else would.

You should be grateful even to have the opportunity to work in news, so you need to work hard to show that gratitude.

Scarcity is often built into competitive or glamorous industries, like entertainment, TV news, publishing, the arts, and more. But a sense of scarcity is also felt deeply when you are an Only.

In the workplace, scarcity can manifest as competition over collaboration, resistance to change, short-term thinking, and a fear of taking risks.[115] But for Onlys, feelings of scarcity might have more layers. When scarcity manifests as a lack of representation—such as being one of the few Black women in a start-up, the only South Asian man in a marketing department, the only woman in a construction company, or the only one with a visible or invisible disability, the only person over fifty in a division—many of us Onlys may feel an added pressure to prove ourselves.

This pressure can stem from being viewed through the lens of stereotypes and feeling the need to work twice as hard as those in the dominant culture to validate our worth. We might feel compelled to exceed expectations to represent our group or culture positively. Additionally, with so few of us in these roles, there can be a sense of needing to "protect our territory," driven by the fear that our presence might be deemed expendable if we don't perform exceptionally.

Professor Dr. Cleopatra Kamperveen, whom you met in Chapter 2.2, shared that people regularly underestimated her. "They didn't have any awareness about how strong I had to be and how hard I had to work to be there in the first place with them." As a young woman of color and a mother of three, she had to work twice as hard and be twice as good as everyone else. "The unspoken message in academia and a lot of professional spaces is that women who have children—or a lot of children—are not serious about their careers or, in my case, not a serious scientist."[116] Dr. Cleopatra became the first woman of color hired on the tenure track in her department, has received nearly $3 million in grant funding, and has been cited in over 1,000 scientific studies.

As an Only, do you feel added layers of pressure because your environment was not built for you? In addition to pressures that come with pursuing goals or building something new, Onlys often expend extra energy navigating invisible challenges that can accumulate and cause significant stress. These challenges include confronting bias, constantly proving yourself—like Dr. Cleopatra—balancing authenticity with assimilation to company culture, and managing external perceptions. While overcoming these obstacles is possible, failing to recognize, release, or heal from them can trap you in survival mode, hindering your ability to truly thrive.

Some Onlys may feel an internal scarcity. They feel that they are not enough no matter how hard they work. One of my on-camera clients, *Architectural Digest* pro designer Brian Brown, now also a brand spokesperson and TV show host, shared that he has always felt the need to prove himself, particularly to his family.

At fifteen, he came out to his mother who accepted his sexuality, but Brian still felt compelled to justify his worth. Raised Catholic, he faced significant guilt and shame and often felt like an outsider, even within the gay community. The feeling of being an Only has been a recurring theme throughout Brian's life. "I'm proud to be gay, but gay isn't who I am, it's not my full identity. There's so much more to me."

After his grandmother and dog passed away and after experiencing some relationship troubles, he used work as an escape rather than deal with his grief. He didn't realize he was burning out until he was rushed to the ER. "I had acute colitis, and because I was working so hard and not taking care of myself, my body shut down. I had no defense system left and couldn't fight off the infection and was bleeding nonstop." Through therapy, Brian realized that his breakdown was related to many other aspects of his life than just work. He needed to take a deeper look inside to fully heal and thrive.

When you are safe but still just trying to survive rather than thrive, it is time for a mindset shift. When you feel like you're not enough or can't get off the hamster wheel of chasing success, it's time to change your path. When you don't have the capacity for abundance or are sacrificing your health, mind, and body, it is time to break free from your past.

FROM SURVIVING TO THRIVING

Going from surviving to thriving is a journey; like any habit or pattern, just *knowing* about it won't actually shift it. To truly thrive, we need to learn how to move from a state of survival to one of abundance and how to catch ourselves when we fall back into old patterns. It's about being aware of when you get stuck and shifting and creating new pathways in your brain and new habits in your life.

That certainly has been the case for me.

Embracing abundance and thriving was not something that came naturally to me; I had to actively create it and continually work on embodying it. I had to reprogram myself and continue to do so every day. Even as I write this book, trying to meet the deadlines, I see myself drifting back into old habits of overwork and forgetting my tools—the exact tools I'm about to share with you. So, this journey isn't about achieving a one-time fix. I'm on this journey with you. You are not alone.

We *all* get stuck.

The key is to understand that you have the power to shift your mindset and practices. It's not an all-or-nothing situation. We must stop this pattern of burnout–success–burnout– success and instead aim for a more balanced and sustainable approach.

It's time to create a new road map and mindset for our future.

You are already successful, but whether you *feel* it or *experience* it depends on how you define success and fulfillment.

Over the next few chapters, I'll show you how to do just that. We'll go through a process of letting go, peeling back layers to get to your true self, and creating the future you want. We will create a new vision and model for your life and goals based on your point of reference, your values, and your rules. You are already successful, but whether you *feel* it or *experience* it depends on how you define success and fulfillment.

First, you will create a new definition of success based on your values, who you are, how you want to be, and what you want to leave behind. Then, we'll discuss why Onlys need to guard our energy and how to navigate spaces to protect our physical, mental, and spiritual well-being. I'll show you how to harness the power of your intuition and healing practices to bring your vision of the future to life.

I'll also discuss how to use discernment—a filter for your life—to help you let go of what you don't want, call in what you do want, and focus on the things that matter.

Finally, I'll share stories of those owning their future and creating their own tables. Their insights will support you in your business and in your everyday life and help you envision what legacy you will leave behind. That is how you harness your Power of the Only and how you own your future.

> **You are *amazing*, just as you are right now.**

HONORING YOU AND YOUR REALITY

Before I walk you through how to own your future, I want to honor you for all that you are.

I see you.

You are *amazing*, just as you are right now.

Being an Only is a gift, but the journey can be exhausting. Sometimes, it may feel like you must override, rewrite, reframe, and fight against everything in your path just to start at the beginning. Everything you feel is valid, and I'm holding space for it.

Too many times, we've been denied, ignored, unheard, and unseen. I spent my life making things work and shoving things down, and it can take a toll. It's not always fair, and it's not always your responsibility, but knowing how to navigate any environment and having the tools and power to do so is worth it.

As I said at the beginning of the book, while there is much in our world that needs to change, the focus here is on you. *You* are the focus of this book. When you are at full capacity—when you are thriving, not just surviving—is when change happens. We can't solve everything, but we can try.

And it starts with you.

Part of owning your future is that you are no longer on autopilot. You get to choose. You decide how you want to navigate a situation, how you want to move forward, and what you want to create, instead of being ruled by invisible societal, cultural, and environmental expectations and barriers. You've earned it. It's time to give yourself grace, create space, and fill it with what *you* need, what *you* desire, and what *you* want your legacy to be.

> **When you are at full capacity—when you are thriving, not just surviving—is when change happens.**

EXERCISE

Ask yourself these reflection questions:

- What role models or societal or familial expectations shaped me? Are there patterns of sacrifice in my life that I recognize as unnecessary now?
- When in my career or personal life did I feel the need to push through discomfort to prove myself? How did I handle it and what did I learn from that experience?
- What are some outdated mindsets or habits I hold on to that might be hindering my ability to thrive? How can I start to shift these mindsets?

Chapter 5.2

CREATE A NEW VISION

There's no better time than now to be who you are.

—BOY GEORGE

Grace Yung Foster (introduced in Chapter 2.1) spent years chasing the life she thought she was supposed to have. "I gave so much of myself to work, to my bosses, to my companies, and what everyone else wanted from me." An adoptee and foster care alum, she dreamed of starting her own family but put these dreams on hold because she felt she first had to achieve a certain level of success. "I believed that I could only have a family if I first reached X salary, X title, X level, X people in my network, X degree."[117]

For a long time, Grace allowed others to define her success. She was lost and unhappy but kept pushing through, working harder and longer hours. "Overperforming only put me in positions where I was taken advantage of." She had spent her life chasing a spot in the homes she lived in, and it was time to change the narrative. "I realized I had to define what it meant for me to have it all. No one else really cared if I achieved it—only I could care enough to give it to myself."

Are you like Grace and chasing others' definition of success? Always focused on what's next? Are you trying to be everything to everyone all the time? Do you have this never-ending to-do list cluttering your brain? Setting goals and achieving them, yet still feeling like it's never enough? Based on societal pressure and metrics, success is usually tied to achievement, and that can be exhausting. The pressure to check off all the boxes starts at an early age. Did you get A's, win awards, go to the right college or university, get a top job or title, get promoted, sell your business, buy a big house, or do all the *right* things?

Just writing this makes me tired!

Would you say you're tired from all this too?

From the conversations I hear, I think we're *all* tired, especially Onlys.

In the beginning, the drive for "more" can propel Onlys forward. As an Only, you might feel under scrutiny, underestimated, or like there is no room for failure. This pressure to prove others wrong can be a powerful motivator. However, there comes a point when what once fueled your success—your perseverance, grit, relentless hustle, the need to be the best, pushing yourself to the limit, always caring for others, and saying yes to everything—can become your greatest obstacles. What protected us or were our strong suits can also hold us back from our true selves and potential unless we create a new vision of what success means to us.

What protected us or were our strong suits can also hold us back from our true selves and potential unless we create a new vision of what success means to us.

When you don't take the time to create a new vision of success that fits your current life stage and continue to chase achievement or other old patterns, you can get stuck. Harvard professor, social scientist, and author of *From Strength to Strength* Arthur Brooks calls it the "striver's curse." Those who strive to be excellent at what they do often wind up "finding their inevitable decline terrifying, their successes unsatisfying, and their relationships lacking."

Arthur began researching why, as people age past sixty-five, some become happier while others grow unhappy. "The people who are on the lower branch of the happiness curve are the ones who did the most earlier, and so they're disappointed that it's finished."[118] He says chasing the same things won't make you happy unless you reframe how you view life's transitions. Those who can step into these transitions with ease and find ways to share their wisdom—what he calls "crystallized intelligence" instead of just striving for more—experience the most happiness as they age.

To own your future, you can't rely on the same patterns over and over again. While it's important to honor the strengths that have served you well, truly owning your future means looking at your current reality—your goals, values, and the specific stages and milestones of your life. It's about recognizing where you get stuck, redefining what success looks like for you now, and being willing to use different tools and strategies to achieve it.

SHEDDING OUR OLD PATTERNS

I stood just outside the air-conditioned ballroom waiting in line with my dad. With flushed cheeks, I started to sway a bit and struggled to keep my balance. Suddenly, I couldn't hold it in any longer. My heart started beating faster and I ran to the first container I saw. I lifted the lid of the hotel trashcan and out it came. As I was throwing up, I could hear the announcer's voice from the ballroom.

"And now, Miss California National Teenager Angela Chee and her father, Joseph!"

I felt better, wiped my mouth with the back of my hand, looked up at my dad, grabbed his arm, and walked in like nothing happened.

When I was fifteen, I entered the Miss California National Teenager competition for scholarship money. As a girl with no pageant experience and a $35 on-sale dress, I never thought I would win, but there I was four months later at nationals in Florida. I had made it through a four-hour pageant. We had been at rehearsals and events all week in the summer humidity. I got sick and had a fever the day before the pageant but I wouldn't let that stop me.

I'm fine!

After I threw up, I had a final dance with my dad, smiled for the cameras, and finally went back to my room and passed out. No one knew what I was going through.

Experiences like these taught me to always be ready, never let them see you sweat, and that the show must go on. I didn't know any other way. If you wanted something, you worked for it and did whatever it took.

End of story.

This mentality set me up for success, especially in my television career, where it was about turning it on for the camera and everyone else. And for me, I wasn't faking it.

I *enjoyed* this pattern.

Or so I thought.

Most of my career was powered by pure drive and determination. I thrived on learning more, doing more, and always going above and beyond. I was up for any challenge. I chose industries where that was the norm and prided myself on how good I was at handling anything that came my way. For years—from school to job after job—I operated in the same high-performance mode, running on adrenaline and cortisol. This mindset was ingrained in me from a young age and it always seemed to work. So why would I change? It felt like a badge of honor. But when I became a new mom, applying my old pattern of success to this new chapter in life backfired.

I was depressed and burned out.

Most of us don't change until we experience too much pain. And sometimes, we must go through painful experiences to grow, but we shouldn't have to burn out and reach total exhaustion before we put our well-being first. We are constantly evolving, but most of us don't take the time to consciously think about how we want our lives to be.

Who are we *now*? How do we feel *now*? What do we want to leave behind? What does success mean to you? Are you building a life you want rather than just checking off boxes or living by someone else's rules? Are you prioritizing the things that matter to you? Can you focus on the joy in the present moment rather than on what's next?

To own our future, we must see, understand, and shed old patterns to create a new vision based on what currently matters to us in our lives.

After my breakdown as a new mom, I had to reevaluate the patterns that were no longer serving me—overwork, constant sacrifice, self-reliance to the point of isolation, and suppressed emotions. I had to consider the new patterns I wanted to cultivate. I'd realized I didn't need to completely abandon my go-getter mindset; we don't have to shed all our strengths. But I'd chosen to focus on joy.

Joy is what I wanted to prioritize.

Finishing my book (life goal), having a peaceful home (I'm raising teenagers), making time for concerts (I realized how much I enjoy live music), real conversations and meaningful connections (I appreciate learning about others and their insights, and that is partially why I started my podcast), watching others shine (I love seeing my clients break through barriers), surrounding myself with beautiful things (flowers, organized spaces), etc.

These are the things that bring me joy.

This new pattern and energy keeps me passionate and moving forward. It allows me to see beyond the typical checklist of success to focus more on fulfillment.

When stress hits, I sometimes slip back into old habits and lose sight of what truly matters. But I've learned how to course correct. By prioritizing how I want to feel and how I want to "be," my to-do list transforms. It's no longer just about achievement or productivity; it's about aligning my actions with what genuinely fulfills me.

STEPS TO CREATE A NEW LIFE VISION

Many Onlys have mastered the art of persevering through tough times, often in environments that weren't designed with them in mind. But the real challenge is to let that drive propel you to your peak, not push you into burnout.

What is that peak?

That is for *you* to decide.

To create a new life vision where you are at your peak, reflect on your values and priorities. These may have shifted as you got older, moved on to a new life stage, or changed circumstances. The following steps will help you consider what's important to you *right now*. Your job is to make some time just for you in a space free from distractions and reflect on your answers for each step.

1. WHAT'S IMPORTANT TO YOU NOW.

- What do you believe in, and why?
- What's important to you at this stage or moment in your life?
- What mindset shifts do you see happening inside of you?

2. PICK THE VALUES THAT ARE A PRIORITY FOR YOU.

- Look at the brief list of values below (or choose your own).[119] Which are your biggest priorities today? Write down whatever resonates with you. There is no right or wrong answer.
- Is there a theme to these values? When you see them, what emotions, ideas, or thoughts do they bring up?

- What story do these values tell you about the new vision of your life?
- Narrow it down to your top three.

VALUES

Acceptance	Efficiency	Integrity	Quality
Achievement	Elegance	Intellect	Radiance
Advancement &	Entertainment	Involvement	Recognition
Promotion	Enlightenment	Joy	Relationships
Adventure	Equality	Knowledge	Religion
Affection	Ethics	Leadership	Reputation
Altruism	Excellence	Learning	Responsibility
Arts	Excitement	Loyalty	Risk: Safety &
Awareness	Experiment	Magnificence	Security
Beauty	Expertise	Making a	Self-Respect
Challenge	Exhilaration	Difference	Sensibility
Change	Fairness	Mastery	Sensuality
Community	Fame	Meaningful Work	Serenity
Compassion	Family	Ministering	Service
Competence	Freedom	Money	Sexuality
Competition	Friendship	Morality	Sophistication
Completion	Fun	Mystery	Spark
Connectedness	Grace	Nature	Speculation
Cooperation	Growth	Openness	Spirituality
Collaboration	Harmony	Originality	Stability
Creativity	Health	Order	Status
Decisiveness	Helping Others	Passion	Success
Democracy	Helping Society	Peace	Teaching
Design	Honesty	Personal	Tenderness
Discovery	Humor	Development	Thrill
Diversity	Imagination	Personal	Unity
Environmental	Improvement	Expression	Variety
Awareness	Independence	Planning	Wealth
Economic	Influencing	Play	Winning
Security	Others	Pleasure	Wisdom
Education	Inner Harmony	Power	
Effectiveness	Inspiration	Privacy	

---

3. LIST THE THINGS THAT WILL HELP YOU LIVE OUT EACH OF THOSE VALUES.

- What is one small thing you can do every day to live out those values?
- What bigger decisions might you need to make in your life?
- On the right side of a piece of paper, write *What I Value* or *Do More* or something like that. Then, write down a list of the things you need to be, do, and feel. Circle it; highlight it!

4. LIST THE THINGS YOU WANT TO AVOID/ELIMINATE.

- What would prevent or block you from what you want and value?
- What habits, emotions, thoughts, things, or actions do you need to drop? How would you avoid them?
- On the left side of the same piece of paper, write *Avoid* or *Stop*. Make a list of the things you need to avoid being, doing, and feeling. Then cross out the entire *Avoid* list.

You now have lists of what you currently value and what you don't, as well as actions, thoughts, and habits that reflect those values. Keep this visible so you can reflect on it frequently. Imagine your new life as if you are living it now. (If your paper got messy from brainstorming, you can rewrite the *Do More* list and use it as a reference for your overall goals.)

Research shows that visualizing your future and your new possible self helps increase motivation by allowing people to identify their goals and develop goal-directed behavior.[120] It also helps improve performance by imagining your future success. When you envision how to bring those possibilities to life, you heighten your emotional engagement and strengthen your ability to plan and act.[121]

The list will serve as a reminder and mental guide to your new life vision. If you start to feel stressed, overwhelmed, out of alignment, stuck, confused, or have any other negative feeling, do more things from the right side of your list. You can adjust this vision at any time and make more than one, but doing this exercise will enable you to think about what you really value at this point in your life.

GIVE YOURSELF PERMISSION

Once you have created and spent time reflecting on your new vision, how do you bring it to life and break through your old patterns?

By giving yourself permission.

Growing up as the eldest child in a South Asian immigrant family, high achievement was a central focus for keynote speaker Henna Pryor. Although her parents provided unconditional love, and she didn't feel that her worth was solely tied to her accomplishments, she still grappled with an all-or-nothing mindset that fueled her drive. "I was very binary in my head. 'I'm either going to be successful, or I'm not. I'm either going to go for this and know it's going to work, or I'm not going to go for it at all.'" It took years to give herself permission to follow her own path and define her own rules. "I wish I had given myself permission earlier than I did, because all my subsequent success as an adult has come from permission of just placing those small bets."[122]

> Once you have created and spent time reflecting on your new vision, how do you bring it to life and break through your old patterns? By giving yourself permission.

Henna secured a position at a prestigious Big Four accounting firm, which made her parents proud. However, she quickly realized that despite outward success, she wasn't genuinely fulfilled. When she decided to leave her traditional CPA role for a commission-based sales position in professional staffing, she faced significant fear and uncertainty. "Raised by immigrant parents, I had always relied on the safety of the known." But once she made that move, she allowed herself to start taking more risks and redefine what success looked like for her. Now, as an executive coach and author of *Good Awkward: How to Embrace the Embarrassing and Celebrate the Cringe to Become the Bravest You*, Henna tells clients not to be afraid to give themselves permission to envision a new vision, especially when they are an Only trying to shift the status quo. "Do it awkward, but do it anyway."

As an Only, you might have felt the same way Henna did as a child. You may feel hesitant to give up your old patterns. It's what you are used to, so you may stick with the same formula because it's comfortable. As humans, we tend to prefer safe and predictable things. These habits may have become so entwined with your sense of self that releasing them feels like losing a part of who you are. You might find it challenging to break free due to emotional attachment or because your environment and social circle reinforce these old ways. However, you don't have to carry everything with you.

That's a lesson that I still struggle with. As a working mom with bold ambitions and a mission to help others, a traveling husband, two teenagers, and aging parents, I have a lot on my plate.

I know you do too.

Deep down, I believe that I am enough, but my body often does not. If our pattern for success is wired one way, learning a new pattern doesn't feel the same and may not register. My brain knows to take in praise, joy, and accomplishment. In fact, I teach it all the time; however, sometimes my brain filters out anything that is "good" or "easy" and doesn't allow my nervous system to rest.

For example, sometimes I overthink things or I don't acknowledge them because I'm used to the struggle. If something comes too easily, my thoughts immediately shift.

It's not worth it.

It doesn't mean anything.
I don't deserve it.
Something is wrong.

I was not wired for things to be good unless I made them good. I had a hard time accepting things as good if I didn't face some form of hardship or pain. I approached everything in my life with the mindset that success required relentless effort and overcoming obstacles; while this perseverance helped me achieve my goals, it also made me doubt the value of ease and contentment. I didn't know *easy*. It was never easy for me, so why would it be easy now? But why does life have to be hard?

We must give ourselves permission to step back, pause, reflect, let go, receive, and reinvent if we are to thrive. Give yourself **space** to feel and be with whatever comes up. Give yourself **thanks** for your past, old patterns, and strong suits because they shaped you into who you are today. At times, they were your protectors to power through, be strong, and prepare for anything. And finally, give yourself **permission** to change. You don't need to do things like you always have to own your future.

I frequently revisited my past while writing this book and reflected on the different phases of my life: the little girl who felt out of place, the teenager striving for perfection, the young professional who never said no, and the new mom who tried to juggle everything. Revisiting these moments evoked a mix of admiration and profound sadness that had me tearing up as I empathized with the struggles I once faced. Instead of pushing these feelings away, I allowed myself to fully experience them, process them, and move through them.

Breaking down invisible barriers from our past is crucial to thriving, but I am not a therapist. The tools in this book are intended as a guide. If you find that these emotions are too overwhelming to handle alone, please seek support from a mental health professional. Ultimately, how you explore your past and utilize these tools is up to you.

YOU'VE ALWAYS BEEN ENOUGH

Steven Bartlett, a British entrepreneur, investor, author, and host of the UK's number one podcast, *The Diary of a CEO*, was born in Botswana to a Nigerian mother and English father and raised in the UK.[123] Growing up as one of the few mixed-race children in his community, living in a rough neighborhood where his family struggled to make ends meet, and dropping out of university at eighteen, he often felt like an outsider both culturally and socially.

Despite taking his social media company public at the age of twenty-seven, becoming one of the richest young people in the UK, and starring on BBC's hit show *Dragon's Den*, he continues to grapple with feelings of scarcity. In a May 2024 LinkedIn post, Bartlett shared, "I've never said this before, but I've started to think that somewhere inside me, there's a young boy who still believes that everything he has could disappear overnight, that he could easily go back to zero—that he's still sprinting away from something. When you start with very little, the 'ghost of losing it all' can haunt you in a way that's both destructive and causes you to be scared of ever letting your foot off the gas."[124] This post came after a week of pushing his physical and mental limits with demanding business obligations and commitments.

Steven's post resonated with me. For too long, I also operated from a place of scarcity rather than abundance, leading me to a life of survival. Thankfully, I spent the last decade reprogramming this scarcity mindset to create a new life vision.

And you can too.

The shift didn't occur overnight; it was a process that unfolded over several years as I uncovered layers of what I had hidden from myself. With years of personal development, therapy, coaching, and grappling with my own breakdowns and burnout, I have learned to prioritize thriving over merely surviving.

I no longer strive to be a perfectionist. I'm comfortable setting boundaries, saying no, and not taking everything on. I'm more at peace with my inner voices because I know where they come from and how to reframe them. I now recognize when I fall into old patterns but instead of just pushing through or past it, I choose to pause, to feel, to process, to ask for help, and more importantly, accept help and see that it's not all on me. Although I still have moments, I learned that there's nothing to prove—there never has been. You don't have to make it hard to be worthy. It's still valuable if it's easy. I am enough. *You* are enough. You've always been enough.

> **You don't have to make it hard to be worthy. It's still valuable if it's easy. I am enough. *You* are enough.**

EXERCISE

- If you did the exercises earlier in this chapter, you took a potentially game-changing step in visualizing how you can thrive as an Only. Take a moment now to review your answers and let them sink in. If you haven't done the exercises, go for it. Think of it as investing in the most important relationship you will have: your relationship with yourself.
- Now that you've contemplated a new vision for yourself as an Only, are your thoughts and feelings any different from before you started reading this book? Internal change can sometimes be hard to measure, but it's happening. Hang on to your new vision. It's your new lighthouse for being an Only.

Chapter 5.3

GUARD AND HEAL YOUR ENERGY

Do not let the behavior of others destroy your inner peace.

—DALAI LAMA

It was a warm summer night. Quarters stuck to my palm as I gripped them tightly, my other hand holding on to my mom's. Grinning, I walked to the corner grocery store with my parents to spend my change on the gumball and toy machines that lined the front of the store. Just as we reached the store parking lot, a loud screech pierced the air, followed by voices chanting, "Chink, ching, chong, chong!" and a shock of cold water hit my face. I screamed.

The quarters fell from my hand and scattered across the sidewalk, some rolled into the street. Blinking and wiping the water out of my eyes, I heard boys laughing and saw my father chasing a van. I stood there with my mom, frozen, dripping wet, and in shock, not knowing what to say or do. I was scared. Someone had sprayed us with water, called us names, and driven off. We didn't talk about it that night, but the words stayed with me and stung like invisible darts of hate that reminded me I was different.

I was six years old.

Racist incidents like this didn't happen to me often growing up, but they *did* happen. Most were more subtle than this, and a few instances didn't even register as racist at the time. These long-forgotten childhood memories resurfaced in the wake of racial hate incidents that surged after 2020. These events not only instilled fear for ourselves and our loved ones but also prompted many of us to reexamine our pasts and process old memories.

You don't have to experience racism or sexism to know this feeling. Just think about the times you've been othered, felt unsafe, or criticized.

As Onlys, we often face many obstacles, big and small, that are beyond our control. Over time, these challenges can wear us down and deplete our energy. Being an Only can lead to feelings of being isolated, undervalued, or misunderstood. You may also experience increased pressure or responsibilities and lack support from your company or peers. Whether being scrutinized or facing direct and indirect bias, feeling the need to advocate not just for yourself but also others, or being asked to take on extra unpaid work or initiatives, these factors can strain your emotional capacity to manage stress and process emotions, affecting your self-esteem, motivation, work, and overall life.

To own your future, you must guard your energy and honor your well-being. Guarding your energy means being aware of your environment, the information you are exposed to and consume, the people you surround yourself with, and what claims your time and attention, then understanding how all of it affects you. It means that as you navigate spaces that aren't supportive, welcoming, or built for you, you can tap into your intuition to block out (not internalize) the negativity around you. It means you decide which emotions you want to experience and which you want to release. By doing so, you can cultivate the energy to appreciate the joy and beauty around you.

I always tell my clients that our energy walks in before we do. Your energy sets the tone for your well-being and influences those around you. Guard it and harness it so it serves you and your goals.

BLOCK OUT NEGATIVITY

"Aren't you a little young?"

"You don't look like the 'typical' founder in our portfolio."

"When pitching to VCs, are you going to be the cute Asian girl or the tiger Asian girl?"

Entrepreneur Misa Chien heard these comments and questions as a young female Asian American founder. She has faced a lot of challenges, from stereotyping during a pitch to offensive comments and unwanted advances. "In my twenties and even into my mid-thirties, I would blame myself for many of the things that happened to me or how meetings ended up. 'Is it something I said? Did I not temper down my femininity enough? Did I somehow miscommunicate my intentions?'"[125]

As Onlys, we often blame ourselves when something unfavorable happens, whether it is sexism, racism, or harassment. Misa said, "The aha moment is when I realized I needed to change the narrative of blaming myself unequivocally every time someone acts unprofessional toward me." She founded The Authentic Asian, an exclusive community of AAPI (Asian American and Pacific Islander) female founders and executives, giving these leaders a supportive space to connect. "There are these invisible barriers that limit us that we need to overcome and I'm tired of doing it alone."

As an Only, you may face being judged, excluded, or underestimated, much like Misa did in her early years. You might encounter interruptions during meetings, have your ideas co-opted, or receive unkind comments.

While ideally we would eliminate ignorance, microaggressions, and other hurdles, it's important to remember that we can't control other people's opinions and actions. It's crucial to stay focused on yourself and not let ignorance, emotional chaos, or bad behavior drain your energy. Being overly consumed by others' negativity, what they say or don't say, or our perception of it diverts our energy from what truly matters. You get to choose. Speak up when necessary, but also know when something doesn't deserve your time or attention.

> **It's crucial to stay focused on yourself and not let ignorance, emotional chaos, or bad behavior drain your energy.**

Protect your mental space.

If we don't block out negativity from others, it literally can kill us. Negativity rewires our brains, making it easier to see the bad and harder to see the good. It's not only our brains that are affected; it's also harmful to our bodies. "Studies show being surrounded by negativity takes up mental space but can also take a toll on the body in the form of high blood pressure, stress, anxiety, headaches, and poor circulation. A five-minute episode of anger is so stressful it can impair your immune system for more than six hours and lead to more serious issues like heart attack and stroke."[126]

Blocking out negativity doesn't mean ignoring problems or disregarding poor behavior toward you or inappropriate or offensive behavior you witness. It's not denying your feelings or pretending that everything is okay when it's not. It's not "toxic positivity" and dismissing others' emotions or bypassing your own. It's good to acknowledge, to understand, and feel the situation, but don't internalize it or blame yourself.

Guarding your energy is claiming your power to decide if, when, and how you will handle situations. If you're on the receiving end of a microaggression or exclusionary or hurtful behavior, *you* have the power to decide whether you want to respond to it, call the person out directly on their behavior, address it through a separate avenue, or ignore it and let it go. Give yourself permission to feel whatever you feel, but *you* decide what you take on, what you don't, and how you are going to move forward. It's important to not let other people's words, perceptions, or misperceptions fuel self-blame and drain your power.

TRUST YOUR INTUITION

To help guard your energy, you must trust your intuition. Over the years, my gut feelings have usually led me in the right direction when it comes to deciding what I do and don't let into my life. The key is finding the balance between trusting your instincts and being too hypervigilant or oversensitive.

The phrase "trust your gut" isn't just a metaphor—it has a scientific basis. Our gut is regulated by the enteric nervous system, often called the body's second brain. This system uses the same chemicals and cells as the brain to help us digest food and alert us when something is off. The gut and brain are in constant communication, and that is why we often get a "gut feeling" about things.[127]

Give yourself permission to feel whatever you feel, but *you* decide what you take on, what you don't, and how you are going to move forward.

Trusting yourself and your intuition means recognizing what works for you in your life at any given moment.

You have the answers, and you can honor what your gut tells you.

Others may offer information and advice, but you have the ultimate authority on how and when it applies to your life. If something doesn't resonate with you, trust that there's often a valid reason. Saying no or choosing a different path isn't necessarily a sign of fear; perhaps you are being realistic and are attuned to your unique experiences and insights. Only you truly understand your journey. While others may have valuable opinions or good intentions, they don't live your life or share your perspective.

Filmmaker Kerry David used to pride herself on taking on everything, but she now knows how to trust herself and guard her energy accordingly. A veteran of the film industry for twenty-plus years, Kerry started her career at Paramount Pictures. It was normal for her to be the only woman in the room, especially in the early years. She eventually founded her own production company after working with Tom Cruise and Nicole Kidman on a variety of films.

"Films are hard to produce. There's ego, money, not enough time, creative differences, artistic chaos." As a female director and producer, Kerry believes it's vital to protect your headspace and trust yourself. "You're trying to put this huge thing together, and you don't need all the outside noise when you have this huge financial burden and a creative project that you want to do the best you can with."[128] By honoring her boundaries and gut and protecting her headspace, Kerry is able to stay focused and channel her energy into making films on important issues that matter to her such as *Breaking Their Silence*, about women on the front lines of the poaching war, and *Open Secret*, a documentary investigating a cover-up and allegations of systemic discrimination and child sexual assault in schools.

In Chapter 3.1, I mentioned how we all take mental shortcuts based on biases or past experiences. It's important to recognize that these shortcuts can become automatic and influence your decisions. Being aware of their impact helps ensure they don't cloud your judgment or override your intuition. Balancing openness with energy protection might seem contradictory, but with the right mindset and tools, it's possible to stay open to new experiences and ideas while protecting your mental energy and well-being.

When should you listen to your intuition?

You'll often feel a strong pull or sense of certainty. At the same time, be mindful that protecting your energy doesn't create barriers to connection, trust, and empathy with others. Ultimately, trusting your intuition is about believing in yourself and recognizing that you are the best judge of your own experiences. Listen to your gut, stay open, and protect your energy wisely.

PROTECT YOUR HEADSPACE FROM THE INFORMATION YOU CONSUME

Guarding your energy is not just about "ignoring the noise" that is often created by other well-meaning (and sometimes not-so-well-meaning) people who want to give their advice or opinions; it's also about guarding your energy from the information you consume. News and social media overload can drain your attention, capacity, and energy.

Today, everything we ever wanted to know is at our fingertips. We can access articles, news updates, blogs, podcasts, entertainment, AI, and more. We can instantly search for anything, connect with anyone, and learn new skills from home. In this interconnected digital information age, we create our own—and others'—realities that are mostly shaped by the media we consume.

It's easy to be overwhelmed and anxious by the twenty-four-hour news cycle and social media landscape. As a former reporter, I value journalism and the importance of staying informed. However, the media's drive for your attention often means headlines are crafted to provoke anger or fear to boost clicks. A study of 23 million headlines from forty-seven major news outlets between 2000 and 2019 revealed a 104 percent increase in anger-inducing headlines and a 150 percent rise in fear-based headlines.[129] Research also shows negative news tends to drive clicks.[130] And now with AI, the information overload is even more intense.

Psychologists are observing a rise in news-related stress, with research linking heavy news consumption on social media to increased symptoms of depression and PTSD.[131] Therapist Steven Stosny, PhD, referred to this phenomenon as "headline stress disorder" after noticing a surge in anger and resentment leading up to the 2016 election. He saw that women are even more vulnerable to this condition because they feel personally affected by many of the issues and are more sensitive to the headlines.[132]

Constant exposure to news can diminish resilience and coping abilities, leading to what psychologists call a "learned helplessness"[133] that occurs when individuals feel powerless to affect outcomes and therefore stop trying. According to Stosny, a sense of helplessness driven by media consumption fosters frustration and anger that can escalate into rage and despair. This cycle contributes to broader social and political polarization, trapping us in siloed perspectives.

All humans are naturally prone to confirmation bias, in which they tend to search for information to confirm their beliefs.[134] Mix that with social media and algorithms—powered by ever more powerful artificial intelligence that usually shows content that aligns with your current beliefs and interests—and you have the state of our world today. This creates echo chambers where existing views are reinforced and alternative ideas are not considered. We are then less likely to encounter different opinions or have conversations with those who think differently.

To protect your mental energy, you must understand this negative cycle, be critical of the information you consume, and take small, everyday actions to gain a sense of agency and control.

Media literacy could help.

Media literacy is understanding and being more critical of how you access, analyze, and evaluate information. It's distinguishing between news sources, opinion sources, blogs, and random noise on the internet. It's a survival skill we all need to guard our energy. When you understand information overload and know how to process it, you're less likely to get sucked into being overwhelmed.

If a headline makes me angry, I try to read the whole article before I make a judgment. If I don't have time to form a real opinion or process it, I don't internalize it and move on until later. If I make the time, I filter it through a series of questions.

Is this a credible source?
What is the objective of this piece?
Who might benefit?
Who could it harm?
Is this information good for me?
What value does it add to my life?
Can I do anything about this issue?

If it's an important topic I want to know about, I may even read several other articles to get a broader perspective. I know we can't do this for every piece of information, but this filter reminds us to have a more critical eye; then, you can decide whether to let it affect you and your energy.[135]

True power belongs to those who can protect access to their mind—those who can focus, be discerning, know what information to take in, what to block out, and what to do about the emotions they ignite.

Another way to protect your mental space is to channel emotions elicited by the information you consume into action. As activist Gloria Steinem says, "The truth will set you free, but first it will piss you off!" Did the information you consume ignite something in you? Is there a way you can become more proactive about the issue? What do you value? What actions can you take to move toward those values or make an impact?

Having the ability to sift through, simplify, and effectively use the abundance of information in the world is more valuable than having access to it. True power belongs to those who can protect access to their mind—those who can focus, be discerning, know what information to take in, what to block out, and what to do about the emotions they ignite.

BE AWARE OF YOUR ENERGY

As I said before, your energy walks in before you do. It sets the tone for your well-being and influences those around you. Awareness of your energy is the first step to guarding it. When you're used to running fast or are in burnout mode, you may not even know your baseline normal. You may *feel* fine, but one extra thing could easily push you over the edge. In short, before you can guard your energy, you need to be aware of your emotional state. The better you become at assessing your energy level or emotional state, the better you'll be able to guard it.

Over the past few years, I've recognized that despite my naturally high energy and fast-paced lifestyle, I need to slow down internally more often. As a middle-aged woman with two teenagers, my emotional capacity isn't what it was in my twenties. It doesn't mean I can't do the same things, but I must be more mindful of when I need to create more internal space.

If I find myself at an emotional intensity level of eight (where one is completely calm and ten is extremely high stress), it might not be the best time to take on new challenges, have difficult conversations, or handle complex situations. It's crucial to wait until I can lower my internal temperature and boost my emotional resilience. A study found that when people label their emotions, functional MRIs showed reduced activity in the amygdala and parts of the brain involved in processing negative emotions.[136] Doing this can help you calm down.

To get better in touch with how you feel and the emotions in your body, try this exercise:

- Close your eyes, put your hand on your heart or mentally focus on your heart, take a deep breath, and just notice.
- How does your body feel?
- What is going through your mind?
- What is going on in your life right now?
- What emotion are you feeling?

- Where do you feel that in your body?
- What events led to this feeling?
- What is this feeling really about?
- What are you holding on to that you need to let go of?
- What do you need right now?

Don't judge it, just feel it. Being aware of your energy will help you decide what you need.

RELEASE NEGATIVITY AND UNWANTED ENERGY

Guarding your energy is not just about protecting it but also about releasing energy that doesn't serve us. Stepping into the Power of the Only can sometimes feel both stressful and isolating. Even when you're making strides and leading the way, you might still be grappling with a range of emotions—such as hurt, anger, frustration, or being overwhelmed— without a clear outlet for that energy. This could stem from daily pressures or specific incidents that challenge you.

You may face tasks or projects that don't align with your values or feel burdensome, or you could be required to take on responsibilities that trigger you or leave you feeling powerless. Even if you have the skills to tackle these challenges, the emotional load can feel overwhelming.

Your emotions are *valid*.

You are *allowed* to feel whatever you feel.

Many of us were not given this permission in childhood; instead, we heard *Don't be silly*, *Keep it to yourself*, or *It's not that big of a deal*. When you feel yourself internalizing the negativity around you, find ways to let go of the energy you don't want to get back to your center.

When I say *let go*, I don't mean ignore it. Research shows emotions can cause physical symptoms like muscle tension and pain; it's called "embodied emotion."[137] Our bodies tell us that something needs attention, but sometimes, these emotions are deep in our subconscious.

If we remain unaware and keep them repressed, they can negatively affect our physical and mental health and overall well-being.[138]

Where do we hold these emotions?

It can vary, but scientists have mapped out where in our bodies we typically feel emotions. Researchers asked participants from both Western Europe and Eastern Asia to indicate on a diagram which parts of their bodies felt "activated" or "deactivated" during different emotional states. Despite their diverse cultural backgrounds, they reported experiencing similar emotions in similar areas of their bodies:[139]

- Anger in the head or chest
- Disgust in mouth and stomach
- Sadness in the throat and chest
- Anxiety in the chest and gut
- Shame in the face and chest

The following is a list of tools I've cultivated through the years to help me release unwanted energy and get back to my center. This is not a substitution for processing your emotions, but it can help you release them. The key is to care for your nervous system and help your body naturally release feel-good chemicals. My descriptions can seem simple, maybe even too simple, but the power behind them is quite complex. Choose any that resonate with you.

Intense Workout: Engaging in an intense workout releases pent-up energy and reduces stress by increasing endorphin levels; natural mood lifters. Research shows that regular high-intensity exercise can improve overall mental health and reduce symptoms of anxiety and depression.[140] Some people love running and can't live without cardio. I prefer yoga, but when I want a more intense workout, I do high-intensity interval training (HIIT) or kickboxing. As a premenopausal woman, research shows I may have elevated cortisol levels,[141] and intense exercise can spike cortisol even more.[142] Therefore, when doing intense workouts (like HIIT), I ensure I don't overdo it and allow proper recovery time. Choose your favorite way to release based on your body.

Dance: Express yourself physically and emotionally through movement to release tension and trapped emotions. Dancing engages the right side of the brain, which allows you to connect to and express your emotions. Research suggests that dancing can boost mood, improve cardiovascular health, and increase social connectedness, making it a great way to release energy and feel good.[143] You can just dance around the room, shake like we did in Chapter 3.2, or try these innovative platforms: S Factor with Sheila Kelley, a conscious feminine movement practice; KINRGY with dancer Julianne Hough, dance and mindful movement inspired by natural elements of earth, fire, water, and air; and The Class, movement to clear the body and connect to the heart. The first time I went to a retreat where they made us dance and move our bodies in public, I was really uncomfortable; now, it's part of several of my keynotes and I'm the one making others move their energy because it works.

Scream in Private: Screaming in a private space or into a pillow can be a cathartic way to release intense emotions and pent-up energy. Vocal expression is known to reduce stress and improve emotional release.[144]

Expressive and Rage Journaling: Release your emotions or rage by journaling. Writing down negative feelings helps you release and let them go. Research indicates that expressive writing can improve mood, reduce stress, and enhance psychological health.[145] Another study found that throwing away or destroying the paper with angry thoughts reduces anger even more and is a simple and effective way to neutralize anger.[146]

Practice Somatic Yoga: Somatic yoga focuses on slow, gentle movements, mindful breathing, and increased body awareness. Research suggests that yoga overall can enhance the mind-body connection, reduce chronic pain, and alleviate symptoms of anxiety and depression.[147] Somatic yoga helps recalibrate the body's response to stress, making it beneficial for healing and releasing unwanted energy. The first time I tried yoga—almost thirty years ago at the gym on the Paramount Pictures lot—I found it strange to move so slowly and deliberately. But soon, I was practicing every lunch break, feeling more grounded and connected with each session.

Massage/Lymphatic Treatments: Receiving a massage or lymphatic drainage treatment stimulates circulation, releases muscle tension, and detoxifies the body. Research shows that massage therapy can decrease cortisol levels, improve immune function, and enhance overall well-being.[148] Lymphatic drainage massage is a form of gentle massage that encourages drainage of the lymphatic system, helping remove waste and toxins from the body and tissues where pent-up energy can be trapped.[149]

Meditation: Regular meditation practices can help release mental clutter and reduce stress, promoting a balanced state of mind. The Mayo Clinic states that meditation can lower anxiety, increase attention span, and improve emotional awareness and regulation.[150] Mental health counselors say when we are emotionally aware and fully present in the now, we can release negative energy from our past.[151] Meditation may not be as effective if you haven't physically released your energy first; that's why I put it closer to the bottom of the list. For some, it may be hard to sit with your thoughts. Guided meditation can make it easier. The first time I tried meditation, I was a new mom and needed a life reboot. I went to a primordial sound meditation retreat at the Chopra Center. I had a hard time trying to quiet my mind and felt out of place. Now, meditation is just part of my daily routine.

Therapy: Sometimes you need a more structured environment to vent, release, and process your emotional burdens. Finding the right therapist is important, and not all therapists and types of therapy are the same. A good therapist can serve any client, but it's nice to have more options for Onlys. Here are resources for therapists who may share your lived experience: Psychologytoday.com, InclusiveTherapists.com, AsiansForMentalHealth.com, LatinxTherapy.com, SouthAsiantherapists.

org, National Queer and Trans Therapists of Color Network (nqttcn. com), TherapyForBlackGirls.com, TherapyForBlackMen.org.[152] *For more on these tools, check out the book resource page at www.AngelaChee.com/ poweroftheonly.*

Like-Minded Social Circles: While I advocate being a part of diverse networks, it's also important to have safe spaces where you have a shared identity or experiences. Like-minded groups can provide support, understanding, and a community for sharing and venting that helps release negative energy and offers positive reinforcement.

The bottom line? Create a toolbox that works for you. Stay open-minded; don't prejudge that something is too hard, too easy, or too weird until you give it a try. Once you release whatever energy you don't want, you are ready to cultivate positive energy in your life.

CULTIVATE THE POSITIVE

I pulled the album out of the sleeve, carefully placed it on the record player, and put the needle on the record. Cue the music.

"When the drumbeats go like . . ."

That's a reference for '80s music lovers; everyone else can look up "Pump Up the Volume" by MARRS (about 2:50 in).

I laid down in front of our wooden stereo console as I stared at the album cover. That's how I spent many hours in the '80s—listening to my favorite songs. Normally, I was waiting for the Top 40 radio countdown, but that day, I had my *own* record. For the first time, it wasn't a read-along storybook. It was *Colour by Numbers* by Culture Club. I loved Boy George and Culture Club. Maybe part of me was drawn to his "Only" spirit, but I loved his soulful voice and creative, free-spirited energy. I even had their poster in my room.

A few years ago, I took my daughter to see him in concert and it was a full-circle moment for me. As a little girl playing the songs over and over by myself at home, I would have never thought I'd see him in concert with my preteen. It wasn't just seeing him in concert that brought me joy; it was nostalgic memories from the past. It was the feeling of a simpler time, the sense of pride seeing how far I'd come and how far Boy George had come. He still sounded great, and his career was thriving after disappearing from the scene for decades.

To guard our energy, we not only need to block out what we don't want—we must cultivate the positive to bring a sense of awe and wonder back into our lives. This allows you to center yourself and recharge your energy. As we get older, we seem to lose a bit of our childhood innocence and awe. Being mindful of what influences you allow into your life and focusing on experiences that bring you joy and fulfillment, like taking a trip down memory lane at a concert, can help you stay resilient, maintain a positive outlook, and avoid becoming drained. There are many ways to cultivate the positive, but the two I enjoy the most are tapping into the power of nostalgia and savoring the beauty in our lives.

THE POWER OF NOSTALGIA

In the last several years, there's been an overwhelming amount of research revealing the benefits of nostalgia—the experience of recalling and a sentimental longing for your past. According to a *National Geographic* article, a variety of studies show nostalgia "increases your sense of well-being, boosts inspiration and creativity, makes us feel more youthful, alert, optimistic and energetic, and even encourages us to take risks and pursue our goals."[153] Nostalgia can also help us regulate our brain activity by acting as a buffer against various psychological and physical threats.[154] Ziyan Yang, a professor at the Chinese Academy of Sciences' Institute of Psychology, says that nostalgic feelings bring a sense of warmth, fondness, and belonging, and people even experience a sort of mental time travel. She says movies and music easily trigger nostalgia and can be very comforting, especially in trying times.

Memories that trigger nostalgia elevate your mood and help you guard your energy by counteracting feelings of loneliness and anxiety. Remembering the past can also give you a sense of belonging and connection. I recently found myself scrolling through "I love the '80s" social media accounts and smiling at seeing retro television and movie clips. I even have a "Memories" playlist. It was fun to share this music nostalgia moment with my teens even though for them, songs from the 2010s are oldies. ☺

To tap into the power of nostalgia, revisit parts of your past that brought you joy or positive feelings. Looking back can be bittersweet because there may be some sadness that the moment is gone, so focus on memories that won't keep you ruminating on the past for too long.

1. Take a walk down Memory Lane. Look at documents, memorabilia, or photographs from your life and career. Research shows reflecting on happy memories can boost your mood and give you a natural dopamine high.[155] It also shows that reflecting on meaningful career moments helped people have a greater sense of meaning at work; it's called organizational nostalgia.[156] Organizational nostalgia is reminiscing about positive work or organizational experiences. When your work feels meaningful, it can help you feel more motivated and engaged and reduce burnout.

2. Curate your own "memories" musical playlist. Choose songs that make you happy and bring back good memories. Research shows people prefer music from their teens and twenties.[157] Music activates the brain's reward system, releasing dopamine and giving you a sense of joy. It also triggers positive memories and emotions.

3. Journal about or revisit a nostalgic memory. Studies show individuals who spend several minutes writing about a nostalgic memory made them feel more open-minded and creative.[158] You can also watch old movies or visit your favorite places from the past, like your old neighborhood.

4. Practice the "three good things" exercise. Notice and write down three events or things that went well each day and reflect on why they happened. Research led by Martin Seligman, known as the "father of positive psychology," shows that reminiscing is not only good in the moment but also can lead to lasting happiness. People who did this exercise every night for a week boosted their happiness and reduced their depressive symptoms for up to six months.[159]

Harnessing the power of nostalgia can help cultivate the positive, balance your emotions, and protect you from the negativity around you. If we don't get stuck in the past, nostalgia can be more than just enjoyable; it can help us move forward and shape our future. So, indulge in those memories and let them guide you toward your next steps!

SAVORING THE BEAUTY IN OUR LIVES

My family didn't buy flowers when I was growing up. My parents considered them a waste of money. Now, embracing a thriving mindset, I override that old programming and purchase flowers to appreciate the beauty in our lives. The vibrant and soothing colors of flowers not only bring joy to our surroundings but also enhance our meals; my favorite café adds edible flowers to their salads, offering both aesthetic pleasure and health benefits. Every time I see those beautiful colors, they make me smile. It's a feeling that might seem abstract, but there's science behind it.

A behavioral research study conducted by Dr. Nancy Etcoff of Harvard Medical School reveals that flowers significantly enhance our well-being. They foster compassion, alleviate worry and anxiety at home, and boost energy and enthusiasm at work.[160] Appreciating flowers is just one of the ways I savor the beauty in life.

Psychologists Fred Bryant and Joseph Veroff say savoring the act of "attending, appreciating, and enhancing positive experiences that occur in one's life"[161] can serve as a buffer to the negative and enhance well-being. Studies show savoring can boost happiness[162] and counterbalance the experience of unpleasant emotions during stressful events.[163]

Appreciating or savoring the aesthetic aspect of things has been used as a healing tool throughout the ages. Ancient and Indigenous cultures used art as part of healing rituals and ceremonies. Ancient Greek, Roman, Islamic, and Asian civilizations designed gardens as places for relaxation, reflection, and spiritual contemplation. Ancient temples and churches often focused on creating spaces that evoked awe and tranquility. Scientific research has caught up to explain why it works; Susan Magsamen, from the Center for Applied Neuroaesthetics at Johns Hopkins School of Medicine, says aesthetic experiences and the arts are hardwired in all of us and are fundamental to our health, well-being, and learning. Her book *Your Brain on Art* reveals research that shows engaging in an art project for as little as forty-five minutes reduces the stress hormone cortisol, no matter your skill level. One art experience per month can extend your life by ten years, and listening to soundwaves can counteract stress.[164]

To tap into the power of aesthetics in your life and curate more positive energy, add a little beauty and art; make engaging in an art practice a part of your daily routine. Savor the beauty and awe of the natural world by going for walks in nature or watching the sunrise or sunset. Appreciate the art of making a meal. Pause as you enjoy your morning tea or coffee. And, of course, keep flowers by your bed or herbs in the kitchen. Smell informs 75 percent of our emotions. You can use the power of smell to cultivate the emotions you want—lavender evokes a sense of calm and relaxation, peppermint enhances mood and invigorates the mind, and the scent of cut green apples reduces anxiety.[165]

What do you want to remember and savor?

PRIORITIZE YOUR ENERGY

Guarding your energy is vital to owning your future. It's the daily practice of blocking out negativity and not internalizing other people's energy. It's about protecting your headspace from the information you consume. It's about trusting your intuition that you know best about what you need and when you need it. It's about learning to be aware of your energy, releasing unwanted energy, and inviting positive energy in. Making a conscious effort to let go of what drains you and cultivate positivity and joy instead will help you navigate any challenge or environment. When you protect and prioritize your energy, you empower yourself to take control and actively create the future you envision.

Making a conscious effort to let go of what drains you and cultivate positivity and joy instead will help you navigate any challenge or environment.

Navigating being an Only is tough, but your challenges don't have to become scars. They can become your fuel. They are your fire. They help you burn through the barriers and pave a path to the future.

They are your superpowers.

EXERCISE

- A wide array of ideas for guarding and boosting your energy was presented in this chapter. Take a moment to notice one or two that were new to you and would represent a stretch. Focus on that growth opportunity and make a tangible commitment to it, whether that be setting an appointment or allocating time to a new activity.

- If you experienced resistance thinking about fostering good energy practices, take a moment to consider your energy level. Have you been fatigued, and if so, for how long? If you have strong energy right now and your gas tank is full, notice that. Or maybe you are somewhere in the middle. This is a good temperature check to take at any time, but if you're feeling resistance and observe that you are fatigued, your tiredness may be causing you to play it safe. New ideas like making your energy a priority are more challenging to take on when you're tired. Your priority is to rest. So that's what I encourage you to do as soon as you're able. How can you increase your rest this week?

Chapter 5.4

BE DISCERNING

Absorb what is useful. Discard what is not.
Add what is uniquely your own.

—BRUCE LEE

I grabbed my wrap tighter around my shoulders to stay warm in the air-conditioned hotel ballroom and wiggled a bit in my chair to stay energized. As I tried to focus on the speaker's words, they started to fade away and sound more like the teacher in Charlie Brown.

Wah, wah, wah, wah, wah . . .

The words he was saying were helpful, but I had heard similar things so many times that they didn't really speak to me anymore. I was used to being the Only in a room and having to reframe a speaker's messages to be useful to me.

But this time, it was different.

I could feel myself shift from a listener to an observer, as if I was hovering above, watching my own experience. This was the beginning of me starting to notice, on a deeper level, that much of the information and advice doled out by gurus, speakers, articles, and blogs and referenced in the media and popular culture are very often the same.

"You can do anything if you just put your mind to it."

"Just have a morning routine!"

"Make a vision board!"

"Just be more confident!"

"Work hard and hustle!"

These are good pieces of advice. I do many of these things to help me succeed. But it's not the whole or the only picture. I was coming to terms with the fact that advice, insights, and ideas from *new* voices were not being heard. Instead, the same voices get the most airtime over and over.

This was the day I realized many rooms don't speak to me.

It was time for a shift.

That's when I started *The Power of the Only* podcast. I wanted to explore new ways of thinking and have conversations with Onlys who were breaking barriers, shifting the status quo, and making positive change. I had no idea that a week later, in March 2020, the world would shut down. I'm sure you remember how we were all forced to change. We had no choice. We went through drastic personal, professional, and societal shifts.

As an Only, I had worked hard to get to the top. I had started to create my own vision of success when I left the news business but was slipping back into my old patterns. Instead of chasing success, I was chasing knowledge. I had spent the last decade learning, growing, healing, and I was *tired*.

It was time to recenter. I blocked the noise that came from gathering more information and strategies that I would inevitably fail to implement. I stopped listening to advice that clouded my internal knowledge and compass instead of creating clarity. I ignored all the information that didn't apply to or serve me. Anything that complicated things or made me feel like it would never be enough was out.

The key to owning my future has been prioritizing my intuitive choices and heeding *my* greater calling: helping others amplify their stories. As a result, I put my heart and soul into my podcast to highlight stories, experiences, and insights of Onlys who deserve more of the spotlight. The ones who are ahead of the curve. The ones who spark innovation and inspire change.

In the previous chapters, you reflected on your values and how you define success for yourself. You created a new life vision. You learned how to guard your energy by blocking out negativity, releasing what you don't want, and calling in more of what you do, all while I told you it's important to stay open and have the capacity to hear, feel, and experience.

Now, you need a filter to bring it all together.

The Onlys who will own the future are the ones who can be discerning about information, people, and energies to embrace. You focus your attention on what truly matters to you and learn to block out all the noise from the past, the future, and external distractions that mute the knowing in your soul. Discernment involves

You focus your attention on what truly matters to you and learn to block out all the noise from the past, the future, and external distractions that mute the knowing in your soul.

understanding what you should carry and what you shouldn't, deciding what aligns with your values and what doesn't, and determining what truly benefits you. It's about setting boundaries with clarity and purpose, ensuring that you remain aligned with your true self and goals. It means being able to say:

I don't agree.
This is not for me.
I've done all I can.
I've had enough.
It's time for me to move on.

It's time for me to do my own thing.

Many rooms are not made for you as an Only, and things may not be set up in your favor. You may not always have the same access, resources, or networks. While this may not be fair, you can still thrive if you have the awareness and tools to discern what applies to you and what doesn't and the agency to decide what you are and are not going to do moving forward.

YOU DON'T NEED TO FEEL WELCOME TO BENEFIT FROM A SITUATION

I usually don't notice that I'm the Only in a room right away. The room could be an internal meeting, a conference, or even a social gathering like a group out for coffee. I think over time, I've gotten used to it and forgotten what it was like because I've built up the skills and tools to navigate it. But there are times when I pull back like I did when I was at the conference and realized the room didn't resonate with me. In those moments, I've had to choose what I take in and what I don't.

When you find yourself in rooms where you don't fit in, you don't necessarily have to take on the burden of changing it or challenging it. Sometimes, you'll find yourself changing the room just by being in it.

This is *especially* important when you find yourself in a room you haven't chosen for yourself. We can't always choose the environments we find ourselves in; some are simply part of our work or life situations, and it's a reality that not all spaces are designed with us in mind. This doesn't necessarily mean the people in these spaces are deliberately excluding us; they may just have blind spots and be unaware of our unique needs. While it might feel like you don't belong or that you're not fully welcome, there's value in participating in these spaces. By staying engaged, you might uncover new insights, gain different perspectives, and move closer to achieving *your* own goals.

When you find yourself in rooms where you don't fit in, you don't necessarily have to take on the burden of changing it or challenging it. Sometimes, you'll find yourself changing the room just by being in it; that's how powerful your presence can be. But there might be times when others aren't supportive or open to change, and that's when you need to tap into your intuition and discernment. Be open-minded, flexible, and curious. If you stand in your power, you know when being in that room is valuable and when it is not, when you can add value and when you can't, and you will have the agency to choose what would best serve you, the situation, and your objectives.

YOU DON'T NEED TO DISAVOW YOUR PAST

As I rolled up to the open field, I could see the news stations and reporters lined up, ready for their live shots. In the distance, I saw the familiar faces of several former colleagues. I was a reporter in Los Angeles and had been sent to my old stomping grounds, Bakersfield, to cover a local story that had made national headlines.

It had only been a few months since I left the Bakersfield news station, and aside from confiding in my best reporter friend, Emily, no one knew I had started working at KCBS-TV. As I stepped out of the massive, fully-equipped satellite news van—accompanied by two photographers, one for shooting and the other for setting up the satellite—we were ready to go live on the spot. After we finished our live shots, I got to spend some time with my old friends. I was greeted with lots of warm faces and questions. It turned out to be a big homecoming of sorts. I had no idea I would ever return to Bakersfield for a story; it was just a coincidence.

It was a coincidence that my soul appreciated.

Although my time as a rookie reporter in Bakersfield was challenging at times, I honor that period, including the people who supported me—like the friends I spent time with after covering the story, as well as those who didn't. I've never burned bridges. Both supportive and difficult experiences have shaped my journey and contributed to who I am today.

Your past is part of your story.

Sometimes we change, grow out of things, get forced out of things, and move on. But that doesn't invalidate our experiences and what we needed at that time. What I needed and the tools I lived by were different when I was a young woman in my twenties than what they are now. The lens through which you see things and your capacity, income, priorities, and focus shift over time.

In the last few years, there has been a reckoning in the world and, for some, within us too. When the #MeToo movement caught fire in 2017, I started to reflect on the years of microaggressions I witnessed and experienced in my childhood and career. People made fun of Asians in front of me and said, "But not *you*, Angela." Boys commented on my body and snapped my bra straps in middle school. I faced sexist and dismissive remarks and witnessed assistants and reporters, both men and women, being screamed at and emotionally abused by their bosses. Knowing others who had worse experiences, I always dismissed mine. Overall, I loved my time in Hollywood and TV news.

Recent events forced me to reevaluate past experiences and feel anger that, as a young person, I had to endure them. It's easy to think that just because others faced worse situations, my own struggles weren't valid or didn't leave their mark.

They did—like tiny paper cuts that add up over time.

Looking at my daughter, I can't bear the thought of her going through similar challenges. Yet, during those times, I learned to ignore the issues, accepting them as part of the norm as many of my generation did. I'm hopeful that future generations will have more awareness and that the fight against all forms of discrimination will continue. While we should address past injustices, we should not dwell on them. Also, certain rooms and experiences that no longer resonate with me now can still hold value, either for me at the time I was there or for others now.

Reflecting on your past actions through your current lens doesn't always work. It's like watching old movies or comedians and realizing the content has not aged well. Or like reminiscing about when certain things considered offensive today were considered okay (even though they weren't okay) and wondering, "What were we thinking?"

Once you experience or learn something, it becomes a part of your awareness and understanding, so it's hard to go back to the status quo. You can't unsee what you've seen or unknow what you know. I feel the same way about mentors I've had or organizations I've supported or learned from but have since outgrown or no longer align with. You can't constantly second-guess decisions you've made or try to rewrite every experience you've had.

Our past doesn't have to define us, but it certainly is a part of us, and we should embrace it. It's important to see, acknowledge, and honor our *whole* selves and who we already are, then discern what no longer serves us and develop what does. It's about embracing your journey, owning all of it, and then adding new chapters. The key question you need to answer to start your next chapter is, "What am I going to do *moving forward*?"

CREATE YOUR OWN TABLE

Despite her early success and fame and Oscar win in 2006, Reese Witherspoon struggled to find satisfying roles in Hollywood and was frustrated by the lack of stories for women. Instead of trying to build something inside a system not made for female partnership, she had to build it outside. She told the audience at her Shine Away event, "After

I did a whole lot of soul searching and a lot of complaining to anyone who would listen, mainly my mother, I realized that if you want to fix the problem, you have to be part of the solution." In 2016, Reese started her own media company, Hello Sunshine, to tell women-driven stories, including TV production hits like *Big Little Lies*, *The Morning Show*, and *Little Fires Everywhere*.

Five years later, it was clear betting on herself paid off. She sold a majority stake of Hello Sunshine to Blackstone-backed Candle Media for $900 million and is continuing to diversify its portfolio. Collaborating with CEO Sarah Harden to raise capital, Reese says she built each piece of the business through female partnership and leaned into all the brilliant women around her who believed in the same dream. "Power in Hollywood has felt like it's been abused in the past and used as a way to keep other people out," she said in an interview with *Time*. With Hello Sunshine, she wanted to create a new type of leadership and culture in Hollywood. "What doors have been closed to women and people of color, and how can we open doors to different communities? It's not just the end product; it's how you make it and whose voices you amplify," she explained.[166]

By being discerning, Reese didn't just elevate other voices—she sparked a ripple effect that empowered others to do the same. Reese's Book Club has been a financial game-changer for many authors. In a SheKnows article, Reese revealed that the author of a book she selected for the club became the first person in her family to buy a home. "The unexpected piece of it all was the economic impact on these authors' lives. She texted me a picture of the key. I burst into tears."[167]

This is the Power of the Only in action. And the power of Onlys helping other Onlys.

Being discerning means recognizing when certain situations aren't changing or are beyond your control. Instead of continually fighting for a seat at the table, you might choose to build your own table, like Reese did. You don't have to wait for everything to change to step into your greatness. This is how we own our future and fully step into the Power of the Only despite the environment or challenges around us.

After spending twenty-two years at Deloitte, Deepa Purushothaman (introduced in Chapter 1.2) felt called to a deeper purpose. She believes work is about more than ourselves, especially for women of color. "Legacy is so important. A lot of us work for success, getting to the top, but we are in this transition point where we can now step in and be the change."[168] Deepa left Deloitte in 2020, founded the re.write, and authored *The First, the Few, the Only: How Women of Color Can Redefine Power in Corporate America.* "After talking to more than 500 senior women of color," she shared with me, "my research found that the pressure to conform is worse as they get higher and they don't know what to do about it. They believe, 'I'll get a seat, I'll get to the table, and then I'll do it my way, I'll bring people up and do it differently,' but there is so much pressure on what it means to be a leader." The old story says we must accept what has come before; the new story gives us permission to challenge the systems around us. At the re.write, an unconventional think tank, Deepa advocates and promotes this new story to the next generation of leaders.

When you leave rooms that no longer suit you, you can make your own room and create new rules—as Deepa is trying to do with the re.write—that will impact not just yourself but others too. You may be the Only right now, but the way to evolve and succeed is to come from a place of abundance to plant seeds, bring people in, and carve a new path for others to follow. When you do, your efforts to step fully into the Power of the Only can have a ripple effect.

Silicon Valley veteran Dave Lu spent his early years chasing success and happiness through security.

Ivy League school? *Check.*

Management consulting job? *Check.*

The right business school? *Check.*

He started his career in tech at Yahoo in the late '90s and went on to other iconic tech companies from Apple to Cisco. "It was a never-ending hamster wheel that I finally got sick of and decided to jump off when I started my first company, Fanpop, at the age of twenty-nine. I just wish I had gotten off a lot sooner."[169] Dave would eventually launch Hyphen Capital, a venture capital firm focused on supporting Asian American founders.

"There's no more impactful way to help someone take the leap and pursue their dream than cutting them a check to break them free from the shackles of their day job and the guilt and doubt of their parents," Dave said. Giving back is how we move from surviving to thriving and owning our future. "We need to take more chances, bet on ourselves and our community, and realize we are playing for future generations. . . . The moment we stop thinking only about what we have, and start thinking about what we could have, is when the change can begin."[170]

When Onlys build their own tables, they not only create new opportunities but also drive innovation that can transform industries and shift standards. This was exemplified by film director Ava DuVernay who we met in Principle 1. By thinking creatively, she redefined film financing. Rather than relying on traditional studio backing for her film *Origin*, she turned to philanthropic organizations like the Ford Foundation and other nonprofits, raising $38 million. Her approach blends philanthropy with social investing, creating a groundbreaking hybrid model.

In an interview with *Forbes*, DuVernay says, "This is social impact investment by people with funds earmarked to create works, organizations, or movements for the social good. The idea that films that are not documentaries can fit into that framework is what is new." Under this model she also had total creative freedom to tell the story how she wanted. "In a time of tension in our industry due to the consolidation of companies, the reimagination of streamers, pandemics, and strikes . . . [it] provides an opportunity for new ways of doing things." And by earmarking funds for socially impactful entertainment, it also amplifies the mission of these foundations.[171]

Like Reese, Deepa, Dave, and Ava, you too can create your own table and, in the process, become a bridge builder to the future you imagine. Whether the table is inside or outside of your current company or industry is up to you. You may not have the option to make your own table, but if you do, bet on you.

Always.

Honor your reality, not what others tell you to do or what may look good. Know you have a bigger vision. That vision may not always turn out exactly as planned. You may have setbacks, you may have to pivot, but ultimately, you have *you*. And if you live by the Power of the Only principles, you and your new table have everything necessary to become more than you ever imagined.

> **Honor your reality, not what others tell you to do or what may look good. Know you have a bigger vision.**

WHEN YOU CAN'T WALK AWAY AND MUST HONOR YOUR REALITY

Sometimes, you might feel a strong urge to change direction but are too deeply entrenched in your current path to simply walk away—or you may not have the option to leave. Or maybe your soul wants to step into something new, but you must honor your reality. Perhaps you are the breadwinner in your family and making a career change is not financially possible currently. Or you'd like to start a new venture or work on a side hustle, but you are the primary caretaker of your kids or aging parents and don't have time to dedicate to the new right now.

Many times, you may not have the privilege to make the changes you want or the financial and emotional support required.

Sarah wrote down a phone number on a piece of paper and said to me, "It's super easy and now I can start sending out my reel. You should call him." An aspiring reporter like me, Sarah shared how she finished her reel in a weekend. Meanwhile, I was working for free at cable stations and going around town *begging* for opportunities to be in front of the camera. Getting a sample reel in the age before cameras were on your phone was not exactly easy. It took me several years to make a solid first reel while others just hired a professional. All you needed was a few thousand dollars: money a newcomer like me didn't have.

When I was trying to break into TV news, lacking financial support or connections meant my path was longer. I worked seven days a week, balancing a weekday job with weekend shifts in news to build my career. I was a bit envious of Sarah, but I had to honor *my* reality.

Sometimes, you can't take the same route as others, but that doesn't mean you won't get there or maybe even end up a bit ahead. About six years after that conversation, I was working at KCBS, and Sarah was still in a small market. Twenty years later, I saw her pop up on national cable news, whereas I'm no longer in the industry. She may have had a shorter route when making a reel, but in the end, it didn't matter; each of us had our own journey.

Trust your own path and be discerning about what works in your life at the moment.

I've had several entrepreneur clients who were advised to "burn the boats"; that is, say goodbye to their current jobs, positions, and roles and go all in to embrace their new business endeavors without looking back. They've been told by some that the only way to be successful is to "Just go for it!"

But that's often not everyone's reality.

Sometimes, your intuition tells you otherwise. It tells you that it is *not* the right time, that going on a new path might mean overextending yourself when you need to be focused on another part of yourself—your health, your relationships, your mental well-being. Your intuition might also tell you that even though you are ready to leave that old room, you don't have the right support (financial or emotional) to open the door to a new one. Knowing when to stay is about knowing what you need.

Nobody knows that better than you.

You have the power of discernment; you know better than whoever is advising you—your partner, friend, or coach—whether it is time to stay or move on or what to do next. Just make sure that when you decide, you are not doing so from a place of fear.

Don't forget: *You* always have the power.

You have the power to go and the power to stay. You can live your life unapologetically on your terms and follow and trust your own path.

YOU CONTROL YOUR FUTURE

Being discerning—knowing when you've outgrown a space, when it's time to challenge the status quo, or when your intuition calls you to stay— can be complex and challenging. It requires a deep self-awareness and the courage to face uncomfortable truths. Growth often brings with it a sense of vulnerability and discomfort as it forces you to confront aspects of yourself and your situation that may have previously been hidden or ignored. This journey of change and growth is not always easy; it can be painful and disorienting.

Yet, embracing this discomfort and allowing yourself to fully experience the process is a crucial part of personal evolution. It's through this struggle that you lay the groundwork for future success. By discerning what truly matters to you and aligning your actions with your core values and desires, you build a solid foundation for thriving. This discernment enables you to navigate your path with intention, adapting to new opportunities and challenges as they arise.

Trust in your ability to steer your own course and own your future. Each decision, whether it leads you to move forward or take a step back, is a step toward greater self-discovery and fulfillment. Embrace the journey with all its ups and downs, knowing that each moment of discernment brings you closer to living a life that is genuinely aligned with who you are and who you aspire to become.

EXERCISE

- Take stock of the various rooms you are currently in. At work, in your social life, perhaps in your advocacy work or personal projects. These rooms are where you've chosen to invest energy. Now, using the lens of discernment, reflect on whether these rooms are serving you today. If not, what changes are you ready to make?
- Building your own table is a big endeavor that starts with the idea that you could create something better than what currently exists. To get the juices flowing on whether you want to do this, consider the things that bother you the most. What aggravates or even angers you enough that you could see yourself taking action to create the new, better version?

That was the last of the Power of Only principles. Now that you've covered them all, what are your ideas about how you can focus on thriving differently?

CONCLUSION

—

I stand near the back of the room and with my fists lightly clenched, rhythmically tapping on my back, then my sides, then my arms. Each move releases stagnant energy as I take deep breaths. I have been doing yoga and other healing practices for decades, but this is my first Qigong class.

Tap, tap, tap, breathe.

Tap, tap, tap, breathe.

As I move through the movement and breath, I'm hit with a sudden, vivid flashback.

I'm ten years old and watching my Po Po, my maternal grandmother, doing these same rhythmic taps as she walks around our neighborhood. Her fists lightly clenched, she pounds her back, then her sides, then her arms. Each step is deliberate and mindful. I see her passing by my friends at the park and I run inside my house to hide. As a girl who just wanted to fit in, I found my Po Po's evening ritual strange and embarrassing.

Back then, I was too young to see the depth of her wisdom and appreciate the power of this ancient healing practice. But just because I wasn't ready to see her wisdom doesn't mean it wasn't there.

As memories of my grandmother flooded my mind, each tap took on a bigger meaning. The shame of dismissing her when I was a kid was released from my body and was replaced with a deep sense of admiration and respect.

My Po Po now lives at a hospital in Taiwan. When I visited her in 2023 with my mom, she was about to turn 100 years old.

100 years of life.

100 years of wisdom.

100 years of being an Only.

Born in Chengdu, China, and orphaned at a young age, my Po Po didn't have access to a lot of opportunities but stepped into her power in her own way. She navigated a tough childhood, experienced war, joined the Air Force, married my grandfather, fled China for Taiwan with several children (including my mom) in tow, worked as a bookkeeper, and raised a family and several grandkids.

I'm not sure when I will see her again. I'm grateful I was able to thank her in person and recognize her strength, resilience, and wisdom.

It often takes time to fully see what was in front of us or inside us all along. Like my Po Po, all of us have so much power and wisdom from our past and present. But to access it, to step into the future we want to create, we need to recognize it and honor it in ourselves and in our ancestors.

My Po Po is part of me. I am a part of her.

Her wisdom lives on, not just in our family, but through everyone she's affected. Just like your wisdom will live on. What you do right now is not just about you. It is all connected.

I know being an Only can be lonely, but now you know you are not really alone and that being an Only is not a weakness but your greatest strength. I hope the stories of other Onlys featured in this book help you feel seen and inspired and that the five principles support you on your journey. Although life as an Only is challenging, you have awakened to new possibilities and gained the awareness, clarity, and tools to navigate, communicate, and thrive in any environment. You can step into your power based on your vision for your life. You recognize you already have everything you need to act, and you get to decide what your next step will be—no matter how big or small.

My life's mission is to help people own their voice and fully see their power, to help them step up, speak up, and create positive change for themselves and the world.

You play a huge role in that.

My greatest joy is hearing the breakthroughs and stories from my clients and readers like you—each person adding to the collective "Only" masterpiece. The young woman who was once terrified of the spotlight but now speaks up for herself at work, reclaiming the parts of herself she had hidden away. The midlevel manager who thought he just wanted to be a more dynamic speaker and ended up healing a part of his past and stepping more fully into his leadership for himself and his team. The successful corporate leader who, no matter how much she achieved on paper, never felt good enough. On the verge of burnout and ready to quit everything, she was able to fully see herself for the first time and give herself permission to create a new vision of success and fulfillment. The entrepreneur who broke through her fear of being seen and fulfilled her life's mission to create a foundation to support others and share her message with the world.

Like Connie Chung, they were all stepping into their Power of the Only. Imagine if Connie Chung hadn't broken through her internal barriers and pushed past her external ones. I still might have found my own way, but the gift she gave me was the one to dream. To see myself where I didn't know there was a possibility I could be. You don't have to make history or be the first at something to have an impact. Realize that *what* you do, *who* you are, and *how* you show up matters. There is a ripple effect. You can be someone's Connie Chung!

You have the power.

You've had it all along.

And now all you have to do is step into it.

ACKNOWLEDGMENTS

Ideas, dreams, goals, movements, and beyond—they start as an individual spark. But it's the energy, belief, and support of those around us that provide the fuel.

Every moment, whether grand or seemingly insignificant, plays a role.

It's time to recognize and honor the people in my life who have shared their wisdom, nurtured my spirit, and listened to my wildest dreams and ambitions. These are the people who supported me not only in writing this book but also in guiding me to this point in my life, enabling me to share these words with you.

Writing a book has always been on my life list. There was no timeline or specific topic—until now. When I first felt the call of the "Only," it began as a gentle tug, then a loud roar, and finally a constant, undeniable pull. I knew it was time. But a book doesn't happen overnight, and it doesn't happen alone.

To my parents, Joseph and Maria, your humble strength, unwavering support, and generous spirit are a part of me. Though I may be the one in the spotlight, it is your courage, sacrifices, and gifts that have allowed me to fulfill mine. 谢谢. I am deeply grateful. To my brother Stephen, thank you for honoring me as your "big sis" over the years, from patiently enduring childhood makeovers to now sharing meaningful conversations.

To my ancestors, I honor your strength and resilience. May my words give voice and peace to the untold stories and burdens you carried.

To my husband Matthew, whom I've known since I was sixteen and who has been listening to my wild dreams for decades. Thank you for holding space for my passionate rants and ideas (which come at all hours of the day or night). I appreciate your loving support as we juggle and build our life and family through challenges, joy, and all the messy in between.

To Aaron and Alexa, who watched me bring my podcast and this book to life from the very beginning as young kids and have now blossomed into teens with dreams of their own, this book is for you too. Thank you for your words of support and for listening to Mom's "life lessons." May you carry them with you as you discover and nurture your own Power of the Only. ♪ "You and me together"♪ forever. I'm so proud of who you both are and honored to be your mom. To Mochi, our cat who passed before I finished the book, thanks for being my late-night writing companion. I love you all.

To Andrea J. Lee, my friend, Asian "sister," and coach—your deep, thoughtful guidance and wise perspectives have profoundly shaped my journey, both personally and professionally. Your support nurtured my healing and work, allowing me to step fully into my Power of the Only. Thank you also for your writing and coaching expertise, which ensured this book remained true to its purpose, served Onlys, and empowered readers to fully explore and apply the principles to their lives.

To AJ Harper, thank you for your magical work, your gift of storytelling, and the beautiful author community you created. To you and everyone in Top Three Book Workshop, thank you for your encouragement, creative spirit, and shared wisdom. It's been an honor to grow, write, and thrive together as we bring our gifts to life. To Laura Stone, our number-one cheerleader: your care and effervescent support bring out the star in everyone.

To Ideapress Publishing and my editing team, I'm deeply grateful for your guidance in bringing my first book to life. Rohit Bhargava, thank you for believing in my vision, listening to my stories from the start, and being an advocate for my work. To Megan Wheeler, Marnie McMahon, Kameron Bryant-Sergejev, Jessica Angerstein, Allison Griffith, Athena Potkovic, and the entire team, I appreciate all your time, expertise, and our creative brainstorms and conversations. It was a joy to work with you. To my gifted editors: Genoveva Llosa, who cared deeply about this book and its readers—thank you for keeping me focused, pushing me when I needed it most, and for bringing everything together. Megan Barnes, your bright energy and polish brought even more impact and clarity to my words.

To my early readers, thank you for taking the time to share your feedback. Writing is lonely and vulnerable. You helped make the book stronger and validated my commitment.

To my clients, thank you for sharing your wins and struggles with me. It's an honor to support you and see you shine. Your stories and breakthroughs impact me deeply and now, they will inspire others.

To my circle of friends, from besties to my book club to moms' groups and family who cheer me on: Thank you for your support, even if you don't always understand what I'm doing. I notice and appreciate every gesture—your interest in my work, your creative input and advice, and your votes of confidence through the years. To my speaker, author, and entrepreneur friends, I appreciate you and love being on this adventure with you.

To my teachers, who have shared their gifts through each stage of my life: Ms. Teri Smith, my seventh grade English/speech teacher, who first encouraged me to own my voice and power and enter my first speech competition, and Ms. Ricki Valencia, my high school activities director, who saw my Power of the Only as a young teen with big dreams with no road map to follow. To all my business and spiritual mentors, your work matters and has a ripple effect.

To my trailblazing podcast guests, I hold your stories close to my heart. Thank you for your willingness to have deep conversations and share your lessons and your impactful work in the world.

And finally, to you, my reader. Despite life's speed bumps, late nights, and my mental blocks, you are the reason I kept writing. May the spirit of the Only inspire you to embrace your unique power and share it with the world.

Thank you all for being a part of this journey. Every comment, email, and kind word has fueled me. My gratitude runs deep. May it spark something within you—and when it does, I'll be here with a smile and a *Woo Hoo!*

To you and your voice,

Angela

WOO
HOO!

Go to **www.AngelaChee.com/WooHoo** to claim your gift.

WORK WITH ANGELA

Own your Only and be YOU, Amplified!—clear, confident, and connected on camera and off.

BOOK ANGELA AS A SPEAKER AND EMCEE

 Learn more about her keynotes, communication/media coaching, workshops, and online programs for you and your organization: www.angelachee.com.

ORDER COPIES OF *THE POWER OF THE ONLY* FOR YOUR TEAM OR ORGANIZATION AND CHECK OUT FREE BOOK TOOLS AND OTHER RESOURCES

 If you would like to buy multiple copies of the book to share with your team, ERG, or organization, we have bulk discounts, bonuses, and special offers, customized to your needs.

Connect with Angela

in linkedin.com/in/angelachee

@angelacheetv

f @angelacheetv

@angelacheetv

ABOUT THE AUTHOR

Angela Chee is a media and communication coach, keynote speaker, host of *The Power of the Only* podcast, and an award-winning former TV news anchor and reporter.

With over twenty years of experience in the media and speaking industry, she combines her deep expertise, personal development insights, and effective coaching strategies to help individuals and organizations own their Only, be YOU, Amplified!, and unlock their full potential.

Angela has worked with top US TV stations, including KCBS-TV, KNBC-TV in Los Angeles, and Fox 6 San Diego. She has hosted programs for major networks, including E! Entertainment and HGTV, and helped launch *Entertainment Tonight China*. Angela was the media mentor on Lifetime's *The Pop Game* and made a variety of media, film, and TV appearances from *The Today Show* to the film *Blades of Glory*, *Heroes*, and more.

Her speaking journey began at the age of fifteen when she became the first Asian American woman to win the title of Miss California National Teenager. Today, Angela is a trusted speaker and emcee for global organizations like Microsoft, Cisco, Intel, JP Morgan Chase, and more. She empowers leaders to amplify their voices, communicate with clarity and confidence, and lead effectively both on camera and off.

Angela lives in San Diego with her husband and two children. She is a healthy foodie who is driven by soul, loves yoga, and all things inspirational.

ENDNOTES

1   Balmer, Crispian. "Avan DuVernay Makes History with Venice Premiere of 'Origin.'" Reuters. Last modified September 6, 2023. https://www.reuters.com/lifestyle/ava-duvernay-makes-history-with-venice-premiere-origin-2023-09-06/#:~:text=VENICE%2C%20Sept%206%20(Reuters),talk%20her%20out%20of%20applying.

2   Chee, Angela, host, *The Power of the Only*. Season 1, episode 16, "The Power of Success—Achieving It and Redefining It on Your Own Terms with Keynote Speaker Vinh Giang." ZenMediaInc, May 26, 2020. Podcast, 50 min. https://angelachee.com/vinh-giang/.

3   Monster. "Monster Poll: Workplace Discrimination." September 6, 2023. https://hiring.monster.com/resources/blog/monster-poll-workplace-discrimination/.

4   McKinsey & Company. "Women in the Workplace 2023 Report." 2023. https://sgff-media.s3.amazonaws.com/sgff_r1eHetbDYb/Women+in+the+Workplace+2023_+Designed+Report.pdf.

5   Chee, Angela, host, *The Power of the Only*. Season 5, episode 34, "The Firsts, the Fews, and the Onlys with Author Deepa Purushothaman." ZenMediaInc, January 12, 2021. Podcast, 50 min., 24 sec. https://angelachee.com/deepa-purushothaman/.

6   Chee, Angela, host, *The Power of the Only*. Season 1, episode 10, "Business Strategist Gina Gomez—The Power of Diversity, Representation, and Facilitating Difficult Conversations." ZenMediaInc, April 14, 2020. Podcast, 38 min., 8 sec. https://angelachee.com/gina-gomez/.

7   Chee, Angela, host, *The Power of the Only*. Season 1, episode 15. "The Power of History, Media, and Representation—Asian Pacific American Heritage Month Special with Nancy Wang Yuen." ZenMediaInc, May 19, 2020. Podcast, 37 min., 25 sec. https://angelachee.com/nancy-wang-yuen/.

8   Vlahakis, George and Jared Wadley. "Study Finds TV Can Decrease Self-Esteem in Children, Except White Boys." IU News Room. Last modified May 30, 2012. https://newsinfo.iu.edu/news/page/normal/22445.html.

9   McIntyre, Rusty B., Réne M Paulson, and Charles G Lord. "Alleviating Women's Mathematics Stereotype Threat Through Salience of Group Achievements." *Journal of Experimental Social Psychology* 39, no. 1 (2003): 83–90. https://doi.org/10.1016/S0022-1031(02)00513-9.

10   Heaning, Erin. "Stereotype Threat: Definition and Examples." Simply Psychology. Last modified October 10, 2023. https://www.simplypsychology.org/stereotype-threat.html.

11   Steele, C.M. and J. Aronson. "Stereotype Threat and the Intellectual Test Performance of African Americans." *Journal of Personality and Social Psychology* 69, no. 5 (1995): 797–811. https://doi.org/10.1037//0022-3514.69.5.797.

12   Spencer, Steven J., Claude M. Steele, and Diane M. Quinn. "Stereotype Threat and Women's Math Performance." *Journal of Experimental Social Psychology* 35, no. 1 (1998): 4–28. https://doi.org/10.1006/jesp.1998.1373.

13   Kray, Laura J., Leigh Thompson, and Adam Galinsky. "Battle of the Sexes: Gender Stereotype Confirmation and Reactance in Negotiations." *Journal of Personality and Social Psychology* 80, no.6 (2001): 942–58. PubMed. https://pubmed.ncbi.nlm.nih.gov/11414376/.

14   Koenig, Anne M. and Alice H. Eagly. "Stereotype Threat in Men on a Test of Social Sensitivity." *Sex Roles* 52 (2005): 489–496. https://doi.org/10.1007/s11199-005-3714-x.

15   Koenig, Anne M. and Alice H. Eagly. "Stereotype Threat in Men on a Test of Social Sensitivity." *Sex Roles* 52 (2005): 489–496. https://doi.org/10.1007/s11199-005-3714-x.

16   Lamont, Ruth A., Hannah J. Swift, and Dominic Abrams. "A Review and Meta-Analysis of Age-Based Stereotype Threat: Negative Stereotypes, Not Facts, Do the Damage." *Psychology and Aging* 30, no. 1 (2015): 180–193. https://doi.org/10.1037/a0038586.

17   Merton, Robert K. "The Self-Fulfilling Prophecy." *The Antioch Review* 8, no. 2 (1948): 193–210. https://doi.org/10.2307/4609267.

18   Keller, Johannes and Denise Sekaquaptewa. "Solo Status and Women's Spatial Test Performance: The Role of Individuation Tendencies." *European Journal of Social Psychology* 38, no. 6 (2008): 1044–1053. https://doi.org/10.1002/ejsp.490.

19   Walton, G. M. and L.G. Cohen. "A Question of Belonging: Race, Social Fit, and Achievement." *Journal of Personality and Social Psychology* 92, no. 1 (2007): 82–96. https://doi.org/10.1037/0022-3514.92.1.82.

20   Cohen, Geoffrey. "Understanding and Overcoming Belonging Uncertainty." Behavioral Scientist. October 10, 2022. https://behavioralscientist.org/understanding-and-overcoming-belonging-uncertainty/.

21   Chee, Angela, host, *The Power of the Only*. Season 1, episode 9. "Psychology Dr. Valerie Rein—Taking Care of Your Mental Health During Crisis: The Power of Shifting from Surviving to Thriving." ZenMediaInc, April 7, 2020. Podcast, 48 min., 10 sec. https://angelachee.com/dr-valerie-rein/.

22   CDC. "Epigenetics, Health, and Disease." Accessed October 25, 2023. https://www.cdc.gov/genomics-and-health/about/epigenetic-impacts-on-health.html?CDC_AAref_Val=https://www.cdc.gov/genomics/disease/epigenetics.htm.

23   Yehuda, Rachel, Nikolaos P. Daskalakis, Linda M. Bierer et al. "Holocaust Exposure Induced Intergenerational Effects on FKBP5 Methylation." *Archival Report* 80, no. 5 (2016): 372–380. https://doi.org/10.1016/j.biopsych.2015.08.005.

24   Dias, Brian G. and Kerry J. Ressler. "Parental Olfactory Experience Influences Behavior and Neural Structure in Subsequent Generations." *Nature Neuroscience* 17 (2013): 89–96. https://doi.org/10.1038/nn.3594.

25   Johns, Michael, Toni Schmader, and Andy Martens. "Knowing Is Half the Battle: Teaching Stereotype Threat as a Means of Improving Women's Math Performance." *Psychological Science* 16, no. 3 (2005): 175–179. https://doi.org/10.1111/j.0956-7976.2005.00799.x.

     Lamon, Ruth A., Hannah J. Swift, and Dominic Abrams. "A Review and Meta-Analysis of Age-Based Stereotype Threat: Negative Stereotypes, Not Facts, Do the Damage." *Psychological Aging* 30, no. 1 (2015): 180–193. https://doi.org/10.1037/a0038586.

26   Torabi, Farnoosh, host, *Yo Quiero Dinero*. Season 5, episode 236. "How to Make Fear Your Superpower." Delish Dlites LLC, October 9, 2023. Podcast, 45 min., 18 sec. https://yoquierodineropodcast.com/podcasts/episode-236/.

27   Chee, Angela, host, *The Power of the Only*. Season 1, episode 4. "Financial Expert Farnoosh Torabi—The Power Building Your Own Brand, Carving Your Own Path, and Staying Ahead of the Curve." ZenMediaInc, March 8, 2020. Podcast, 1 hr., 1 min., 1 sec. https://angelachee.com/farnoosh-torabi/.

28   Chee, Angela, host, *The Power of the Only*. Season 2, episode 37. "The Power of Positivity and Tenacity with 'Chopped' TV Show Creator Dave Noll." ZenMediaInc, February 23, 2021. Podcast, 53 min., 24 sec. https://angelachee.com/dave-noll/.

29   Chee, Angela, host, *The Power of the Only*. Season 2, episode 53. "The Power to Shape the Future with Keynote Speaker and Futurist Crystal Washington." ZenMediaInc, November 16, 2021. Podcast, 47 min., 54 sec. https://angelachee.com/crystal-washington/.

30   Chee, Angela, host, *The Power of the Only*. Season 4, episode 77. "The Power of Being Underestimated and How to Fully Step into Your Only with Caulipower Founder Gail Becker." ZenMediaInc, September 6, 2023. Podcast, 45 min., 20 sec. https://angelachee.com/gail-becker/.

31   Wikipedia contributors. "Seven Generation Sustainability." Wikipedia. Last modified April 30, 2024. https://en.wikipedia.org/wiki/Seven_generation_sustainability.

32   Tanner, Kristi. "Becoming a Transitional Character: Changing Your Family Culture." BYU Forever Families. Accessed October 25, 2024. https://foreverfamilies.byu.edu/becoming-a-transitional-character-changing-your-family-culture.

33   Carla Harris. "Author." Accessed November 6, 2024. https://www.carlaspearls. com/author.

34   Chee, Angela, host, *The Power of the Only*. Season 4, episode 80. "How to Stop Hiding and Embrace the Power of You with Author and Board Director Tricia Montalvo Timm." ZenMediaInc, December 19, 2023. Podcast, 54 min., 51 sec. https://angelachee.com/tricia-montalvo-timm/.

35   Cherry, Kendra. "How Groupthink Impacts Our Behavior." Verywell Mind. Last modified June 19, 2024. https://www.verywellmind.com/what-is-groupthink-2795213.

36   Segal, Elizabeth A. "Why We Need Diversity." Psychology Today. July 16, 2019. https://www.psychologytoday.com/us/blog/social-empathy/201907/why-we-need-diversity.

37   Liu, Deborah. *Take Back Your Power: 10 New Rules for Women at Work*. Zondervan, 2024.

38   Liu, Deborah, "Fireside Chat with Deborah Liu (CEO of Ancestry)" (online event, The Authentic Asian Circle, January 12, 2024). https://www.theauthenticasian.com/event-details-registration/fireside-chat-with-deborah-liu-ceo-of-ancestry.

39   Chee, Angela, host, *The Power of the Only*. Season 4, episode 78. "The Power of the Pack with Female Quotient CEO and Founder Shelley Zalis." ZenMediaInc, October 10, 2023. Podcast, 53 min., 50 sec. https://angelachee.com/shelley-zalis/.

40   Wikipedia contributors. "Bakersfield, California." Wikipedia. Last modified October 25, 2024. https://en.wikipedia.org/wiki/Bakersfield,_California.

41   Wikipedia contributors. "Bakersfield, California." Wikipedia. Last modified October 25, 2024. https://en.wikipedia.org/wiki/Bakersfield,_California.

42   Yung F., Grace. "I Was Chasing a Life I Thought I Was SUPPOSED to Have." LinkedIn, April, 2024. https://www.linkedin.com/posts/graceyungfoster_adoptee-fostercare-solareclipse-activity-7183109528110952449 zLRB?utm_source=share&utm_medium=member_desktop.

43   Chee, Angela, host, *The Power of the Only*. Season 4, episode 80. "How to Stop Hiding and Embrace the Power of You with Author and Board Director Tricia Montalvo Timm." ZenMediaInc, December 19, 2023. Podcast, 54 min., 51 sec. https://angelachee.com/tricia-montalvo-timm/.

44   Montalvo Timm, Tricia. *Embrace the Power of You: Owning Your Identity at Work*. Page Two, 2023.

45   Binnion, P.F. and R. Das Gupta. "Prophylactic Antiarrhythmic Drug Therapy in Acute Myocardial Infarction." *Cardiovascular Clinics* 7, no. 2 (1975): 203–217. PubMed. https://pubmed.ncbi.nlm.nih.gov/145/.

46   Chee, Angela, host, *The Power of the Only*. Season 1, episode 20. "How to Tap into Your Power of the Only to Create Individual and Institutional Change with

Dr. Cleopatra Kamperveen." ZenMediaInc, June 30, 2020. Podcast, 40 min., 56 sec. https://angelachee.com/dr-cleopatra/.

47 Mooney, Jonathan. "Some Things About Me—About Jonathan." Jonathan Mooney. Accessed October 25, 2024. https://www.jonathanmooney.com/about.

48 Chee, Angela, host, *The Power of the Only*. Season 1, episode 23. "Krish O'Mara Vignarajah—From Refugee to Gubernatorial Candidate to CEO: The Power of Authenticity, Taking Risks, and Redefining Leadership." ZenMediaInc, August 11, 2020. Podcast, 45 min., 16 sec. https://angelachee.com/krishanti-vignarajah/.

49 Müller-Pinzler, Laura, Nora Czekalla, Annalina V. Mayer et al. "Negativity-Bias in Forming Beliefs About Own Abilities." *Scientific Reports* 9, no. 14416 (2019). https://doi.org/10.1038/s41598-019-50821-w.

50 Pilat, Dan & Krastev, Dr. Sekoul. "Why Do We Fail to Accurately Gauge Our Own Abilities?" The Decision Lab. Accessed October 25, 2024. https://thedecisionlab.com/biases/dunning-kruger-effect.

51 Pilat, Dan & Krastev, Dr. Sekoul. "Why Do We Fail to Accurately Gauge Our Own Abilities?" The Decision Lab. Accessed October 25, 2024. https://thedecisionlab.com/biases/dunning-kruger-effect.

52 Chee, Angela, host, *The Power of the Only*. Season 1, episode 2. "Business Mentor Ali Brown—The Power of Answering Your Calling and How to Step into Your Legacy Work." ZenMediaInc, March 8, 2020. Podcast, 40 min., 57 sec. https://angelachee.com/ali-brown/.

53 Chee, Angela, host, *The Power of the Only*. Season 2, episode 37. "The Power of Positivity and Tenacity with 'Chopped' TV Show Creator Dave Noll." ZenMediaInc, February 23, 2021. Podcast, 53 min., 24 sec. https://angelachee.com/dave-noll/.

54 Cleveland Clinic. "Dopamine." Last reviewed March 23, 2022. https://my.clevelandclinic.org/health/articles/22581-dopamine.

Cleveland Clinic. "Serotonin." Last reviewed March 18, 2022. https://my.clevelandclinic.org/health/articles/22572-serotonin.

Cleveland Clinic. "Endorphins." Last reviewed May 19, 2022. https://my.clevelandclinic.org/health/body/23040-endorphins.

Henley, Casey. *Foundations of Neuroscience*. Open Edition. Michigan State University, 2021. https://openbooks.lib.msu.edu/neuroscience/.

Optimum Health Institute. "The Science of Celebration." *Optimum Health*, November 23, 2018. https://www.optimumhealth.org/blog/the-science-of-celebration.

Lewis, Robert G., Ermanno Florio, Daniela Punzo, and Emiliana Borrelli. "The Brain's Reward System in Health and Disease." *Circadian Clock in Brain Health and Disease* 1344 (2021): 57-69. https://doi.org/10.1007/978-3-030-81147-1_4.

55   Spoon, Marianne. "Keeping Up That Positive Feeling: The Science of Savoring Emotions." University of Wisconsin-Madison News. July 22, 2015. https://news. wisc.edu/keeping-up-that-positive-feeling-the-science-of-savoring-emotions/.

Heller, Aaron S., Carien M. van Reekum, Stacey M. Schaefer et al. "Sustained Striatal Activity Predicts Eudaimonic Well-Being and Cortisol Output." *Psychological Science* 24, no. 11 (2013): 2191–2200. https://doi. org/10.1177/0956797613490744.

56   Deschene, Lori. "40 Amazing Everyday Successes That Are Worth Celebrating." Tiny Buddha. 2014. https://tinybuddha.com/blog/40-everyday-successes-to-celebrate/.

57   French Gates, Melinda. "Melinda French Gates Reflects on Personal Growth, Commitment to Advocacy." Interview by Gayle King. CBS News, June 18, 2024. Video, 09:23. https://www.cbsnews.com/video/melinda-french-gates-reflects-on-personal-growth-commitment-to-advocacy/.

58   Alexander, Kerri Lee. "Melinda Gates." National Women's History Museum. 2019. https://www.womenshistory.org/education-resources/biographies/melinda-gates.

59   French Gates, Melinda. "Melinda French Gates: The Enemies of Progress Play Offense. I Want to Help Even the Match." *New York Times.* May 28, 2024. https://www.nytimes.com/2024/05/28/opinion/melinda-french-gates-reproductive-rights.html?unlocked_article_code=1.vU0.zJn_.lw80pe38kIEi#LI.

60   McLeod, Saul. "Freud's Theory of the Unconscious Mind." Simply Psychology. Last modified January 25, 2024. https://www.simplypsychology.org/unconscious-mind.html.

61   Richards, Blake A. and Timothy P. Lillicrap. "The Brain-Computer Metaphor Debate Is Useless: A Matter of Semantics." *Frontier Computer Science* 4, no. 810358 (2022). https://doi.org/10.3389/fcomp.2022.810358.

62   Korba, Rodney J. "The Rate of Inner Speech." *Perceptual and Motor Skills* 71, no. 3 (1990): 1043–1052. https://doi.org/10.2466/pms.1990.71.3.1043.

63   Tony Robbins. "Are You Living Your Primary Question?" Accessed October 25, 2024. https://www.tonyrobbins.com/living-primary-question.

64   Emoto, Masaru. "Profile of Masaru Emoto." Office Masaru Emoto. Accessed October 25, 2024. https://masaru-emoto.net/en/masaru/.

65   Chee, Angela, host, *The Power of the Only*. Season 1, episode 19. "The Power of Breaking Through Your Fear of Being Seen and How to Be Ready for Any Opportunity with Dr. Ann Shippy." ZenMediaInc, June 16, 2020. Podcast, 32 min., 31 sec. https://angelachee.com/ann-shippy/.

66   Dwyer, Karen Kangas and Marlina M. Davidson. "Is Public Speaking Really More Feared Than Death?" *Communication Research Reports* 29, no. 2 (2012): 99–107. http://dx.doi.org/10.1080/08824096.2012.667772.

67   Öhman, Arne, Katrina Carlsson, Daniel Lundqvist, and Martin Ingvar. "On the Unconscious Subcortical Origin of Human Fear." *Physiology & Behavior* 92, no. 1-2 (2007): 180–185. https://doi.org/10.1016/j.physbeh.2007.05.057.

68   Croston, Glenn. "The Thing We Fear More Than Death." Psychology Today. November 29, 2012. https://www.psychologytoday.com/us/blog/the-real-story-risk/201211/the-thing-we-fear-more-death.

69   Pietrangelo, Ann. "What the Yerkes-Dodson Law Says About Stress and Performance." Healthline. October 22, 2020. https://www.healthline.com/health/yerkes-dodson-law.

70   Sauer, Megan. "Simone Biles Tells Herself These 3 Words Before She Competes—Everyone Should Try It, Ivy League-Trained Expert Says." CNBC Make It. August 2, 2024. https://www.cnbc.com/2024/08/02/simone-biles-tells-herself-3-words-to-get-ready-to-compete.html.

71   Kross, E., E. Bruehlman-Senecal, J. Park et al. "Self-Talk as a Regulatory Mechanism: How You Do It Matters." *Journal of Personality and Social Psychology* 106, no. 2 (2014): 304–324. https://doi.org/10.1037/a0035173.

72   Kross, Ethan. "When I Become You." In *Chatter: The Voice in Our Head, Why It Matters, and How to Harness It.* Penguin Random House, 2021.

73   Holzman, P.S. and C. Rousey. "The Voice as a Percept." *Journal of Personality and Social Psychology* 4, no. 1 (1996): 79–86. https://doi.org/10.1037/h0023518.

74   Lee, M., M. Drinnan, and P. Carding. "The Reliability and Validity of Patient Self-Rating of Their Own Voice Quality." *Clinical Otolaryngology* 30, no. 4 (2005): 357–361. https://doi.org/10.1111/j.1365-2273.2005.01022.x.

75   Gilovich, T., V.H. Medvec, and K. Savitsky. "The Spotlight Effect in Social Judgment: An Egocentric Bias in Estimates of the Salience of One's Own Actions and Appearance." *Journal of Personality and Social Psychology* 78, no. 2 (2000): 211–222. https://doi.org/10.1037/0022-3514.78.2.211.

76   Cuncic, Arlin. "The Spotlight Effect and Social Anxiety." Verywell Mind. Last modified August 28, 2023. https://www.verywellmind.com/what-is-the-spotlight-effect-3024470.

77   Gilovich, T., K. Savitsky, and V.H. Medvec. "The Illusion of Transparency: Biased Assessments of Other's Ability to Read One's Emotional States." *Journal of Personality and Social Psychology* 75, no. 2 (1998): 332–346. https://doi.org/10.1037/0022-3514.75.2.332.

78   Raposa, Elizabeth B., Holly B. Laws, and Emily B. Ansell. "Prosocial Behavior Mitigates the Negative Effects of Stress in Everyday Life." *Clinical Psychological Science* 4, no. 4 (2016): 691–698. https://doi.org/10.1177/2167702615611073.

79   Cleveland Clinic. "Vital Signs." Last modified March 15, 2023. https://my.clevelandclinic.org/health/articles/10881-vital-signs.

80   Jelinek, Joslyn. "Can Shaking Your Body Help Heal Stress and Trauma? Some Experts Say Yes." Healthline. March 5, 2021. https://www.healthline.com/health/mental-health/can-shaking-your-body-heal-stress-and-trauma.

81   Trivedi, Gunjan, Kamal Sharma, Banshi Saboo et al. "Humming (Simple Bhramari Pranayama) as a Stress Buster: A Holter-Based Study to Analyze Heart Rate Variability (HRV) Parameters During Bhramari, Physical Activity, Emotional Stress, and Sleep." *Cureus* 15, no. 4 (2023). https://doi.org/10.7759/cureus.37527.

82   Merriam-Webster.com Dictionary. "Imposter Syndrome." Accessed October 31, 2024. https://www.merriam-webster.com/dictionary/impostor%20syndrome.

83   Ravindran, Sandeep. "Feeling Like a Fraud: The Imposter Phenomenon in Science Writing." The OPEN Notebook. November 15, 2016. https://www.theopennotebook.com/2016/11/15/feeling-like-a-fraud-the-impostor-phenomenon-in-science-writing/.

84   Clance, Pauline Rose and Suzanne Ament Imes. "The Imposter Phenomenon in High Achieving Women: Dynamics and Therapeutic Intervention." *Psychotherapy: Theory, Research & Practice* 15, no. 3 (1978): 241–247. https://doi.org/10.1037/h0086006.

85   Jamison, Leslie. "Why Everyone Feels Like They're Faking It." *The New Yorker*. February 6, 2023. https://www.newyorker.com/magazine/2023/02/13/the-dubious-rise-of-impostor-syndrome.

86   Chee, Angela, host, *The Power of the Only*. Season 5, episode 80. "How to Stop Hiding and Embrace the Power of You with Author and Board Director Tricia Montalvo Timm." ZenMediaInc, December 19, 2023. Podcast, 54 min., 51 sec. https://angelachee.com/tricia-montalvo-timm/.

87   Tulshyan, Ruchika & Burey, Jodi-Ann. "Stop Telling Women They Have Imposter Syndrome." *Harvard Business Review*. February 11, 2021. https://hbr.org/2021/02/stop-telling-women-they-have-imposter-syndrome.

88   "Makers Conference" (The Beverly Hilton, California, February 27–29, 2024).

89   Chee, Angela, host, *The Power of the Only*. Season 5, episode 82. "The Power of Connection and Mindset with Professional Speaker Frank Kitchen." ZenMediaInc, February 28, 2024. Podcast, 36 min., 59 sec. https://angelachee.com/frank-kitchen/.

90   Cooks-Campbell, Allaya. "What Is Code Switching and How Does It Impact Teams?" *BetterUp*, March 1, 2022. https://www.betterup.com/blog/code-switching#:~:text=Sometimes%2C%20when%20we're%20around,be%20a%20very%20positive%20experience.

91   Chee, Angela, host, *The Power of the Only*. Season 1, episode 22. "Tony Chatman—How to Be a Trailblazer Not a Token." ZenMediaInc, July 28, 2020. Podcast, 1 hr., 0 min., 13 sec. https://angelachee.com/tony-chatman/.

92   Hewlett, Sylvia Ann. "The New Rules of Executive Presence." *Harvard Business Review*. January-February 2024. https://hbr.org/2024/01/the-new-rules-of-executive-presence.

93   Filipkowski, Jenna. *Executive Presence: Desired but Ill-Defined* (Human Capital Institute, 2020). https://tracom.com/wp-content/uploads/2020/02/HCIReportTalentPulseTRACOM.pdf.

94   Costigan, Amelia. "The Double-Bind Dilemma for Women in Leadership (Infographic)." Catalyst. February 16, 2024. https://www.catalyst.org/research/infographic-the-double-bind-dilemma-for-women-in-leadership/.

95   Chee, Angela, host, *The Power of the Only*. Season 5, episode 81. "The Power of Clarity and Stepping into Your Leadership with Jennifer McCollum, CEO & Author of 'In Her Own Voice—A Woman's Rise to CEO.'" ZenMediaInc, January 30, 2024. Podcast, 43 min., 14 sec. https://angelachee.com/jennifer-mccollum/.

96   Anne Chow in conversation with the author, May 22, 2024.

97   Stephens, Greg J., Lauren J. Silbert, and Uri Hasson. "Speaker–Listener Neural Coupling Underlies Successful Communication." *PNAS* 107, no. 32 (2010): 14425–14430. https://doi.org/10.1073/pnas.1008662107.

Greg J. Stephens, Lauren J. Silbert, and Uri Hasson hasson@princeton.edu Authors Info & Affiliations Communicated by Charles G. Gross, Princeton University, Princeton, NJ, June 18, 2010 (received for review April 30, 2010) July 26, 2010 107 (32) 14425–14430 https://doi.org/10.1073/pnas.1008662107.

98   Sridharan, Mithun A. "Rule of Three." Think Insights. August 16, 2022. https://thinkinsights.net/consulting/rule-of-three/.

99   Pilat, Dan & Krastev, Sekoul. "The First Impression Bias." The Decision Lab. Accessed October 25, 2024. https://thedecisionlab.com/reference-guide/psychology/the-first-impression-bias.

100 Cleveland Clinic. "5 Ways to Stimulate Your Vagus Nerve." *Health Essentials* (blog). *Cleveland Clinic*, March 10, 2022. https://health.clevelandclinic.org/vagus-nerve-stimulation.

101 Brixius, Kasey. "10 Surprising Benefits of Jumping Jacks to Know." Nutrisense. January 24, 2024. https://www.nutrisense.io/blog/benefits-of-jumping-jacks.

102 Harvard Mahoney Neuroscience Institute. "Dancing and the Brain." Harvard Medical School. Winter 2015. https://hms.harvard.edu/news-events/publications-archive/brain/dancing-brain.

103 Rees, Mathieu. "What to Know About Jaw Tension and Anxiety." Medical News Today. July 16, 2024. https://www.medicalnewstoday.com/articles/jaw-tension-anxiety#is-there-a-link.

104 Fancourt, Daisy, Lisa Aufegger, and Aaron Williamon. "Low-Stress and High-Street Singing Having Contrasting Effects on Glucocorticoid Response." *Frontiers in Psychology* 6, no. 1242 (2015). https://doi.org/10.3389/fpsyg.2015.01242.

105 Kreutz, Gunter, Stephan Bongard, Sonja Rohrmann, Volker Hodapp, and Dorothee Grebe. "Effects of Choir Singing or Listening on Secretory Immunoglobulin A, Cortisol, and Emotional State." *Journal of Behavioral Medicine* 27 (2004): 623–635. https://doi.org/10.1007/s10865-004-0006-9.

106 Chee, Angela, host, *The Power of the Only*. Season 1, episode 12. "Christina Blacken—How to Disrupt the Status Quo, Break Through Stereotypes, and Build Connection Using the Power of Story." ZenMediaInc, April 28, 2020. Podcast, 48 min., 17 sec. https://angelachee.com/christina-blacken/.

107 Jess Pettitt in discussion with the author, March 4, 2023.

108 Chee, Angela, host, *The Power of the Only*. Season 1, episode 12. "Christina Blacken—How to Disrupt the Status Quo, Break Through Stereotypes, and Build Connection Using the Power of Story." ZenMediaInc, April 28, 2020. Podcast, 48 min., 17 sec. https://angelachee.com/christina-blacken/.

109 Jess Pettitt in discussion with the author, March 4, 2023.

110 Carucci, Ron. "How to Build Bridges Between the Most Bitterly Divided People." *Forbes*. September 23, 2019. https://www.forbes.com/sites/roncarucci/2019/09/23/how-to-build-bridges-between-the-most-bitterly-divided-people/?sh=3219b4565ecd.

111 "Is Your Campus Community Feeling Isolated and Polarized?" ConnectEffect. Accessed October 29, 2024. www.connecteffect.us.

112 Chee, Angela, host, *The Power of the Only*. Season 1, episode 8. "COO, Mortgage Bankers Association and mPower Founder Marcia Davies—The Power of Inclusive Leadership, Communication, and Community in Navigating Uncertain Times." ZenMediaInc, March 31, 2020. Podcast, 52 min., 39 sec. https://angelachee.com/marcia-davies/.

113 Dinesh, Shradha & Parker, Kim. "More Than 4 in 10 US Workers Don't Take All Their Paid Time Off." Pew Research Center. August 10, 2023. https://www.pewresearch.org/short-reads/2023/08/10/more-than-4-in-10-u-s-workers-dont-take-all-their-paid-time-off/.

114 Chee, Angela, host, *The Power of the Only*. Season 1, episode 9. "Psychologist Dr. Valerie Rein—Taking Care of Your Mental Health During Crisis: The Power of Shifting from Surviving to Thriving and the Key to Women's Happiness and Fulfillment." ZenMediaInc, April 7, 2020. Podcast, 48 min., 10 sec. https://angelachee.com/dr-valerie-rein/.

115 Benton, Lizzie. "The Silent Threat of Scarcity Mindset in the Workplace." Liberty Mind. May 24, 2023. https://libertymind.co.uk/the-silent-threat-of-scarcity-mindset-in-the-workplace/.

116 Chee, Angela, host, *The Power of the Only*. Season 1, episode 20. "How to Tap into Your Power of the Only to Creative Individual and Institutional Change with Dr. Cleopatra Kamperveen." ZenMediaInc, June 30, 2020. Podcast, 40 min., 54 sec. https://angelachee.com/dr-cleopatra/.

117 Yung F., Grace. "If It Were All to Go Away Tomorrow, Here's What Matters." LinkedIn, October, 2024. https://www.linkedin.com/posts/graceyungfoster_career-motherhood-adoptee-activity-7249056501930016768-Bq85/?utm_source=share&utm_medium=member_desktop.

118 Farr, Adrienne. "Break Free of 'the Striver's Curse.'" Oprah Daily. April 22, 2022. https://www.oprahdaily.com/life/health/a39789195/albert-brooks-strivers-curse-happiness/.

119 "Positive Psychology Toolkit: List of Values." Positivepsychology.com. Accessed October 28, 2024.

120 Oyserman, Daphna, Deborah Bybee, and Kathy Terry. "Possible Selves and Academic Outcomes: How and When Possible Selves Impel Action." *Journal of Personality and Social Psychology* 91, no. 1 (2006): 188–204. https://doi.org/10.1037/0022-3514.91.1.188.

121 Ruvolvo, Ann Patrice and Hazel Rose Markus. "Possible Selves and Performance: The Power of Self-Relevant Imagery." *Social Cognition* 10, no. 1 (2011). https://doi.org/10.1521/soco.1992.10.1.95.

122 Chee, Angela, host, *The Power of the Only*. Season 4, episode 72. "Henna Pryor—Workplace Performance Coach & Keynote Speaker on the Power of Awkwardness." ZenMediaInc, February 7, 2023. Podcast, 45 min., 46 sec. https://angelachee.com/henna-pryor/.

123 Steven Bartlett. "Home." Accessed October 25, 2024. https://stevenbartlett.com/.

124 Bartlett, Steven. "This Shot Taken by Will Lindsay-Perez Sums Up One of the Hardest Few Weeks of My Life in Recent Times… Let Me Explain." LinkedIn, May, 2024. https://www.linkedin.com/posts/stevenbartlett-123_mentalhealthweek-activity-7195774621327998976-TEZA?utm_source=share&utm_medium=member_desktop.

125 The Authentic Asian. "About." Accessed October 25, 2024. https://www.theauthenticasian.com/about.

126 Stillman, Jessica. "Chronic Negativity Can Literally Kill You, Science Shows." *Inc.* October 13, 2016. https://www.inc.com/jessica-stillman/science-the-negative-people-in-your-life-are-literally-killing-you.html.

127 Harvard Mahoney Neuroscience Institute. "The Gut and the Brain." Harvard Medical School. Winter 2017. https://hms.harvard.edu/news-events/publications-archive/brain/gut-brain#:~:text=The%20enteric%20nervous%20system%20that,brain%20when%20something%20is%20amiss.

128 Chee, Angela, host, *The Power of the Only*. Season 1, episode 3. "Filmmaker Kerry David—The Power of Film, Storytelling, and Passion." ZenMediaInc, March 8, 2020. Podcast, 1 hr., 1 min., 57 sec. https://angelachee.com/kerry-david/.

129 Rozado, David, Ruth Hughes, and Jamin Halberstadt. "Longitudinal Analysis of Sentiment and Emotion in News Media Headlines Using Automated Labelling

with Transformer Language Models." *PLOS ONE* 17, no. 10 (2022). https://doi.org/10.1371/journal.pone.0276367.

130 Robertson, Claire E., Nicolas Pröllochs, Kaoru Schwarzenegger, Philip Pärnamets, Jay J. Van Bavel, and Stefan Feuerriegel. "Negativity Drives Online News Consumption." *Nature Human Behavior* 7 (2023): 812–822. https://doi.org/10.1038/s41562-023-01538-4.

131 Price, M., A.C. Legrand, Z.M.F. Brier et al. "Doomscrolling During COVID-19: The Negative Association Between Daily Social and Traditional Media Consumption and Mental Health Symptoms During the COVID-19 Pandemic." *Psychological Trauma: Theory, Research, Practice, and Policy* 14, no. 8 (2022): 1338–1346. https://doi.org/10.1037/tra0001202.

132 Stosny, Steven. "Overcoming Headline Stress Disorder." Psychology Today. March 4, 2017. https://www.psychologytoday.com/us/blog/anger-in-the-age-entitlement/201703/overcoming-headline-stress-disorder.

133 Huff, Charlotte. "Media Overload Is Hurting Our Mental Health. Here Are Ways to Manage Headline Stress." *Monitor on Psychology* 53, no. 8 (2022): 20. American Psychological Association. https://www.apa.org/monitor/2022/11/strain-media-overload.

134 Cherry, Kendra. "What Is Confirmation Bias?" Verywell Mind. May 19, 2024. https://www.verywellmind.com/what-is-a-confirmation-bias-2795024#citation-4.

135 Chee, Angela, host, *The Power of the Only*. Season 1, episode 29. "The Power of Media Literacy—An Inside Look at How the Media Works and How to Be a Critical Thinker and Creator." ZenMediaInc, November 3, 2020. Podcast, 17 min., 57 sec. https://angelachee.com/media-literacy/. If you'd like to take a deeper look at how the media works and how to be a more critical thinker and creator, check out episode 29 of my podcast.

136 Lieberman, Matthew D., Naomi I. Eisenberger, Molly J. Crockett, Sabrina M. Tom, Jennifer H. Pfeifer, and Baldwin M. Way. "Putting Feelings into Words: Affect Labeling Disrupts Amygdala Activity in Response to Affective Stimuli." *Psychological Science* 18, no. 5 (2007): 421–428. https://doi.org/10.1111/j.1467-9280.2007.01916.x.

137 Davey, Steven, Jamin Halberstadt and Elliott Bell. "Where Is Emotional Feeling Felt in the Body? An Integrative Review." *PLOS ONE* 16, no. 12 (2021). https://doi.org/10.1371/journal.pone.0261685.

138 Patel, Jainish and Prittesh Patel. "Consequences of Repression of Emotion: Physical Health, Mental Health, and General Well Being." *International Journal of Psychotherapy Practice and Research* 1, no. 3 (2019): 16–21. https://doi.org/10.14302/issn.2574-612X.ijpr-18-2564.

139 Murnan, Amy. "Can Emotions Be Trapped in the Body? What to Know." Medical News Today. August 21, 2023. https://www.medicalnewstoday.com/articles/emotions-trapped-in-the-body.

Nummenmaa, Lauri, Enrico Glerean, and Riitta Hari. "Bodily Maps of Emotions." *Proceedings of the National Academy of Sciences* 111, no. 2 (2013): 646–651. https://doi.org/10.1073/pnas.1321664111.

140 Borrego-Mouquinho, Yolanda, Jesús Sánchez-Gómez, Juan Pedro Fuentes-García, Daniel Collado-Mateo, and Santos Villafaina. "Effects of High-Intensity Interval Training and Moderate-Intensity Training on Stress, Depression, Anxiety, and Resilience in Healthy Adults During Coronavirus Disease 2019 Confinement: A Randomized Controlled Trial." *Frontiers in Psychology.* 12, no. 643069 (2021). https://doi.org/10.3389/fpsyg.2021.643069.

141 Woods, Nancy Fugate, Ellen Sullivan Mitchell, and Kathleen Smith-DiJulio. "Cortisol Levels During the Menopausal Transition and Early Postmenopause: Observations from the Seattle Midlife Women's Health Study." *Menopause* 16, no. 4 (2009): 708–718. https://doi.org/10.1097/gme.0b013e318198d6b2.

142 Rose, Alexandra. "The Cortisol Creep: Is HIIT Stressing You Out?" Healthline. April 14, 2021. https://www.healthline.com/health/fitness/the-cortisol-creep.

143 Fasano, Robin. "Releasing Trapped Emotions." Spirituality & Health. October 25, 2024. https://www.spiritualityhealth.com/articles/2020/09/24/releasing-trapped-emotions.

144 Ward, Fiona. "Women Everywhere Are Doing 'Screaming Therapy' as a Healing Way to Release Anger and Trauma." *Glamour.* November 23, 2022. https://www.glamourmagazine.co.uk/article/screaming-therapy.

145 Ollennu, Amerley. "We're Angry and It's Harming Our Mental Health. Is Rage Journaling the Answer?" *Stylist.* 2022. https://www.stylist.co.uk/health/mental-health/rage-journaling-anger/802643.

Pennebaker, James W. "Expressive Writing in Psychological Science." *Perspectives on Psychological Science* 13, no. 2 (2017). https://doi.org/10.1177/1745691617707315.

146 Kanaya, Yuta and Nobuyuki Kawai. "Anger Is Eliminated with the Disposal of a Paper Written Because of Provocation." *Scientific Reports* 14, no. 7490 (2024). https://doi.org/10.1038/s41598-024-57916-z.

147 Woodyard, Catherine. "Exploring the Therapeutic Effects of Yoga and Its Ability to Increase Quality of Life." *International Journal of Yoga* 4, no. 2 (2011): 49–54. https://doi.org/10.4103/0973-6131.85485.

148 Marsolek, Amy. "Can Massage Relieve Symptoms of Depression, Anxiety, and Stress?" Mayo Clinic Health System. July 20, 2022. https://www.mayoclinichealthsystem.org/hometown-health/speaking-of-health/massage-for-depression-anxiety-and-stress.

149 Eske, Jamie. "How to Perform a Lymphatic Drainage Massage." Medical News Today. Last modified November 6, 2023. https://www.medicalnewstoday.com/articles/324518.

150 Mayo Clinic Staff. "Meditation: A Simple, Fast Way to Reduce Stress." Mayo Clinic. December 14, 2023. https://www.mayoclinic.org/tests-procedures/meditation/in-depth/meditation/art-20045858.

151 Peoples, Dr. Kat. "Living in the Now: Using Mindfulness to Release Negative Energy from the Past." *Attaining Positive Mental Health Through Philosophy* (blog). *Philosophical Healing*, May 9, 2024. https://philosophicalhealing.com/2024/05/09/living-in-the-now-using-mindfulness-to-release-negative-energy-from-the-past/.

152 Sahaj Kaur Kohli. "Therapy Databases." Accessed October 28, 2024. https://sahajkaurkohli.com/therapy-databases.

153 Campbell, Olivia. "Feeling Nostalgic? Your Brain Is Hardwired to Crave It." *National Geographic*. July 28, 2023. https://www.nationalgeographic.com/science/article/nostalgia-brain-science-memories.

154 Yang, Ziyan, Tim Wildschut, Keise Izuma et al. "Patterns of Brain Activity Associated with Nostalgia: A Social-Cognitive Neuroscience Perspective." *Social Cognitive and Affective Neuroscience* 17, no. 12 (2022): 1131–1144. https://doi.org/10.1093/scan/nsac036.

155 Bryant, Fred B., Colette M. Smart, and Scott P. King. "Using the Past to Enhance the Present: Boosting Happiness Through Positive Reminiscence." *Journal of Happiness Studies* 6 (2005): 227–260. https://doi.org/10.1007/s10902-005-3889-4.

156 Leunissen, J.M., C. Sedikides, T. Wildschut, and T.R. Cohen. "Organizational Nostalgia Lowers Turnover Intentions by Increasing Work Meaning: The Moderating Role of Burnout." *Journal of Occupational Health Psychology* 23, no. 1 (2018): 44–57. https://doi.org/10.1037/ocp0000059.

157 Loveday, Catherine, Amy Woy, and Martin A. Conway. "The Self-Defining Period in Autobiographical Memory: Evidence from a Long-Running Radio Show." *Quarterly Journal of Experimental Psychology* 73, no. 11 (2006): 1969–1976. https://doi.org/10.1177/1747021820940300.

158 Van Tilburg, Wijnand A.P., Constantine Sedikides, Tim Wildschut. "The Mnemonic Muse: Nostalgia Fosters Creativity Through Openness to Experience." *Journal of Experimental Social Psychology* 59 (2015): 1–7.

159 Seligman, Martin E.P., Tracy A. Steen, Nansook Park, and Christopher Peterson. "Positive Psychology Progress Empirical Validation of Interventions." *Journal of the Norwegian Psychological Association* 42, no. 10 (2005): 874–884. Psykologi. https://psykologtidsskriftet.no/fagartikkel/2005/10/positive-psychology-progress-empirical-validation-interventions.

160 Goldsmith, William M. "A Bouquet a Day: Study Finds That Living Around Flowers Reduces Stress." *The Harvard Crimson*. October 26, 2006. https://www.thecrimson.com/article/2006/10/26/a-bouquet-a-day-a-new/.

161 Bryant, Fred B., and Joseph Veroff. *Savoring: A New Model of Positive Experience.* 1st Edition. Psychology Press, 2007. https://doi.org/10.4324/9781315088426.

162 Jose, Paul E., Fred B. Bryant, and Bee Teng Lim. "Does Savoring Increase Happiness? A Daily Diary Study." *The Journal of Positive Psychology* 7, no. 3 (2012): 176–187. http://dx.doi.org/10.1080/17439760.2012.671345.

163 Ramirez-Duran, Daniela. "Savoring in Positive Psychology: 21 Tools to Appreciate Life." PositivePsychology.com. February 5, 2021. https://positivepsychology.com/savoring/.

164 Magsamen, Susan and Ivy Ross. *Your Brain on Art: How the Arts Transform Us.* Random House, 2023.

165 Time Out. "Things You Never Knew About Smell." September 27, 2011. https://www.timeout.com/chicago/things-to-do/things-you-never-knew-about-smell.

166 Feldman, Lucy. "Hello Sunshine: Shifting the Narrative." *Time.* April 26, 2021. https://time.com/collection/time100-companies/5953581/hello-sunshine/.

167 Burtt, Kristyn. "How Reese Witherspoon's Book Club Has Been a Financial Game-Changer for Authors." SheKnows. May 18, 2024. https://www.sheknows.com/entertainment/articles/3026699/reese-witherspoon-book-club-finances-authors/.

168 Chee, Angela, host, *The Power of the Only.* Season 2, episode 34. "The Firsts, the Fews, and the Onlys with Author Deepa Purushothaman." ZenMediaInc, January 12, 2021. Podcast, 50 min., 20 sec. https://angelachee.com/deepa-purushothaman/.

169 Lu, Dave. "Bamboo Ceiling? Build Your Own House." *Hyphen Nation* (blog). *Dave Lu,* May 29, 2020. https://www.davelu.com/p/bamboo-ceiling-build-your-own-house-283970a193f5.

170 Lu, Dave. "How the Immigrant Scarcity Mindset Holds Us Back." *Hyphen Nation* (blog). *Dave Lu,* November 27, 2023. https://www.davelu.com/p/how-the-immigrant-scarcity-mindset.

171 Feldman, Dana. "How Ava DuVernay Raised $38 Million for 'Origin.'" *Forbes.* Last modified December 21, 2023. https://www.forbes.com/sites/danafeldman/2023/12/20/how-ava-duvernay-raised-38-million-for-origin/.